All the Presidents' Pastries

Twenty-Five Years
in the White House

enjoy my story

All the Presidents' Pastries

Twenty-Five Years in the White House

A Memoir

Roland Mesnier,
with Christian Malard

Translated from the French
by Louise Rogers Lalaurie

Flammarion

Translated from the French by Louise Rogers Lalaurie
Copyediting: Chrisoula Petridis
Design and Typesetting: Thomas Gravemaker
Jacket illustration: Ruth Marten
Proofreading: Anne Korkeakivi
Color separation: Penez Éditions
Printed in the United States by RR Donnelley

Distributed in North America by Rizzoli International Publications, Inc.

Originally published in French as *Sucré d'état*
© Flammarion, SA, Paris, 2006

English-language edition
© Flammarion, SA, 2007

www.editions.flammarion.com

07 08 09 3 2 1
ISBN-10: 2-0803-0559-X
ISBN-13: 978-2-0803-0559-6
Dépôt légal: 02/2007

Contents

PROLOGUE

FRIDAY, JULY 30, 2004. Late afternoon. I'm leaving. Retiring. Slipping away. For the last time, I cross the closely guarded threshold of the White House as executive pastry chef. Sad? Yes. No one leaves a home to which they have devoted twenty-five years of their life without a sharp tug at the heartstrings. Particularly when the home in question is the presidential palace of the most powerful nation on Earth. During all those years it was my enormous privilege, and heavy responsibility, to serve five presidents whose names have already passed into the history books. Five presidents, each of whom, in his own way, wrote a page of the history of the United States of America, and the world: Jimmy Carter, Ronald Reagan, George Bush Senior, Bill Clinton, and George W. Bush. I was close to them all, in my capacity as pastry chef—responsible for producing healthy, sumptuous desserts for them and their guests, delicacies to delight the eye and titillate the taste buds. The final flourish of so many state dinners, and an essential part of their success. This book will, I hope, introduce the reader to the simple, warm-hearted, ordinary people who chose to shoulder the unimaginable burden of high office. I knew their tastes and preferences, their weaknesses. Ronald Reagan's sweet tooth and Bill Clinton's allergies. Inevitably, too, I collaborated closely with their wives, the First Ladies, who as the all-powerful chatelaines of the White House, presided—some more than others—over the selection and presentation of the desserts. Rosalynn Carter and Hillary Clinton, the Democrat First Ladies, each played an active role in state affairs. Nancy Reagan, Barbara Bush, and Laura Bush, the Republican First Ladies, confined their authority to the running of the White House. An accident of personal temperament or a political dividing line?

~

But now it's over. I will no longer be scolded by Nancy Reagan for forgetting to submit a menu for her approval. Never again will Hillary Clinton ask me—the night before, or at lunch for teatime the same day—to prepare a pastry buffet for thirty people. No more public congratulations, no more affectionate signs of gratitude and esteem, such as I was honored to receive. No longer will I find myself creating a dessert for an official dinner for 300 guests, while simultaneously making preparations for the state governors' banquet (150 guests) and the Congress barbecue (3,000 guests), or the many festivities at Christmas and New Year's. I will no longer witness the great succession of state visits, from Mrs. Thatcher to Menachem Begin, President Mitterrand, Her Majesty Queen Elizabeth II, Ariel Sharon, Yasir Arafat, Queen Beatrix of the Netherlands, President Sadat, King Hussein of Jordan, and the crowned heads of Morocco, Spain, and many more. I will no longer be party to the White House gossip: how and why Prince Charles had no idea what to do with a tea bag; how Chancellor Kohl of Germany was unable to fit into a normal-sized car, or why George Bush Senior was so preoccupied with golf that he forgot his morning suit for the wedding of his youngest daughter, Doro, at Camp David.

On the day of each new presidential inauguration, a family moves in to the White House—husband, wife, and children, sometimes even grandchildren, favorite pets and all. A family with its habits and traditions to be respected, its particular tastes in food, which must be taken into account, and its own very individual style, each so different from the last: the friendly Carters, the punctilious Reagans, the relaxed Clintons, the approachable Bushes, father and son. People who have always made me feel like one of the family.

~

Politics? Naturally, the affairs of state aren't cooked in the White House kitchens. *The White House Pasty Chef* won't reveal any state secrets. But the aftershocks of great world events were felt in the day-to-day routines of the White House, from the euphoria following the signing of the Camp David accords in 1978, to the freeing of the Tehran hostages, a cause for which President Carter fought to the very last moments of his presidency. And from the desolation following the Oklahoma City bombing in 1995 to the terror and alarm of September 11, 2001. I was there, and this book records these events as I experienced them.

I hope, too, that my story will be a ray of hope. Look where I came from, and how far I have come. There is life after the White House, but there was a life before the White House, too, one that will also be told here: a life of endless work, learning, apprenticeships, and hard-won success. Because you can do anything if you have the will to succeed. The secret is simple: love what you do and work, work, work.

~

I cross the White House's magnificent gardens one last time. Yes, I feel sad. And lost. Like a leader who has lost an empire, an actor leaving the stage, a pilot setting his flight case down on the ground. It's time to open the cage and let my memories fly out to you, the reader.

CHAPTER I

"Douce France, cher pays de mon enfance…"

(Charles Trenet, 1943)

I discovered my vocation on a summer's day in 1956, at the age of twelve. My parents had decided to send me to stay with my older brother Jean for part of the summer vacation. Jean was a pâtissier—a baker and pastry chef—in the town of L'Isle-sur-Doubs, twenty miles from our family home in Bonnay, a tiny village of just 150 inhabitants. There was no money for any other sort of vacation. We were poor: my father worked on the railroads, my mother guarded the grade crossing in the village, and we were nine children: two girls and seven boys. When I saw Jean's pastry ingredients—the sugar, flour, eggs, and the rest—and better still, when I mixed them all together, I felt quite dizzy. The aromas from the oven were intoxicating. Pastries back then were made with nothing but fresh, seasonal ingredients. My stay coincided with the season for *cerises aigres* (sour red cherries) and the dark pink fruits were baked every day in hundreds of delicious tarts. There were soft, sweet brioche loaves, too, and croissants, meringues, cream-filled *choux* buns, and the whole panoply of delicious pastries, decked out in their party best. I still dream of them today! On Saturdays and Sundays, especially after Mass, people would stand in line outside the shop. Often, they would be waiting for it to open. And for us, it was like living in an enchanted sugar garden.

I had made my decision. I would be a pastry chef. But I had my doubts, too: would I have the physical strength to stand for such long hours in the pastry kitchen, working at a trade that afforded so few days off?

II

My brother and I started work at 5 a.m., and the days were very long. Would I be capable of doing what Jean had done, of working so hard and building a successful business? He had endured a tough apprenticeship, softened by the companionship of a girlfriend named Thérèse, whom he later married. He had completed his compulsory military service in Madagascar, and was tempted to stay there, such that at the end of his time in the army he wrote to my mother, asking her to send out his battery of patisserie utensils. Thérèse put her foot down, so he came home to France and a job in the pastry shop where I spent that summer of 1956. My brother was a very hard worker, and a staunch conservative. One of the old school. I admired him enormously. I would watch as he worked his pastry decorations with incredible dexterity, making it all look so simple. I told myself I would never be able to match his skill. He was an artist who played an immensely important role in my life.

I wondered, too, if I would have the will to give up the things I enjoyed so much: playing soccer, going to the river, having fun with friends. My mother cherished the hope that I might take holy orders. She was a deeply religious woman, who would have done anything to attain the apotheosis of her Catholic faith: a priest in the family. I had other ideas. Unintentionally, my mother was also nourishing my dreams of a career in patisserie. She was an excellent cook and the creator of many splendid desserts, especially in summer. Every time she baked an ovenful of tarts, I breathed again the sublime aromas of my stay in L'Isle-sur-Doubs. There was one final deciding factor. You'll be working in the food trade, I told myself. You'll never go hungry.

～

We were a tightly knit family, despite the inevitable squabbles between brothers and sisters. We took our example from our parents. My father worked from dawn till dusk, every day of the week, with never a weekend off, just the occasional fishing expedition on a Saturday or Sunday. When he was not working to serve the SNCF (France's state-owned railroad system), he was chopping wood or cultivating his vines. We made our own wine, and the days of the grape harvest were an unforgettable treat, full of laughter and impatience. It was rough stuff, but we were proud of it.

My mother never drank alcohol. Her whole life long, she never set foot in a cinema. She turned her first electric light switch (the old-fashioned kind that you had to literally "turn on") at the age of fifty-five, and she always walked everywhere she went. On exceedingly rare occasions she took a bus or train. My father never drove a car, never knew any means of getting around other than his Mobylette moped or his bicycle.

On Sundays, he allowed himself a glass of Pernod—because it was Sunday—and he would send us to fetch cold water from the village fountain, about a mile from the house. There were no ice cubes, of course, because we had no electricity and no refrigerator. For us, the cool water from the deep spring feeding the fountain was the drink of kings compared with our own well, whose water was neither cool nor pleasant-tasting.

We also kept chickens, rabbits, goats, and sheep. Our vegetables and fruit came from our own kitchen garden. We were, in effect, wholly self-sufficient. But it was punishingly hard work. Everyone chipped in. Thursday, when there was no school, was the day for tending the garden, cleaning out the rabbit hutches and the chicken coop, and taking away the accumulated droppings. Everyone did what they could. My sister Geneviève laundered great loads of washing for the entire family when she was barely fourteen or fifteen years old. My father would preserve quantities of fruit in barrels. In my youth, the law still permitted the distilling of alcohol for one's own private consumption (the so-called *privilège des bouilleurs du cru* [grower-distillers' privilege]). My father would go to the neighboring village each autumn, where there was a pot still, and make his own fruit brandy, known as *goutte* (literally, "a drop"). He would stay there for three or four days, and we would take food and clean clothes to the little hut where he stayed.

~

The winters were long. My father would slaughter one or two goats ahead of the worst weather, and my mother would cook the meat and preserve it in sealed jars. It was a cruel business; I don't like to think of it now, but we needed food for the table in the coldest months. Our winter vegetables consisted of *cocos*, round white beans which my mother shelled and preserved, potatoes, and pickled cabbage, stored in a stinking barrel in the cellar. We had to eat.

Our little house offered no comforts. There was no heating other than the wood-fired stove, and no running water—we had to fetch what we needed from the well in all weathers. The laundry was housed in a covered shelter, where our clothes and bed linen were boiled. There was, as I have said, no electricity. And the house was very crowded—not only with people, but also rats, who occupied the cellar, from where they had colonized the entire building. After nibbling through the baseboards around the bedroom walls, they had gouged gaping holes in the floor, and lived in the space between the bedroom floors and the dining-room and kitchen ceilings. At night we could hear them fighting, nibbling, scuttling everywhere. We tried to catch them, of course, but they were cunning creatures, and seldom allowed themselves to become trapped. Ours was a house "of rats and men," and there were at least as many of them as there were of us.

We slept four to a room, two to a bed, in two little bedrooms under the eaves. Eight altogether, upstairs. The ninth child slept in the dining room downstairs, next to my parents' bedroom, which was a decent size. There were no toilets, just a wooden shack behind the chicken coop. Visiting the toilet at night was a major expedition; in winter, when it snowed, or in driving wind and rain, it was best to make sure you went before getting into bed. Often, it was so cold inside that the windows were covered with a thick layer of ice inside. We placed hot bricks in the beds to warm them up.

For light, there were oil lamps or carbide gas lamps. These were cylindrical in shape; water fell drop by drop from the top of the cylinder onto a piece of calcium carbide placed at the bottom, releasing a gas that rose up and was forced out through a small spout. By striking a match in front of the spout, it was possible to obtain a tiny flame, by the light of which I did my homework at night. The light was extinguished by cutting the supply of drops of water. The system produced a feeble light, but it was less dangerous than the oil lamps, which could set the entire house alight if ever one was dropped. The carbide gas lamps were allowed upstairs, but not the oil lamps.

~

My mother, as I have said, guarded the village's railroad crossing. It was her job to clear the tracks by lowering the barriers as soon as she received the signal that a train had left the next station up or down the line. There were eight trains a day, which made her task quite complicated. In those days, the local cows were taken to pasture early in the morning, then brought back to the pens over lunchtime, and taken out again until early evening. This meant four journeys daily, every one of which coincided, alas, with the passage of a train. Whenever my mother went to close the barriers, she would find the farmer pleading with her to let him pass with his cows—there was plenty of time, he would argue, even though the little tinkling bell told my mother something quite different. When she finally stopped work, it was with an enormous sense of relief—no more hay wagons, or cows, not to mention her own children, whom she would count and recount feverishly, for fear that we might be playing on the tracks. Not forgetting that other hazard of the day, the burning coal embers that flew out of the steam furnaces and could set fire to the grass on the embankments either side of the line. When this happened, every man in the village was called out to beat the flames with bundles of sticks, and quench the fire before it reached our house. We lived in deadly fear of seeing our home consumed by these fires, which were sometimes halted just a few steps away, and always just in time, thank God.

And so life was hard but happy. We had little, but wanted for nothing, since you can't miss what you've never had—a truism I have never forgotten. Our father and mother looked after us magnificently well, creating strong, warm, family ties, so that we felt supported and fulfilled, despite our shabby clothes, handed down—as in every large family—from one child to the next. Clothes were for keeping warm, and that was that.

My mother was always doing something. She rose at 5 a.m. each morning, went to bed at 9:30 p.m. each night, and never stopped in between. If she found a few minutes to sit down, she would mend socks or stitch a shirt or knit. She seldom bought anything in a store. Essential purchases were made on trips to the nearest town, when she would strive to find the best quality and the lowest possible price. On Sundays, she rose at 4:30 a.m. to start preparing the family meal, which began in time-honored fashion with a pot-au-feu, served with tomato sauce. Next came another meat dish, usually from our own small-holding: a chicken, rabbit, or leg of lamb. And to finish, a mountain ham served with lettuce. Not forgetting the homemade desserts: rhubarb tarts that were so delicious there was never enough, or her wonderful mocha cake, the like of which I have never tasted anywhere else. For this exceptional cake my mother made her own butter cream and her own coffee extract. Our Sunday feasts were all the more bountiful thanks to the contributions from my brother Gabriel, a baker, who would come home on weekend visits bringing good, fresh bread, brioches, and sometimes even cakes. My brother Jean did the same once he began work at the patisserie. And little by little, as the years went by, our lot improved.

I have forgotten to mention my mother's walnut wine, made to her own recipe. The nuts had to be gathered while their shells were still soft, so that these could be pierced with a needle before being soaked in wine, with sugar and seasoning. The result was an absolutely delicious aperitif. And then there was the *liqueur du pendu*—hanged man's liquor, the "hanged man" being an orange pierced all over with cloves, which my mother suspended from a thread in a jar of liquor for several months at a time, so that the flavor and fragrance of the citrus fruit were transferred to the alcohol. Not to mention her rabbit pâté, made by marinating large pieces of meat and preserving them in jelly. Or the hundreds of frogs that my father would collect from the riverbank in springtime—the centerpiece of a great family feast, which everyone came to share. Or the snails, which I gathered in season with my father and brothers, early in the morning before going to school, in the nettles along the railroad.

~

I was appallingly badly behaved throughout my last year at school, leading up to the *certificat d'études*, a diploma that up until 1959 was taken by French children at fourteen years of age.

I could see the moment of decision fast approaching. When you're thirteen years old, the future is an ocean. You can't wait to dive in but you hesitate in fear, on the brink. Fraught with indecision, I retaliated by abandoning my schoolwork and acting up in class. A new trick or joke every day, to the delight of my classmates: from the thumbtack placed point upwards on the teacher's chair, to the fine art of sticking blotting-paper bombs to the ceiling, or putting carbide in my fellow pupils' ink-wells (which had the effect of turning them into miniature fireworks). Best of all was the time I sneaked out on the pretext of a visit to the toilet, in order to catch a chicken in the neighbor's yard and let it loose in the classroom, to wild laughter. I was punished virtually every day, and every day I thought up new ways of drawing attention to myself. I was also very interested in the opposite sex, and never missed an opportunity to go and see the village girls kneeling on the stones around the basin in the public washhouse, the *lavoir*, beating and scrubbing the laundry. Young boys today will never know what they are missing.

We reached the end of June 1958 and the dreaded *certificat d'études*. Five pupils in my class were taking the examination, and our teacher predicted that four of us would pass without any difficulty, while a fifth candidate would fail. Guess who? We decided to cycle together from Bonnay to Moncey—the administrative town for our district, a few miles away—where the exams were to be held. On that day, a guardian angel came to sit on my shoulder and has never left me since. I summoned all the means at my disposal, concentrated fiercely, and worked hard at all the tests set before us. I was conscious of nothing but the white sheet of paper in front of me. After lunch, which we took all together at the local restaurant—rabbit and pasta, I remember it to this day—I applied myself to the task once again, with renewed vigor. By the end of the day I had a furious headache. I had completed the tests, but was no more confident of my results than I had been when I started. We returned home to our village and waited, nervous and anxious.

Eight days later, we cycled back to Moncey for our results, armed with fifty centimes to pay for our diploma, assuming we had passed. I went along for the ride, but didn't bother to take the money, convinced that I had failed. But when I looked at the bulletin board, my name was on the list of those who had passed. A miracle! I couldn't believe my eyes. One of the girls in our group had failed, however. Our teacher was right—one candidate would have to take the exam again, but not the one he had predicted. My friend gave me her centimes so that I could pay for my certificate. She never let me pay her back, yet she had every reason to feel bitter—during all our years together at school, she had always worked harder and obtained better grades than me.

I was deliriously happy. I had my *certificat d'études*! Now, I would have to make a decision about my future. Should I stay in Bonnay? I wanted to, but what could I do in a tiny village of 150 souls, whose distractions consisted of one hotel and restaurant, three bars and three ninepins lanes, plus a grocery store, bakery, and butcher's, a tobacconist, two cheese shops, two schools, a barbershop (providing shaves for people and sheep), and a church? I knew that the time had come to fly the family nest—that it was up to me to vacate some space in our tiny, still heavily populated house. One less mouth to feed and one less body in bed would make a big difference. I asked my mother to find me a place as an apprentice pastry cook in Besançon, a fine, large town about ten miles away. I had been there several times, staring wide-eyed with disbelief at the splendid shops. There were several patisseries in Besançon, which was a very well-to-do, bourgeois place. My mother had planned to go to town that very afternoon. She would take the bus at 1:30 p.m. and be home at 7:30 p.m. Meanwhile, my fate would be decided.

I took a last walk through my beloved fields and woods, and along the banks of the Ognon River—the countryside I loved so well. Even today, almost fifty years later, I can still feel the breezes and showers on my face, breathe the scent of the leaves, the grass, the water. My life was going to change. I was full of hope and fear in equal measure. I came back from my walk in the late afternoon, but I couldn't eat a thing. I kept staring at the clock, ticking slowly or too quickly. I was desperately ill at ease. What if I turned out to be a bad apprentice, just as I had been a bad pupil at school? What would become of me then?

7:30 p.m. Time to meet my mother at the bus stop. My heart is thumping. The bus arrives five minutes late—five hours by my reckoning. My mother is loaded with shopping. I help her with a few bags, and walk beside her, asking nothing, because I have all but changed my mind. I can't leave my village, my countryside, my river, my friends, on a mere whim. We walked in silence for 300 feet or so, before my mother says, "I have found you a place. You start on July 8."

The crowning misery. July 8 is my birthday. I will be fourteen, and instead of celebrating with my friends, I'll have to tear myself away from everything I love. I don't know what to say. I can't tell my mother that I've abandoned the idea after all she has done for me.

After a few minutes, I ask in a choked voice, "Where? On the main street?"

"Yes. Pâtisserie Maurivard, formerly the Pâtisserie Bonnot. It's a fine shop. I'll take you there next week, to meet the boss."

And that's that. The dice are thrown. I feel hot and cold. I don't know whether to laugh or cry at the prospect of fending for myself. It's an exhilarating and frightening experience, to suddenly find yourself the master of your own destiny.

~

A few days later, as planned, my mother took me to Besançon. I was very nervous. I had no idea of what I was expected to say, or how I should behave.

"Above all, be polite and don't act the fool," advised my mother.

We arrived and I met Madame Maurivard, my employer, and Madame Annie, her sister-in-law, who worked in the shop. I stared around me without the slightest idea of what I was looking at. The cakes and pastries here were far more sophisticated than those in my brother's patisserie.

I felt afraid, very afraid. The boss himself, Monsieur Maurivard, arrived. He seemed huge and impressive. I felt even more frightened. I was introduced to him and to the pastry chef, Raymond Ligney, Annie's husband and Monsieur Maurivard's brother-in-law. Everyone seemed quite young. The bosses had two young daughters, Sylvette and Marie-Christine. Madame Maurivard's mother was also part of the team—as cook, cleaner, and nanny to the children. A real family business. And I can't leave out the dog, named Gold, a superb collie. I wasn't the only apprentice. Another boy had started a few months earlier. The new faces, the strange new atmosphere, unlike anything I have known before, were simply terrifying. My mother tried to comfort me on the way home. The Maurivards seemed like very nice, kind people; they would take good care of me.

As arranged, I started on July 8. I arrive on the bus, with one piece of luggage—a little *cuir-bouilli* suitcase reinforced with twine. The suitcase contains some clean laundry, a pair of trousers, and a toothbrush. And five francs of pocket money given to me by my mother.

As soon as I arrive at the shop, Madame Maurivard leaves me in the charge of her mother, Madame Fantou, a very stiff, rigid, old-fashioned type. She takes me to what will be my bedroom for the next three years—assuming I pass the first test (I am on trial until September 1).

Noon and my first meal with my new family. The girls are there, home from school just a short walk away from the house. Everything is strange and new. I don't dare eat, I am paralyzed with shyness. Everyone asks questions, which terrifies me even more. I try to answer as best as I can.

After lunch, two hours of free time. I take the opportunity to acquaint myself with my bedroom, shared with the other apprentice. Two narrow, hospital-style beds, a wardrobe, a table, two chairs, a window opening onto the stairwell. No heating, no washbasin. We wash in the pastry kitchen, or at the tap in the yard at the back of the building. Scrubbing the wooden stairs leading to our employer's apartment is part of our work routine. At 2 p.m. I go down to the pastry kitchen for the first time. Raymond the pastry chef gives me a blue apron and shows me the sink, full of saucepans and patisserie utensils, waiting to be washed. He asks me to heat some water on the gas (there is no hot water tank). Then he asks me to do the dishes.

~

It's September 1. My contract is about to be signed in the presence of my parents. My father makes a point of asking my boss to make sure I work very hard. There's no place for sentiment or pity. In his scheme of things, I'm a man already, with a duty to do well and work hard like everyone else. Suddenly, I feel desperately empty, lonely, and forsaken. I am an orphan, about to lose my parents. I fight back the tears. Everyone in our family has been taught to keep their emotions at bay. Today, I want desperately for my mother to take me in her arms one last time, for my father to give me more than a handshake. But we take our leave without fuss, our emotions walled up inside.

CHAPTER 2

A Bittersweet Apprenticeship

My first year as an apprentice pastry chef was devoted to domestic chores: washing dishes, scrubbing the pastry kitchen, scraping the baking trays, cleaning the shop windows, taking my employers' little girls to school, running errands.

The errands were far from disagreeable. They were a chance to get out and about, and to avoid other less pleasant tasks. Often, I was asked to go on foot to deliver a cake packed in a basket to a customer who would be waiting for it at a particular time, sometimes on the other side of town. These deliveries resulted in tips, which added to my apprentice pay (five francs per month, plus room and board). Some customers were very generous, others not at all. I learned that it takes all kinds. But Sundays were always the best: I began my deliveries at 9:30 a.m. and finished at around 1 p.m., with enough tips to pay for a trip to the movie theater in the afternoon once the dishes were done, provided that Madame Fantou didn't decide at the last minute to find another urgent task for me, such as scrubbing the stairs. In which case, no trip to the movie theater.

There were also regular errands to fetch supplies for the pastry kitchen: fresh fruit, plums, prunes, milk, lemons, and chocolate. Anything that might be needed suddenly and unexpectedly, always at the last minute. For this, Madame Maurivard provided me with a float from the petty cash, and it was up to me to write down what everything had cost and any cash payments that I received for the return of prepaid deposits on glass bottles. But when it came to settling up with Madame Maurivard, after dinner, late in the evening (I finished work at around

8 or 9 p.m.), I was hardly ever able to balance my account. Not that I was taking any liberties with the cash—even if such a plan had occurred to me, I would have been perfectly incapable of carrying it out—I was just too tired to do the math. My honor was at stake, the honesty that I had learned from my parents, in a family of nine, where none of us ever had cause to question the integrity of another sibling. This made me all the more nervous and anxious when it came to settling the account with Madame Maurivard. Often, I had forgotten to note down some small expense or receipt in cash, in the general haste, and with all the absent-mindedness (it has to be said) of my fourteen years—an age when the mind is not always fully concentrated on the task in hand. Sometimes, there was too much cash left over, and I was unable to say where it had come from. One evening, Madame Maurivard declared in exasperation: "You won't go to bed until you've balanced the account."

A hard task indeed! I finally remembered that various deposits had been repaid to me, and I was able to justify the excess cash. Madame Maurivard's outburst was hard to swallow at the time, but later I came to understand that lessons like these forge the character, and shape us for life.

~

On Mondays, the shop was shut. On that day, about once a month, and within the limits of my meager funds, I took the bus home to have lunch with my parents. I remember my first trip home. Above all, I wanted to give my family the impression that I adored what I was doing, that I had found the perfect job, that everything was absolutely fine—although this was far from the case. My mother had bought me a shirt. I was touched by this affectionate gesture and happy that she had not forgotten me. But behind my show of optimism, I wondered how long I would last with the Maurivards. The work was really very hard. I was extraordinarily tired, and had little or no free time of my own. In reality, I was dragging myself from bed to work, and from work back to bed, day in, day out.

The other apprentice had decided to give up, after his first year in the patisserie trade. He wanted his youth back. His departure came as a blow to me—we had become friends, and now he was abandoning me. I asked myself what would happen if I did the same. But if I decided to return home, my parents would bring me back to the shop the very same day. Giving up was impossible, unthinkable. I had to finish what I had started.

My bosses filled the newly vacated post with another apprentice who arrived, like all apprentices, in a state of acute anxiety. I became, ipso facto, the senior boy, so that Monsieur Maurivard and the pastry chef had no choice but to put me to work in the pastry kitchen itself. From now on, my chores were carried out by the new apprentice. And so I began work as a pastry chef, starting with the simplest tasks: garnishing tarts, making a few small cakes. From that moment, I rediscovered my enthusiasm for the work. The aromas and sensations of 1956, and my stay with my brother Jean, came flooding back. My enthusiasm grew as I learned more and more from Raymond, the pastry chef. I tried my hand at a few artistic creations of my own, such as decorative chocolate borders for the desserts. Raymond demonstrated his confidence in me, as did Monsieur Maurivard. Things seemed to be looking up. I was so pleased that I gave up any idea of returning home. My parents visited me at the shop from time to time, and checked on my progress with the Maurivards. Monsieur Maurivard gave favorable reports of my work on the whole, but his praise was never wholehearted. There was always scope for more progress: I needed to stick more closely to the rules, rectify certain mistakes. Monsieur Maurivard was an exacting boss, and he instilled his perfectionism in his pupils.

One day, when business was slow, he decided to let me make the croissants on my own. I prepared the dough twenty-four hours in advance, then rolled it out, cut and shaped the croissants, and baked them. When I took them out of the oven, I felt I had accomplished a great feat—I had scaled the Everest of patisserie.

~

Monsieur Maurivard was an accomplished pastry chef. He had worked in Switzerland, where he learned the art of chocolate-making, and then at the Hotel Lutétia in Paris, where he met his wife. The newlyweds returned to Besançon and bought the Pâtisserie Bonnot, where Monsieur Maurivard had served his own apprenticeship. The Maurivards' establishment was not the biggest patisserie in Besançon, but it was the best. Monsieur Maurivard was younger than most of his fellow pâtissiers, and enjoyed a head start in the profession as a result. He taught me a great deal. Many of the recipes I use today were handed down from him. And there is not a single day when I don't thank him and his wife for their tough, rigorous training. The soft dough of youth needs to be worked vigorously if it is to rise properly. A good boss will give his young trainees firm direction, know how to correct their mistakes, and always be ready to listen and help. Monsieur and Madame Maurivard watched over us constantly; we weren't free to do as we pleased. We did what the bosses wanted, in the way they wanted it done.

Working for the Maurivards was an extraordinary stroke of luck. Other patisseries in Besançon were, it seemed, less agreeable places to work. Many apprentices were beaten by their bosses. I attended an evening class in pastry theory (I had the practical side well in hand by now) and often my fellow students would arrive with black eyes or limping. Neither I, nor my parents, would have stood for this. Being taught by the boot, or the fist, is no way to learn.

In truth, the Maurivards brought me up, just as my parents had. They gave me a great deal of good advice about how to conduct my life. The extraordinary rectitude that they applied to their own lives, and the raising of their children, was a great example to me. One day, when I was working alone in the pastry kitchen, as I did every day in preparation for the *Certificat d'Aptitude Professionnelle* (CAP), one of the girls, Marie-Christine, came and asked—or rather ordered—in a very superior way: "Give me an ice cream, right now."

"That's no way to talk to anyone." I scolded her for her rudeness. She ran off crying to her mother, who brought her back down to the pastry kitchen straight away, to get the full story.

"Madame," I explained, "Marie-Christine spoke to me as if I was no better than a dog. I'm not a dog. She should have asked me politely for an ice cream, in the proper way." Madame Maurivard turned to her daughter, gave her a loud and thorough scolding, and demanded that she apologize to me straightaway. The Maurivard children were expected to show the same standard of behavior as we apprentices: politeness at all times and respect for others.

My life would doubtless have turned out quite differently if I had not encountered this family. Monsieur Maurivard gave me that extra "something" that is so essential to success, and from Madame Maurivard I learned how to get along with people and make a good impression. She was a consummate professional, classy, always ready to chat with customers, always smiling and approachable. Many customers visited the shop regularly, in the late afternoon, for nothing more than a pleasant chat. The Maurivards have remained staunch friends ever after, always keeping in touch with my news. Later, whenever I was in Besançon, I would always stop by for a visit, and have always been welcomed like one of the family. We are still friends, and I owe them an enormous debt of gratitude.

~

I continued to make deliveries, adding to my modest pay, so that in my second and third years with the Maurivards, I was earning 100 or 150 francs per month—vast riches compared with my first pay of just the five francs per month. I was able to buy a nearly new bicycle from my brother Jean, who had no more need of it, and made my rounds on two wheels now. One Sunday in winter, I skidded on a patch of black ice, sending bike, rider, and cake in three different directions. An old lady who was passing at the time commented sourly that, next time, I should try riding even faster. The cake was, of course, destroyed. I had to return to the patisserie and fetch another, and was reprimanded in the process. The bicycle brought its share of further troubles, too. Once, I went home for a long weekend and thoughtlessly left it standing on the sidewalk in Besançon, just as I did on my errands. When I returned, the bike had gone. No one had noticed anything. I went to the police station, and a lieutenant (who turned out to be Monsieur Maurivard's brother) asked me a great many detailed questions. I felt almost guilty for having let myself be the victim of such a theft. The inspector concluded that he would see what he could do. But time passed, and there was no news of the bicycle. Until one day, during the family meal, Marie-Christine gave the game away: the bike was in the attic, under a pile of boxes. The Maurivards had taken it indoors for safe keeping, and Monsieur Maurivard had conspired with his brother, the lieutenant, to teach me another valuable lesson.

~

But now the end of the third year of my apprenticeship was approaching. And with it, the CAP. Traditionally, the examinations were held in the biggest patisserie in Besançon, run then as now by the Baud family. There were twenty-two candidates. The day was every bit as intense as for the *certificat d'études*. We each had to make a cake, prepare puff pastry dough and a selection of desserts, make chocolates and molded chocolate figures or shapes, and prepare a *choux* pastry dough. A vast program! I worked hard, focusing my energies and concentration to be sure of success. I had to prove to the Maurivards, and my family, that I was capable of being a pastry chef, and an excellent one at that. My hard work paid off. I was awarded second place and a silver medal. When I heard the result, I felt as proud as a peacock. Monsieur Maurivard was delighted, too. My success was proof, if proof were needed, of his excellent training.

~

The time had come to plan for my future. Thanks to the CAP, I was now a qualified pastry chef and could command a much higher salary than the Maurivards were able to pay. With a heavy heart, I resigned myself to leaving their household and looking elsewhere. I wanted to work in a big pastry kitchen where I could learn modern "production line" techniques. The teacher at our evening classes, Monsieur Beligat, ran just such an operation. Here, I worked for the first time with twelve other pastry chefs and apprentices, with particular responsibility for the *entremets*, sweet small dishes served between courses, traditionally reserved for the best chef on the premises. I was flattered to be appointed, and my monthly salary was a princely 30,000 old francs (roughly 50 dollars)—a great deal for me. With my first wages, I went to a local hardware store and bought my first radio—it was white, and cost exactly 30,000 francs. On weekdays, I also prepared the shop's range of petits fours and cakes for the weekend. A great many were needed—the shop was besieged with customers. The boss, who had worked in Switzerland, was a motorbike fanatic and the owner of a splendid machine with a big engine, on which he offered to drive me home to my parents during the weekend. During the week, we took our meals with the family, as at the Maurivards', and were exceedingly well fed. We slept four to a room and shared a wash basin. In the pastry kitchen, at the top, next to the flour sacks, was a shower. Undreamed-of luxury! But after six months, I felt that I had learned all there was to learn with Monsieur Beligat and decided to look elsewhere. Where indeed? Why not Paris? There, I thought, I would learn everything there was left for me to know.

~

It so happened that one of my aunts lived in Paris. Her friends the Godots kindly agreed to rent me a room while I waited to find a place of my own.

I started looking for a job right away, and approached a specialist agency, the Saint-Michel. I was asked if I had already worked in Paris, and was immediately relegated to the bottom of the list when I answered no. As far as they were concerned, a pastry chef who had never worked in Paris was completely ignorant. There was no likelihood of working in the sort of patisserie I dreamed of: I was offered the worst jobs, the ones no one else wanted, and almost always out in the suburbs. Then one day, quite by chance, I was offered a job at the Régence, a restaurant and patisserie on Place du Théâtre-Français in the very center of Paris. I accepted right away. The Régence was a well-known brasserie, frequented by the likes of Sylvie Vartan, Johnny Halliday, and others from what later came to be known as the world of showbiz. Despite this, the pâtissiers were, it seemed to me, nothing out of the ordinary. Their creations were run-of-the-mill, traditional, and unadventurous. I was not happy at the Régence.

Life in Paris wasn't easy, either. After leaving the Godots, I rented a room in a small hotel nearby, for 100 francs a month. It was basic to say the least: no heating or hot water, just a washbasin with cold water, and this during one of the coldest winters imaginable. The Godots leant me a small electric heater, which helped take the chill off the air when I was getting undressed for bed or washing. Every morning, before leaving for work, I locked it in the wardrobe (the hotel's rules forbade the use of electrical equipment in the bedrooms). Alas, one day I forgot to hide it and was thrown out by the manager that very evening.

I took refuge with the Godots, who generously agreed to have me back while I looked for a new place, despite the limited space in their small apartment, which was directly above their electrical business. I was in no hurry, if the truth be known. The Godots had a very pretty daughter my own age, Michèle. We spent hours talking together about each other's plans and dreams. Sometimes, we went to the movies together. But time was passing and I had to move on. I found a room near Bastille, in the house of a widow whose husband had been a pastry chef. There was heating, and hot water: it was a moderately comfortable existence.

The problem was simply that I disliked Paris and felt I was wasting my time there. There seemed to be no scope to learn anything new, to progress. I made pilgrimages to the shop windows of the great pâtissiers of the day, Gaston Lenôtre or Fauchon, but these only made me feel more melancholy still. I could never hope to work in such a place. No one would want a country boy from Bonnay.

~

One day, I confided in the executive chef at the Régence—a man who was almost invariably bad-tempered and rude to me. Every morning I would enter his domain to fetch the big basins in which I prepared my *crème pâtissière* (confectioner's custard, twenty liters at a time). And every morning, he never missed an opportunity to be as insulting as possible: "Here he comes, the stupid midget. Come to steal my saucepans again? Get lost before I kick your ass!" The same story, day in, day out.

But this time, to my great surprise, he was friendly and approachable. We had finished work, and I was changing in the cloakroom. The executive chef was there, too. Outside work, he had evidently decided to change his tone.

"How's it going?" he asked.

I replied that I was not at all satisfied, that I badly wanted to learn more, and that the Régence was not the place to do it.

"Listen," he said kindly, "you should go to Germany. The patisseries are excellent. And they make superb marzipan figures. Go and get a job there."

As it happened, there was a German chef by the name of Paul Gauweiler working at the Régence. We had become friends, and I confided my new dream, inspired by the head chef's advice. I wanted to work in Germany. Could he give me any advice?

"It depends on where you want to go," said Paul. "You've got to decide which town you want to work in first." Which didn't help me much.

And so, one evening, when I was feeling particularly low, I went to a nearby bistro and started drinking. I drank too much. I had no idea what to do next. I had reached a turning point. Which way to go? I wanted to learn. I was determined to show the world what I could do, to become a truly great pâtissier. Drunk as a skunk, I took a sudden decision—the kind that is only ever taken in a state of advanced drunkenness. I went out and bought a map of Germany, took it back to my room, grabbed a pencil, and declared that I would go wherever the point of the pencil pierced the map.

The sharpened pencil stuck in northern Germany, on a place marked Hanover.

Hanover it was, then.

CHAPTER 3

Hanoverian Cuisine

My departure for Hanover was painful. With the exception of Lucien Vannier, the executive chef, everyone tried to dissuade me.

"What do you want to go there for? You don't speak the language, you don't know anyone. It's madness."

My German friend had no patisserie contacts in Hanover, but had given me the address of one of his friends, Franz Hocker, a salesman for McCormick tractors. No one in Paris could understand that I wanted to learn about other kinds of patisserie, that I wanted to make a name for myself, and that this would mean making certain sacrifices. I had to leave, even if it meant leaving my friend Michèle and her family, who had been so kind.

I went from bistro to bistro, gathering Dutch courage, but still managed to buy my ticket, and pack my flimsy little *carton bouilli* suitcase. I set off for Germany on August 8, 1962. The train pulled out of the Gare du Nord at 8 p.m. At the Belgian border, the customs officials were astonished to find me traveling alone—I wasn't eighteen yet—in an almost deserted night train, with just one cheap suitcase. They asked for my ID. They wanted to know why I was traveling to Germany and where exactly I was headed. I said I was going to Hanover. Did I have work there? I replied that I would be staying with a family, the Hockers, although this was far from certain. I could see that the scales were about to tip and not in my favor. I begged them. The guards made me promise that I would write to my parents as soon as I arrived in Germany. They would let me pass, they said, although they had their doubts. In theory, I should have been sent back to France, because I was underage. My guardian angel had saved me once again.

~

The train was extraordinarily slow, like all trains at that time. We crossed Belgium and part of the Netherlands, and made a stop in Düsseldorf, where we waited almost all night, in an unheated carriage, before continuing on to Hanover, where I arrived at 10 a.m. the following day. Here I was, in a city of grim façades, beneath gray skies, speaking not a word of German, with no work, no money (or very little), and nowhere to spend the night. I decided to go straight to Franz Hocker's address and showed the slip of paper to a taxi driver, who delivered me to his front door. My ring was answered by a blond man with thinning hair, in his early thirties. He asked me who I was and what I wanted.

"Monsieur, my friend Paul Gauweiler tells me that you speak French."

"Fluently. I often go to France on business. What do you want?"

I summoned up all my courage and took the plunge: "Monsieur, you must help me. I beg you."

My guardian angel can't have been far away, because Franz Hocker opened his door and invited me in. He introduced me to his wife, a very pretty woman, tall and blond, also in her early thirties. They had two charming little girls, aged about seven and four. This was a happier, more innocent time than our own. Times have changed. Today, Herr Hocker would almost certainly have called the police. I had been traveling all night. I was unwashed, unshaven, dressed scarcely any better than a tramp, with a suitcase to match. And here was Franz Hocker, chatting politely and asking if he could be of any help. I explained who I was, that I had come from Paris, that I was a pastry cook, and that I dreamed of working in Germany.

"Monsieur, I want to get a job in the best patisserie in Hanover, and I need a place to stay. My friend told me that you might be able to help. I hope that you can."

Herr Hocker and his wife assured me that I could stay with them while I found a room. I could hardly believe my ears. Such kindness really did exist. Either that or my guardian angel (Mickaël, as I later came to call him) was truly a champion seraph among seraphs.

"Tomorrow morning," added Franz Hocker, "I'll take you to the finest patisserie in Hanover to meet the pastry chef. I don't know him personally, but we'll see how it goes. And in the meantime, you'll stay with us and eat with us. You can sleep in the girls' room."

The following morning, we drove to the Opern Konditorei, a patisserie near the opera where I met Hermann Heising, a big, fat man with a cold stare, huge glasses, and a loud voice. A quite terrifying individual. He didn't understand a word of French, so Franz Hocker acted as our interpreter, with the result that I was asked to come back the following Sunday and work for a day to show what I could do. If my work proved unsatisfactory, Herr Heising would put me on the Monday morning train back to Paris.

~

On Sunday, I arrived at the appointed time, 6 a.m. The patisserie was closed. Not a soul in sight. I waited for three long hours until 9 a.m., sitting on the sidewalk. When the boss finally arrived, he was smiling slightly. I had just passed my first test: proving that I really did want to work in his establishment. He took me to a small room off the main pastry kitchen and showed me the machines used for melting chocolate, together with the fillings for the Opern Konditorei's homemade chocolates—the sweet centers waiting to be covered with their chocolate coating. My first task. This was a great stroke of luck—I had learned the very same technique with the Maurivards. The big, fat chef left me to get on with the job for several hours, came back to inspect the results and gave me a hearty slap on the back while telling me all manner of things, none of which I understood. Finally, he took a piece of paper and wrote "6 a.m." This, I understood, was the time at which I was to start work on Monday. After that I was free for the rest of the day. Apparently, my work had proved satisfactory.

On Monday, I was flung in at the deep end. There were more than twenty pastry cooks working at the Opern Konditorei. For the first time since the end of my apprenticeship, I felt that I had found what I was looking for, a place where I could learn a great deal. For the first time, too, seeing the superb quality of the Opern Konditorei's pastries and the many skills I could learn there, I felt that I stood a chance of making a real name for myself as a pastry cook.

After three weeks, I found a place to stay and was able to vacate the room I had been occupying with the Hockers, my friends, who had kindly put me up and looked after me for so long. Friends whose kindness and generosity I have never forgotten.

My new lodging, in the suburbs of Hanover, was a room in the house of a charming elderly couple who ran a small grocery store. They were delightful people who often invited me to eat with them, an offer I always refused for fear of bothering them and not wanting to seem to be taking advantage of their generosity. My room was warm and pleasant, and I was allowed to use the kitchen as well as the bathroom. Nonetheless, food remained a problem. My salary covered my rent and my journeys to and from work by monorail, but this left me with the equivalent of just one dollar per day for dinner (lunch was provided at the patisserie, in the form of a singularly unappetizing soup made with the leftovers from a nearby restaurant). The cheapest evening meal cost at least two dollars, which I didn't have. I had one or two tricks up my sleeve: I would take an apple from the patisserie when I left work; on the way to the station, I would stop in a sort of coffee shop, which housed an array of slot machines. I played a tiny amount of cash and, if I won, I could eat something—a potato salad, or on a really lucky day, a sausage or two, even a glass of beer. More often than not, however, I lost and was left to munch my apple.

I had so little money that I was unable to buy clothes and was forced to hang onto the ones I had, which were thoroughly worn and threadbare. My only shoes were a pair of wooden clogs, which I wore without socks, winter or summer. And heaven knows, the winters were cold in northern

Germany. It was snow and ice, ice and snow. Sometimes—for entertainment—I would visit other patisseries. There were a great many in Hanover, and several of them were quite splendid. I took notes, made sketches, and copied these out neatly when I got home. I filled dozens of notebooks with useful information, which I have used throughout my career.

The pastry chef, Herr Heising, managed his team with an iron fist. One day, an apprentice made a stupid mistake. His meringues failed to rise and when I asked him why, he replied that "he" (meaning Herr Heising) had told him to do it that way. Herr Heising overheard, sought out the unfortunate apprentice and boomed: "Who is this 'he'? Here, it's 'Chef' or 'Herr Heising.'"

And he slapped the boy with his huge hand. The young apprentice never referred to his boss as "him" or "he" again.

Herr Heising's chief problem was the liter of rum he drank every day. This tended to make the latter part of the day rather difficult, which was a great shame, because he was a good pâtissier. At the time, he was considered to be one of the finest pastry chefs in Germany and had written a number of books, which he presented to me as gifts. He was married with two children, but spent almost no time with his family. He was wedded to the rum. Like so many pastry chefs at that time, drink was his only leisure. To the extent that we sometimes found him asleep in his office chair in the morning.

Herr Heising took a great liking to me, despite his tough exterior. Perhaps this was because I tried so hard to learn German. As the only foreigner working at the patisserie, I quickly realized that if I wanted to understand the job, I would have to learn to speak Herr Heising's language as soon as possible. I understood, too, that my fate was in his hands. It was essential that I worked to his satisfaction. I rose to the challenge. Herr Heising kept me back in the evenings after work, and taught me skills that he did not reveal to the others. He also saw that I was always hungry and would sometimes sneak a chicken leg or a cutlet from the kitchen and place it under a plate on my worktop, so that the others wouldn't see.

All in all, I was very lucky. My colleagues at the patisserie were kind and friendly—they appreciated my efforts to learn their language as quickly as I could. After three months, I even felt confident enough to answer the telephone. Sometimes, they invited me to come and drink with them after work, whenever they could afford to pay for me, because I had warned them that I was unable to pay for myself.

~

Christmas 1962, and there was no disguising my loneliness, until a friend invited me to come and stay with his parents in Kassel, south of Hanover in the province of Hessen, two hours away by train. The young German, who worked in the kitchens at the Opern Konditorei, had spent holidays in France and spoke a little French, which was rare in northern Germany. Thanks to him, I was happy to visit a new town and see new sights. I discovered a charming family. My friend and his parents all brought me breakfast in bed on Christmas morning. I was speechless: no one had ever done anything of the kind for me before. We spent three very happy days together, ate hearty meals, and visited the sights.

I returned to work at the patisserie before the end of the year. Everyone was working double time to prepare for the New Year festivities. All the pastry chefs wanted a day off on January 1, which is an important holiday in Germany when everyone celebrates, eats, and drinks a great deal. The patisseries were filled to bursting with the national specialty, the marzipan figurines that I had heard so much about. The windows looked more like toy shops, with superb figures, each more impressive than the last. But there was a problem. No one wanted to work on the night of December 31, but on January 1 it was customary for everyone to buy so-called *Berliner Kugeln* (Berlin balls) fried in oil, to bring good luck for the coming year. The Opern Konditorei sold around 10,000 *Berliner Kugeln* and pastries on January 1 alone. On the night of December 31, there were still 1,500 *kugeln* to be made. I have always relished a challenge and, as no one else wanted to give up their evening, I offered to make the *kugeln* on my own, together with some other pastries. I began at around 3 p.m. and next morning at 8 a.m. the 1,500 *kugeln* were ready. I was doubly happy: I had given my coworkers their much sought-after night off, and I had proved to everyone, including myself, exactly what I was capable of.

~

But life is never all glory. My time in Hanover was marked, too, by an unforgivable blunder. My rented room was near the family home of Paul Gauweiler, my German friend in Paris. Occasionally, I would visit his mother and brother. One day, they told me that Paul would be coming home on holiday soon and that he would be bringing his girlfriend with him, a girl I knew very well. She worked at the Régence, too, and had a solid reputation as a seductress and man-eater. Paul, on the other hand, was a man of impeccable integrity, and a talented pâtissier, greatly respected at the Régence and widely reproached for going out with the girl in question. Young and foolish as I was, I blabbed the gossip to Paul's family. A few days later, having completely forgotten what I had said, I visited the family and was greeted at the door by Paul's mother, his brother, and Paul himself. I had barely said "hello" when the girlfriend whose reputation I had slandered appeared from nowhere in a fine fury and administered two ringing slaps to my face. I was horrified at being humiliated in front of everyone, with no explanation as to why. I burst into tears on the spot. Paul took me back to my place, and we discussed the matter. The girl shouldn't have hit me, but I shouldn't have gossiped about her to Paul's family either. We said goodbye and didn't speak again until he telephoned me at home in Virginia, forty years later, on November 2, 2004. When I heard his voice, there were tears in my eyes again. He explained that he had had a great deal of difficulty tracking me down after the attacks on September 11, 2001 because the subsequent Anthrax mail scandal caused disruptions

to the delivery of staff mail in the White House. He runs a small patisserie on the outskirts of Los Angeles. And perhaps I'll go and see him
there one day.

~

On the way to the monorail station there was a fine restaurant with a
basement dining room. The windows at street level displayed a superb
array of pâtés, sausages, and hams. Every time I saw them, I told myself
that one day, when I had a little money, I would go into the restaurant,
and order myself one of their platters of cold cuts.

On one of my days off, when I had a little money saved up, this was
the very first thing I did. The restaurant was a typically German establishment: the waiters wore traditional outfits, the beer flowed freely,
and there was a friendly, jolly atmosphere. The head waiter looked me
up and down as I approached. I looked nothing like his usual clientele,
with my bare feet in wooden clogs and my shabby, uninspiring clothes.
All the same, he showed me in and sat me in a little room all to myself,
as if he thought I might have the plague. I ordered my food, washed
down with a pot of beer. I still remember the flavor of the sausages and
salt pork, which the Germans prepare with such skill. I was so eager
to eat something really good and so hungry that I devoured everything
on the platter, down to the last salad leaf. As I ate, the head waiter
stopped at my table every now and then, nodding with approval as I
wolfed down the sausages and ham. He probably thought I had just
been released from prison.

~

One of the great local specialties in Hanover is the *baumkuchen*, which
literally means "tree cake." This is a batter cake cooked on a spit: properly prepared, the resulting delicacy can stand up to three and a half feet
high and weigh around sixty-five pounds. The cake forms the center-

piece for weddings, christenings, birthdays, and other festive occasions. I wanted to learn how to make one. Herr Heising offered to teach me one Sunday when we had the kitchen to ourselves. My first attempt was unsuccessful. Towards the end of the cooking process, the entire piece fell off the spit. About 150 eggs—and goodness know how many pounds of butter—were lost, broken, strewn all over the floor. Herr Heiser said: "Never mind, we'll come back next Sunday and try again." We did, and this time the *baumkuchen* was a magnificent success.

~

After a year in Hanover, I asked my boss if he knew of any other towns where I could work and learn more about German cakes and pastries. Herr Heising had a friend in Hamburg, by the name of Kranke, and one Sunday morning, we went to see him. The Kranke Konditorei was a family affair, like so many patisseries in France. The father, mother, and two sons all worked in the business, which consisted of two shops, one in the center of Hamburg and one on the outskirts. The Kranke family was well-known for its marzipan figures, and one of the sons was an expert in this, as well as in chocolate-making. They hired me straightaway and after working my two weeks' notice in Hanover, I arrived in Hamburg. It was 1963. I had a job as an assistant pastry chef and a salary of 170 marks per week. I was significantly better off, which delighted me no end. I could work overtime on Sundays, which brought in another 30 marks, and best of all I lived on the premises with my employers.

Late at night, after work, I would stay on in the pastry kitchen, alone, to practice the art of blown and pulled sugar. A quantity of sugar is cooked in a pan with water, glucose, and lemon juice until it melts to form a thin caramel. This is poured out onto an oiled marble worktop, and left to cool until it turns slightly opaque, a process known in French as *satinage*. With the addition of food coloring, it is possible to obtain a host of different colors and shades. Working with sugar in this way is probably the most difficult pastry skill of all, but it produces the most beautiful results. Sugar is a vibrant, living substance, and with it you can recreate almost anything that exists in nature. I was totally fascinated by this, and I worked at it again and again. But after months of practice, the only thing I was able to produce, after endless hours of work, was a sugar vase containing a single rose.

After a few months, I found myself a room near the Hamburg fish market, where I lodged with a mother, her divorced daughter—an attractive woman of about forty—and the latter's son, aged about seventeen. I was allowed to use the kitchen and the family bathroom, and found my hosts to be charming and kind. The daughter was particularly attentive. I would go so far as to say that on a few occasions, she even tried to seduce me. When she invited me to a restaurant, she evidently hoped that we would sit a little closer together. And when we were walking along a street, she would take my arm, as if we were a real couple. These familiarities made me uncomfortable. To a young man of twenty, a woman of forty can seem old.

One day, I discovered that someone had been searching through my things. The money I had saved for a trip home to France to see my family, part of which I had hoped to give them if it was needed, was gone. I went to see the mother of the family, to explain what had happened. Naturally enough, she refused to believe me. I knew, however, that the boy was smoking heavily and often went out without his mother knowing. He had probably stolen the money. The family wouldn't hear of it and asked me to leave. When I told Frau Kranke about it, she suggested that I come back to stay at the patisserie in the meantime.

During the course of that year, I lived better than I had ever done before. I had quite a few friends and was able to go out in the evenings—at long last, I was finishing work no later than 8 p.m. In short, I was a contented young man.

But I had to continue my professional training. I had met a teacher at the patisserie college in Hamburg, and asked him to find me a place in London. One day, he invited me to lunch at his house and showed me a letter he had received from England. The letter stated that a patisserie in Soho would be happy to take me on and that I could start as soon as I liked. Once again, I was off to another country, leaving my friends behind, starting from scratch.

CHAPTER 4

At the Savoy

I stepped off the boat at Folkestone at about 8 a.m. on March 7, 1964, speaking not a word of English. It was then that a strange incident occurred, which I have never been able to explain. As soon as I presented myself to the immigration officials, with my little *carton bouilli* suitcase and my entry papers for the United Kingdom, a woman intervened and ordered me into a freezing room with walls painted a horrible shade of green. There, she told me to strip naked. I obeyed. I was in a foreign country, I couldn't speak English. I was scared of these people, scared of everything.

I undressed and sat on a bench. The woman went out, leaving me alone and shaking with cold. Nothing happened. I sat waiting for almost an hour. Then the woman came back and without a word of explanation indicated that I should put my clothes back on and pass through customs, where my papers had been inspected and my suitcase opened. I passed the frontier with no idea at all of why I had been detained.

~

I took the train to London, got into a taxi and arrived at the patisserie from which I had received the letter confirming my new job. I spotted a small hotel and booked a room beforehand, then presented myself at the shop, where I asked to see the woman in charge. I proffered the letter to a cold-looking lady who took it, and denied ever having made such an offer, even though it was there in front of her in black and white. Was I too late? Perhaps the post had been filled in the meantime? Perhaps the woman was put off by my age or my appearance? Perhaps she was simply not a woman of her word? It was hard to tell, particularly when neither of us spoke the other's language.

And so I found myself on a London street, knowing no one, and without a word of English. I thought for a while and remembered what Monsieur Maurivard had told me about the Savoy, the finest hotel in the world. The Savoy employed a host of pastry chefs, a professional elite who could work wherever they chose after this.

All things considered, and in spite of my very uninspiring appearance, I decided to take a taxi to the Savoy. The doorman, who was decked out in gleaming buttons and braid like an admiral, gave me a frosty stare. I didn't dare approach him. What to do? I studied the menus displayed outside the hotel and walked slowly up and down Savoy Court, the little side street off the Strand that leads up to the main entrance—the only thoroughfare in London where traffic must drive on the right. A new doorman relieved the admiral at the end of his tour of duty. He was every bit as decorated his predecessor, but younger and friendlier-looking. I attempted to explain what I wanted, with a great deal of mime and gesturing. I pointed to the menu, drew an imaginary chef's toque in the air above my head, play-acted a chef slaving over his hot oven. The Savoy turned out to have two restaurants. The smartest, the Grill, had an à la carte menu. The other dining room catered mainly for functions and produced quantities of pastries.

Eventually, I managed to see the head chef of the Grill, an Italian by the memorable name of Silvano Trompetto who—what a stroke of luck—spoke perfect French. He took me straight to his office.

"My boy," he asked. "What can I do for you?"

I told him that my sole ambition was to work as a pastry cook, and that I would be overjoyed to work at the Savoy. I showed him my folder, which contained the fateful letter from the woman at the Soho patisserie, together with letters of recommendation from all of my former employers: Messrs Maurivard and Beligat in Besançon, the Régence in Paris, the Opern Konditorei in Hanover, and the Krankes in Hamburg.

It was an impressive set of credentials. Trompetto picked up the telephone and called the Savoy's personnel department. I understood nothing of what he said, apart from something about a "super, super certificate," which made my heart beat a little faster.

After a few minutes' conversation, Trompetto hung up and said: "I will give you a job as a pastry cook on my staff. But there's a problem. You won't be able to get a visa to work in England straightaway. There are a certain number of formalities to complete. Go back to France. We'll send the papers to your family address, and you'll be back here in five or six weeks."

I left, as happy as if I'd won the lottery. The Savoy was a legendary establishment, often referred to with awe by all of my employers during my time as an apprentice. And I was going to work there! I broke into a run and literally jumped for joy in the street. My life had taken a decisive turn.

~

When I arrived in the courtyard of the retirement home to which my parents had moved after leaving their little SNCF house, my mother couldn't believe her eyes. She was overjoyed to see her prodigal son returning home, and the entire family came to greet me, celebrate my success, and hear about everything that had happened since I had left home. There were new arrivals, too: brothers- and sisters-in-law who had joined the family since my departure, and little nephews and nieces. Not forgetting our neighbors in the village, because news travels fast.

The local mayor got to hear of my return, too, which was less welcome news. I should have completed my military service by now; my call-up papers had been sent out, but I had ignored them, since I was working abroad. There was no way out of it, and I spent three days at the barracks in Mâcon, before joining the 35th Motorized Infantry Regiment in Belfort.

I informed the Savoy about this complication, and asked if they would mind keeping the job for me until the end of my military service, convinced that they would not. In response, Trompetto sent me a kind letter stating that this was no problem at all; I simply had to notify them two months before my demobilization. To say I was pleased would be a gross understatement.

The reality of military service in Belfort quickly dampened my spirits, however.

~

There is little point in dwelling on this period. I made some good friends and got on with soldiering to the best of my ability, not wishing to appear lazy or unequal to the task.

CHAPTER 5

The Sugar Palace

My military service was coming to an end, and I contacted the Savoy in London once again, as arranged. I left the barracks on December 21, 1964. I was in London by January 1, 1965, and started work on January 2 or 3. The hierarchy at the Grill had changed in the meantime. Signor Trompetto had been promoted to the post of executive chef in the hotel's other dining room and the Grill was now run by a new chef, Louis Virot.

The pastry kitchen at the Savoy Grill employed seventeen chefs. The head pâtissier was an Englishman by the name of Brian Clark. Our workspace was tiny, but we worked three eight-hour shifts in a full twenty-four-hour day, so that there were never more than five or six chefs on duty at any one time. From the outset, I was fascinated by the perfect, clockwork organization of the place and its cosmopolitan atmosphere (which applied to the staff just as much as to the clientele). The waiters, cooks, pâtissiers, and bellboys came from all over the world: Swiss, Germans, Chinese, Japanese, and a great many French, too. Not to mention the dishwashers from Pakistan. Ho Chi Ming had once worked as a pastry cook in the very same kitchen at the Savoy Grill. The mix of languages, cultures, and colors was extraordinary. I knew right away that the Savoy would be the launch pad for my ambitions and dreams, although I was still far from thinking about the White House.

Meanwhile, I was getting used to my new life. Never before had I seen such elaborate discipline, such refined food, such accomplished service. I was earning nine pounds a week, which was next to nothing, but at least we were fed. The meals were plain, but things improved when our French colleagues were on duty and took the trouble to send over a rich, savory stew for us. There were plenty of Frenchmen on the staff at the Savoy, and in the pastry kitchen, which was a great advantage for me in this strange new country. It was also a disadvantage when it came to learning English, since we always spoke together in French. I signed up for English classes at the Alliance Française, but made slow progress, giving into the temptation to speak French with my colleagues every day at work.

~

After lodging for a time with a family in the London suburbs, I moved into a small shared apartment with two French friends from the Savoy, Michel and Jean-Marc. We didn't spend a great of time "at home"—the apartment was in the basement, like so many apartments in London, and consisted of two bedrooms, one of which was also the living room. There was no TV, just a small radio. The heating worked on a coin-fed meter and since we had scarcely any money, we were forced to go without and took the precaution of closing off one room when the temperatures became truly arctic.

Happily, we had girlfriends: French au pairs with whom, of course, we spoke French. Best of all, our English boss Brian Clark spoke impeccable French, which was thus the lingua franca in the Savoy Grill's pastry kitchen, too.

~

The Savoy was not only the finest grand hotel in the world. It was also a magnet for the wealthiest and most famous guests on the planet. Every evening, the dining room glittered with just as many dignitaries as later graced the White House. In the mid-1960s, these included the Kennedys, Onassis and his girlfriend of the time, Maria Callas, Elizabeth Taylor, Fred Astaire, Gary Cooper, and a whole supporting cast of stars, often from Hollywood. Not forgetting Charlie Chaplin, who rented an apartment at the hotel all year round with his family; I was often asked to prepare his favorite dessert (bananas with raspberry cream), taking extraordinary pains, as you can imagine. Later, I often served this striking combination of flavors to guests at the White House to great acclaim. Some stars were, of course, notable for their eccentricities. One day, a celebrated, beautiful, ultrafeminine lady arrived at the Savoy Grill wearing a white transparent minidress with nothing underneath. The head waiter suggested, with enormous tact, that she might like to come back with a few more clothes on. I wonder if he would dare say the same thing today.

The hotel was also frequented by billionaires such as Calouste Gulbenkian. An Armenian-born businessman, he was a noted collector of paintings and objets d'art, and a passionate lover of petits fours. Gulbenkian would often entertain ten or fifteen business associates at lunch at the Savoy; each time, the climax of the meal was an immense platter of petits fours decorated with a beautiful pulled-sugar centerpiece, chocolates, and most important of all, an array of ultra-thin *tuile* cookies. When the platter arrived, Gulbenkian would take one of the *tuiles* and drop it onto the table. If it failed to break, he would send the entire platter back to the kitchens. His visits made me sweat with anxiety. To make matters worse, every table at the Savoy was laid with a soft, protective covering underneath the tablecloth; so that the *tuiles* would only break if they were as light and fragile as a snowflake.

Another guest, a French lady, insisted on brioches being delivered to her room every morning at 6 a.m. The duty pâtissier would have to get up in the middle of the night to have everything ready on time, and the lady in question would then take her brioches to church to have them blessed before eating them for breakfast.

I was amazed to see that all the food served to the guests, including the pastries, was presented on silver platters; hot dishes were covered with a silver cloche to keep them that way. Never before in my career had I seen such refinement—it was beyond my wildest imaginings. I had no idea that such splendors existed. And this was just one of the many signs of opulence at the Savoy in the mid-1960s. Today, if one guest asks for roast chicken, he or she will be presented with the cut of their choice, on a plate, with a selection of two or three vegetables: would Sir or Madam prefer the breast, wing, or thigh? Back then, however, the whole roast bird was escorted to the table, with its sauce, vegetables, and a basket of soufflé potatoes garnished with watercress. The guest was served in fine style by the head waiter himself, who was—needless to say—a skilled carver. The chicken, or what was left of it, remained under its silver cloche on the serving table nearby until the guest had finished his plate, when the head waiter would offer him a second helping, carved with the same ceremony and elegance. Whatever was left at the end of the meal went into the hotel larder, to be used cold in salads.

And the Peach Melba! This essentially simple dessert was the object of infinite care and attention. First, a fine ripe peach was selected from the storeroom, peeled, and lightly poached in syrup. The trick was to extract the pit without breaking the fruit, which was then placed in a glass bowl inside a second bowl, of silver, decorated with ivy leaves. This was only the beginning. The space between the two bowls was filled with crushed ice; three scoops of fresh vanilla ice cream were placed in a third bowl with whipped cream, and in a fourth bowl, the Melba sauce (a purée of wild strawberries, raspberries, and redcurrants). Finally, a fifth bowl of plain glass was filled with toasted, sliced almonds. The whole splendid platter was then transported to the table, after which the bowl of ice cream was placed before the lucky diner. The peach was carefully removed from its bowl and placed on top of the ice cream. Next, the Melba sauce and almonds were served as desired by the guest. A time-honored ritual, bordering on the sacred.

It was extraordinary to see that the head waiters in those bygone days were just as skilled in the culinary arts as the chefs themselves. It was the waiters who carved and flambéed dishes at the table; often, they even prepared the sauces right there on the spot, and all without dipping so much as a finger in the brew.

Guests at the Savoy were well versed in the great classics of fine cuisine and patisserie. They didn't come to eat heartily, but to appreciate gourmet food. Often, they became experts or at the very least knowledgeable connoisseurs of the protocol and finer points of service. The Savoy's house rule, the bedrock of its reputation, was never to refuse anything a client saw fit to request, regardless of what was on the menu, in either the Grill or the restaurant, at any time of the day or night.

~

Brian Clark, the head pastry chef, was a great artist but paradoxically not a great innovator. He knew comparatively little about the preparation of creamy, smooth, sumptuous, richly flavored desserts, preferring to concentrate on the aesthetic aspects of patisserie. He made the finest pulled-sugar sculptures I have ever seen, from sugar of exceptional quality.

One year, he created an Indian-style head for an exhibition at the Olympia in London, entirely in blown sugar. This is a technique that makes no use of molds. The sugar is blown and shaped on the end of thin, straw-like tube held in the mouth, like a master glassblower. The result was simply extraordinary: the eyebrows, lips, and eyes were all astonishingly lifelike, right down to the pupils. There was a turban and jewelry. Thinking about this remarkable piece, I feel the same admiration now as I did then. The other pieces in the exhibition were just as impressive, and I found myself wondering if I would be capable of such wonders myself, one day.

Naturally, Brian Clark encouraged me to continue experimenting with sugar sculpture as I had done in Hamburg. My working day finished at midnight, after which I would stay on in the pastry kitchen, alone, to cook the sugar and practice shaping it. I showed my creations to Brian the following morning, when he would inspect them and suggest improvements. After a few months, I was producing compositions good enough to be seen by the guests. Every day, the hotel made around fifty such pieces to decorate the platters of petits fours, chocolates (made on the premises), and miniature pastries. My newfound skills were put to good use, and sugar sculpture became my personal specialty. We made parrots, swans, peacocks, baskets of roses, and sugar fruit. The compositions often had to be repaired: guests could never resist breaking off a leaf or a petal to taste.

~

During those years, my devotion to the art of sugar sculpture meant that I arrived at the Savoy early every morning and left very late at night. All of which led to a dreadful incident, the memory of which still fills me with horror today. I left the Savoy at about 4:30 a.m. and was waiting for the first of my two bus rides home. It was raining, and I didn't have an umbrella (a fatal error in London). I crossed the little park at the back of the hotel and waited at the bus stop on the Embankment, beside the Thames. The rain fell harder and harder, and I spotted a public toilet with a covered entrance that would provide some shelter. I decided to wait under the shelter for the bus, which was approaching in the distance. Suddenly, two men appeared from nowhere, wearing long coats, and demanded to know what I was doing. I told them that I was waiting for my bus, that I was returning home from work. They shouted that they didn't believe me, grabbed hold of me, dragged me into the toilets, and slammed me against a wall, asking again and again what I was doing there, although I had already told them. I said that if they came with me to the hotel, I could show them the card I used to clock on and off, proving that I had indeed just finished work. They refused to listen, doubtless convinced that I was involved in sex trafficking of some sort or drugs. Finally, they rammed my head into the wall several times and left. I was in deep shock, completely horrified. When I finally got back to my room, I found it impossible to sleep. How could such a thing happen to me, who worked so hard, and was involved in nothing outside my professional life?

The following morning, I went to see the head chef and told him about the incident. "What can we do about it, son?" he said. "We don't know anything about the two men, who they are, or where to find them. There's nothing to be done." I was deeply affronted. I felt the outrage of an innocent man falsely accused of some terrible atrocity. To be manhandled with such violence left me with a sense of shame that still upsets me today. I have never found a satisfactory explanation for it or discovered who the two men were. The incident has remained with me, like a dark stain.

Happily, my nocturnal working life had its compensations, too. Late at night, I was lucky enough to sample the celebrated Savoy omelette named in honor of the English novelist Arnold Bennett, a lightly cooked concoction of a dozen eggs and herbs, cut lengthwise to a depth of about two inches, and stuffed with crab and lobster in hollandaise sauce. The top was sprinkled with caviar, and the whole thing washed down with a glass of champagne or two.

~

As time went on, my fascination for sugar sculpture, and the resulting decorations, came to the attention of the pastry chef at the Savoy. He suggested that I take part in a small competition to be held in the seaside resort of Torquay in the southwest of England. The piece had to be transported by train. I had to remain on duty in London, and Brian Clark offered to take my creation—a basket of fruit made entirely of blown and pulled sugar—with him to the event. I won a bronze medal at my very first professional competition. I was overjoyed. A few months later, Brian Clark allowed me to come with him to an exhibition in Cambridge. This time, I produced a far more elaborate, refined piece: a basket with several tiers, in a whole range of shades, full of sugar flowers and decorated with ribbons. Result: a silver medal. My confidence was redoubled. I worked hard to try and win more prizes. Brian Clark had given me a terrific boost by encouraging me to enter the competitions and offering his invaluable advice. Thanks to him, I felt a special excitement that I had never experienced before.

One day, I created a magnificent swan in white sugar with unfurled wings. An apprentice chef came to see me in the kitchens, saw the bird and exclaimed how beautiful it was, banging his fist on the table for emphasis. The table wobbled, the swan bounced very slightly, fell, and broke into hundreds of pieces. I froze. Hours of painstaking labor had gone into the piece, which had been reduced to smithereens in an instant. I held my tongue, fearing to say something I might regret, and went back to work.

~

Our working relationships were not always rosy. The Savoy pastry kitchen employed an Italian chef called Marcello, who was much older than me and very proud of the gold medal he had won at the exhibition at the Olympia. The rest of the staff was proud of it, too, and it had gone to his head. He was, in any event, a man who had a very high opinion of himself, disliked hard work, and was content to rest on his laurels. He demanded a show of respect from young men such as myself—and we were happy to provide it. When Brian Clark was absent, Marcello always treated me badly, criticized my work, and took every opportunity to make hurtful comments. About six months after my arrival at the Savoy, I found myself on duty with him one evening. It was summer, and things were relatively quiet. Marcello had opted to station himself at the front of the kitchen, passing orders out to the waiters as they called for them: desserts garnished with fruit, pre-prepared platters of petits fours, and decorative sugar baskets to place on the platters. I was busy making chocolates and petits fours for the next day. Marcello settled in a corner and buried himself in a pile of Italian magazines he had brought with him to work. When the waiters arrived asking for this or that, Marcello didn't move a muscle. It was up to me to interrupt my own work and serve them. Once, twice, three times. On the fourth occasion, I exploded. Had Marcello come to work or to put his feet up and get some rest? By way of a reply, he took his handful of magazines and threw them in my face.

I was furious, and went straight to the sous-chef, who was in charge of the kitchen that night, while the executive chef was away. I said I was going straight home. There was no way I could continue working at the Savoy under such conditions. I would come back in the morning to fetch my utensils, and hand in my resignation. The following morning, someone had already spoken to the executive chef before my arrival. I informed him that I was handing in my notice: "Coming to the Savoy was a big mistake. I can't work in such conditions, I'm leaving." The chef simply said, "Go and get changed and get on with your work. Don't worry about a thing."

We never saw Marcello again. He disappeared. Sank without a trace. Vanished into thin air. The chef had fired him on the spot. When he showed up in the afternoon for his shift, his time card had been taken out of its slot next to the time clock. He had to ask someone else to fetch his utensils, because no one would let him enter the hotel premises.

The chef had taken an on-the-spot decision to fire a man who had worked at the Savoy for seven or eight years, and to keep me, a virtual beginner. This made me proud and gave me added confidence. But I also needed to prove that I was worthy of his choice. Nonetheless, I felt uneasy that someone, even someone as disagreeable as Marcello, had lost their job because of me. All I wanted was to work in peace.

Happily, I made some good friends at the Savoy, too. One of these was Jean Laffont, the fish chef, a first-class worker with a prickly temperament. The other chefs found him difficult to get along with, but not me. I took a liking to this human cactus, and he to me. One day, I arrived too late for lunch and faced the prospect of working my entire shift on an empty stomach. Jean came to find me in the pastry kitchen and asked if I was hungry. Of course I was hungry! He brought me a plate of scampi, which he prepared just for me. It was simply superb. I still thank him for it today. I saw him quite recently. We have kept in touch over the years.

He works in Dallas. The last time we met, he brought along a photograph of the kitchen staff from the Savoy, taken when we were both still working there. We were astonished, greatly amused, and not a little melancholy to see how we used to look back then.

The man who taught me how to run a busy kitchen and marshal a team of chefs was Louis Virot, the head chef at the Savoy Grill, who had taken over from Signor Trompetto, the man who hired me. Virot had a staff of eighty or so under his command, including cooks, pastry chefs, and dishwashers. He managed them all with magisterial authority. If someone needed putting in their place, he would handle the task with extraordinary tact and dexterity. Boys who had failed to carry out their appointed tasks were picked up by their trouser belts and given a thorough two-minute tongue lashing. After which, it was back to work with a smile.

Answering directly to the chef were four sous-chefs, responsible for inspecting the plates and platters before they left the kitchen. And each separate section of the kitchen had its own head chef: the fish chef, the vegetable chef, the soup chef, the sauce chef (with a complete staff all his own), the *rôtisserie* chef (in charge of the roasts), and the grill chef. There was also a chef in charge of the storeroom, a *chef cafetier* in charge of the coffee, and a chief buyer, whose job it was to ensure that the storeroom were kept stocked with the finest quality produce and supplies. Not forgetting, of course, the head pastry chef and the *aboyeur* (barker), whose job it was to call the orders on the slips torn off the waiters' notepads into a microphone. The slips were then stamped to record the time at which they entered the kitchen, which in turn enabled us to check the time taken to prepare the orders before they were served.

This quasi-military hierarchy was under the command of the executive chef—an all-powerful figure akin to a chief of staff (it is surely no accident that the word "staff" applies to both hotel kitchens and the armed forces), beneath whom were the "colonels" and "captains" and a host of young assistant chefs and apprentices, the foot soldiers of the culinary army. The executive chef was responsible for the menus, which changed daily at every meal, ambitious menus featuring thirty different vegetables, as many different meat and fish dishes, not forgetting the soups and desserts. The executive chef prepared the shopping list of provisions each morning, with the help of two secretaries, who were in charge of keeping the accounts. Every evening, before service began for dinner, he would make an inspection tour of the kitchen, tasting every sauce and anything that had been prepared in advance, and checking his staff's uniforms. Anyone with a stained jacket or unpolished shoes was sent back to the changing rooms and would only be readmitted to the kitchen once they were spotlessly clean. Failure to comply meant you were sent home and lost a day's wages. Military discipline indeed!

In a great establishment like the Savoy, every meal service resembled a military campaign, to be won at all costs or risk the reputation of the hotel. Our enemies were not, of course, the guests, but negligence, clumsiness, and lack of organization. And time! Time that had to be conquered in order to serve every dish promptly and to perfection. I never tired of watching as the kitchen prepared for combat. In the evening, before the first desserts and pastries were ordered and served, I would take a few minutes to step out of the pastry kitchen and watch the other chefs at work. Almost all of the diners would arrive at the same time for the evening sitting, and as soon as the proverbial starting gun was fired, the cooks launched into a frenzy of activity, scurrying left and right, calling in loud voices to tell everyone else what they needed, what they were doing, what they were sending out. Meanwhile, flames could be seen emerging from the ovens and stove tops. Everyone was busy, tossing ingredients in a heavy pan or reducing a sauce. There were the massive silver platters, too, with their superb decorations. And the hustle and bustle of the waiters, carrying heavy dishes on outstretched arms, from the kitchens to the dining room on the floor above. Once upstairs, the mood shifted from military campaign to theatrical performance. A culinary ballet.

Often, the Savoy Grill would serve 400–450 covers in the evening and 150–200 covers at lunchtime. About 600 meals every day! The Savoy opened its doors on August 6, 1889, under the directorship of its founder, Richard d'Oyly Carte. The hotel's front entrance, in Savoy Court, is located just off the Strand while at the back quiet, leafy gardens extend towards the Embankment and the River Thames. In 1889 the hotel occupied a brand new, state-of-the-art building, equipped with sixty-seven bathtubs (one for every two rooms), a revolution in its day. The Savoy was able to generate its own electricity and had its own water supply. During the Second World War, the Savoy operated a policy of business and service as usual during the blackouts, attracting a faithful crowd of wealthy clients, who were delighted and reassured to be able to pursue their luxurious lifestyles—to some extent at least—in such apocalyptic times.

Sometime after opening his establishment, Richard d'Oyly Carte recruited a new director, a man who went on to become a legend in the hotel world: César Ritz. Ritz himself hired another legend, the chef Georges-Auguste Escoffier, who went on to become the director of London's Carlton Hotel until his retirement in 1925. When I first arrived at the Savoy, we were still working in Escoffier's original kitchens. The equipment had been updated, of course, but the ovens were his, and the layout remained the same, with a very low ceiling and no air conditioning, so that in summer the workspace was a veritable furnace, a Sahara, a Gobi Desert for the poor chefs who rushed to fetch a cool drink between dishes. Towards the end of my time at the hotel, a new ventilation system was being installed.

Escoffier was the inventor of the modern hotel kitchen and its organization. The departmental structure with its military hierarchy of chefs is his legacy. It was Escoffier, too, who devised the uniforms that allow each member of the squad to be identified by rank and role, starting with the hierarchy of chefs' toques, the tallest and biggest hat being reserved for the executive chef, after which they decrease in height and volume, from sous-chef to section head, first *commis*, *commis*, and apprentice. As in the army, it's impossible to confuse an officer in the kitchen with a private.

And so the Savoy's distinguished history dates from the very beginnings of modern catering and cuisine, all of which adds to its extraordinary charm and unrivaled professionalism, both in the kitchen and throughout the hotel. The Savoy is a temple to the very real art of fine hospitality.

Spring 1967, and I was beginning to feel the need to spread my wings a little. I began to make contacts. One of our au pair friends, a very pretty girl named Michelle who went on to become a flight attendant, was the daughter of a hotelier with a chain of establishments in the Ivory Coast. She indicated that he might be able to offer me a job, and invited me to come and meet her parents, who received me with great kindness. I explained that I was looking for a post as a head pastry chef, and that I was enthusiastic about the prospect of working in Africa.

After this, I returned home to visit my parents, a holiday I will always remember as a last breath of adolescence, with all the craziness that that implies. Naturally, I paid a visit to the Maurivards in Besançon.

On my return to London, I received a letter from a certain Edmond Gurret, the executive chef at a hotel in Bermuda, the Princess. He was looking for a pastry chef, and Michelle's father had mentioned me.

I had no idea where Bermuda was, so I asked around, but no one else was too sure, either. When I finally discovered the tiny dot on the map, in the North Atlantic, I was very excited. I answered Monsieur Gurret's letter straight away, with my certificates and letters of recommendation, and indicated that I was very, very interested in the job. A few weeks later, I received a reply. I was too young to be hired as a head pastry chef, but he was happy to offer me the post of sous-chef.

With all the folly and temerity of youth, I replied that I was not interested in the post of sous-chef, since this was my current rank at the Savoy. I posted the letter and told everyone that I had just lost the chance of a job in Bermuda. But I was wrong. A few weeks later, I received another letter, informing me that the hotel was prepared to take me on as head pastry chef, provided I served a trial period of several months after which, if I failed to meet the requirements of the post, I would have to agree to be downgraded to the rank of sous-chef, or leave the hotel. The conditions were stringent, but I decide to take the challenge.

Towards the end of my time in London, I found myself living alone in the flat I had shared with my friends Jean-Marc and Michel. Both had returned to France, and the rooms that had once been so full of life, and the laughter of young girls, now rang very hollow. I was waiting for my passport to Bermuda. My time in London was up. One of our friends, Valérie, and I decided to celebrate by going out to a restaurant: a rather melancholy outing, since we were saying goodbye, after so many good times together.

Returning home from the Savoy that evening, I was delighted to see Valérie standing on the sidewalk outside my flat. But the poor girl was in tears. I took her inside. What had happened? She told me that the owner of the flat had come and insulted her, hit her, and told her that she had no business here any more.

I was horrified. Valérie had done nothing wrong. She had simply been waiting for me in my flat, which our landlady had no right to enter, and certainly not in order to insult and attack one of my friends. I went to find the wretched woman, who threatened to throw me out at the same time, just a few weeks before I was due to leave London, with no possibility of finding another flat for such a short time. Disaster! Not to mention the fact that I had paid my rent until the end of the month, and there was precious little money left. Finally, after lengthy negotiations with my landlady, during which I swore not to receive a single visitor in my last weeks, she agreed to let me stay until I was due to leave.

Valérie and I went to the restaurant as planned, but our hearts weren't in it.

CHAPTER 6

An Island Paradise

And so I left the Savoy in London, and returned to France to say good-bye to my parents ahead of what promised to be a long trip. After that, back to London for the flight to Bermuda. Except that upon my arrival at the check-in desk, I discovered that no one is allowed to fly to Bermuda without a return ticket—a thoroughly British precaution designed to prevent legal difficulties on the island, which is a British Overseas Territory. If I committed any crimes or misdemeanors during my stay, I could be sent home at no cost to the authorities. I asked how I was supposed to obtain my return ticket, and was told that it should have been supplied by my employer at the Princess Hotel. I was in a difficult situation, with no idea how to obtain the return ticket in time to start my new job in Bermuda. I decided to go back to the Savoy and ask Brian Clark to lend me the money for the ticket. I would pay him back as soon as I received my first paycheck in Bermuda. He lent me the money—about thirty-five pounds sterling—and I dashed back to the airport, just in time to catch the flight.

This was my first time on a plane. In the late 1960s the flight attendants were all blessed with stunning, movie-star good looks. The seats were wider and more comfortable than they are today, with passengers now crammed in like sardines for economic reasons. The food was excellent, and so was the wine. Everyone was given free British Airways postcards, and I wrote one to a friend: "You can't imagine! I'm thousands of feet up in a plane. The sky is blue, the sun is shining. It's like paradise."

My first flight was an incredible experience for me, especially when the plane began its descent, toward the clear, deep blue waters of the Atlantic.

The Princess was a magnificent hotel in a perfect setting in the Bermudan capital, Hamilton: there were gardens, palm trees, fountains, and the seashore with yachts and fishing boats. There was a jetty for bigger ships including the *Franconia*, which pulled up every week with a cargo of tourists and a Bermudan steel band beating out its rhythms on oil drums. The fragrance of the flowers overwhelmed you as soon as you stepped ashore. Staff at the Princess, including the directors, all wore matching uniforms: a smart blue blazer and badge with a shirt, tie, and shorts for the men and dresses for the women. The hotel itself had a nickname, the Pink Palace.

I went to the reception desk and was given a room in the hotel. I had dinner in the dining room on the first night, and was introduced the following morning to my future colleagues: the director general, a Swiss man by the name of Bodo Von Alvensleben, his assistant Walter Sommer, and, of course, the executive chef Edmond Gurret. I was given lodgings in the building reserved for hotel staff. We slept two to a room, with a shared toilets and washbasins on the landing. It felt a little like returning to barracks. I was shown the pastry kitchen, which was brand new, like the hotel itself (it had been renovated and reopened two years earlier), and thoroughly well equipped. I met the head pastry chef whom I would be replacing. Monsieur Rosier was returning to France. He showed me around town, we talked and had lunch together, after which I was introduced to some of the pastry chefs on my staff. There were five pâtissiers and two bakers, who worked at night.

A few days later, I started work as the head pastry chef at the Princess. I was in for a surprise, not to say a big disappointment. I had come from the Savoy, where everything was perfect, with impeccable, luxurious silver service. The Princess, at the time, was a far less distinguished establishment, in terms of comfort, service and—alas—food.

The Princess boasted a small brasserie-style restaurant, run by a

Frenchman, Michel Galand, plus two dining rooms: the Three Crowns, named for the plaster decorations on its ceiling, serving between 800 and 950 covers daily, and a smaller à la carte restaurant, serving between 100 and 120 covers. The latter was very expensive, but offered a stunning view of the sea and crystal chandeliers. Sadly, the food leaving the kitchens—under plastic cloches—was cafeteria fare at best. The kitchens were much smaller than those at the Savoy, and the oven was placed against a wall. The pastry kitchen produced standard cakes cut into individual portions and served with frozen sauces. Nothing was freshly made.

I was faced once again with a seemingly impossible challenge. I thought seriously about giving up. Racking my brains for a solution, I would walk out to a small bistro on the outskirts of Hamilton, popular with the local black community, and think long and hard over a beer. After a month, I decided to stay on and fight to improve things. It was hard, but this was another good reason to stick at the task in hand. Before leaving London, I had gone into St. Martin-in-the-Fields Church to pray. I had the will and determination to succeed, and now I begged my guardian angel to show me the way. I would transform the pastry kitchen at the Princess into a little Savoy! And since the director was a great fan of sugar sculpture (my abilities in this direction were one of his main reasons for hiring me), I would make it a house specialty, to his undoubted satisfaction. And so I got to work. I changed the menus, brought in new dishes, made a feature of the sugar sculptures. Little by little, we made noticeable progress. We organized elegant functions with menus to match the Princess's lofty ambitions (at least, in the case of the desserts). The director was delighted. And so was I.

Better still, my sugar sculptures had scored a notable success: upon my arrival in Bermuda, every pastry chef on the island swore that it was impossible to produce blown and pulled sugar in the local climate. Bermuda boasted ninety percent humidity. Just a few days after my arrival, the director asked me to make a large, rectangular cake for a going-away party for one of his team. I wanted to make some sugar decorations, but quickly understood the extent of the problem I faced. I began to cook the sugar as usual, with glucose and lemon juice, before pouring the caramel onto the oiled marble surface to cool and harden, not too much. It had to stay malleable, so that it could still be pulled with the hands to form the glutinous mass from which the creations are sculpted. But it was impossible to pour it out of the casserole. The sugar had not caramelized. Once I was able to pour it on the marble, it would not harden and therefore could not be handled. This was worrying. I had insisted on the post of head pastry chef at the Princess, and now my first creation was a failure. I had to find a way of working the sugar, or face being fired and humiliated. Suddenly, I had an idea. I would change the recipe. By taking out some of the glucose, the sugar became harder and malleable enough to make a ribbon that I could tie in an attractive bow around the cake. It wasn't my finest creation, but I presented it as it was, hoping that the party guests would approve, which they did. In fact, it was an extraordinary triumph, given that everyone had said it was impossible to work sugar in this way in Bermuda. Subsequently, I improved the recipe little by little until I was able to produce sugar sculptures every bit as fine as those at the Savoy.

The staff in the hotel kitchens—and the pastry chefs—were from many different countries, but above all there were plenty of French, Swiss, and Germans, as well as some Italians. The dining-room staff, on the other hand, was almost all Italian. The Bermudans, for their part, eschewed the punishing hot work of the kitchens and other dining services in the hotel, preferring more "decorative" functions, like extras on a film set.

Spurred on by my success, I decided to take part in a culinary exhibition held each year in Bermuda: a prestigious event that attracted all the international cooks and pastry chefs who were working in Bermuda. Everyone had said it was impossible to produce blown and pulled sugar here, so that was what I would do. The pastry chefs on the island were astonished at my success with the stubborn substance, and at my decorative creations. I won the gold medal, and repeated my success the following year. I was always striving to do better, and so I set myself the improbable goal of competing in three of the competition's four or five categories—sugarwork, celebration cakes, and frozen desserts—with the aim of winning three gold medals. The problem was that at the same time, I was also supposed to be preparing for the hotel's annual birthday celebrations, for which I planned to create a sugar model of the Princess. My second-in-command was a German chef, much older than me, and very jealous of my success. He clearly hoped that I would fail, and did everything he could to ensure I did just that. Two or three weeks prior to the event, he left the hotel for good, taking three of my pastry cooks with him.

The Princess's pastry staff consisted of six chefs, including myself, which left us with precious few hands on deck. I was like the French marshal Soubise, who lost his army and was caricatured looking for them in the dark with a lantern. It was clear that I couldn't carry both projects on my own. Meanwhile, I hired my friend Yvon—my fellow apprentice at the Maurivard patisserie—to work in the pastry kitchen with me. His presence was a comfort in the face of the mass desertion, but it was not enough to get things moving again. For weeks and months I scarcely left the pastry kitchen. I worked harder than I had ever worked before. And I achieved everything I set out to do: a model of the Princess in sugar and three gold medals.

All of which encouraged the hotel's director to send me to compete in an annual exhibition in New York, an event even more prestigious than the show in Bermuda. One thing led to another.

Happily, not all of my collaborators were as dastardly as the German pastry chef. I made a great friend by the name of Joe Klein, also German, who was the hotel butcher—a colossus with a fist of iron, and the original gentle giant. He often came to see me in the pastry kitchen. Because I was very young—still only twenty—and very thin, he would pick me up by the seat of my pants with one hand and lift me over the worktop. He owned a big boat and often organized night fishing parties, to which he invited his friends. Ten or fifteen of us would set off, with a hefty cargo of wine and beer, in search of sharks. Big chunks of meat slung overboard on hooks proved to be highly effective as bait. The sharks we caught were lashed to the boat with ropes around their necks. We would return to port at around 2 a.m. with a dozen or so fish, each measuring about six to nine feet in length. Next morning, Joe Klein would cut out their jawbones, which were worth a small fortune. He sold these to the tourists and threw the rest back into the sea.

One year, the celebrated French ocean explorer Jacques Cousteau came to Bermuda with his son Philippe and their entire organization to record the songs of the whales passing close to the islands on their migration route each spring. From my house, perched on the rocks, I could see the water spouting from their blowholes. The Cousteaus rented Joe Klein's boat. Joe was my neighbor, and we held a beach barbecue in honor of Jacques Cousteau's son. One of life's little gifts.

Bermuda presented me with another—incomparable—gift, too. On my day off (I think it was a Monday), I used to walk on the seafront with a friend of mine, looking for girls to pick up, as young men will. One day, very exceptionally, the weather was overcast, and the beach was deserted. We stood there like a couple of spare parts, unsure what to do with ourselves. Then we noticed a girl sitting all on her own, on the sand. My friend said, "Leave her to me, I'll go and talk to her."

To which I replied, "Go on, then, she's all yours."

I watched from a distance as he engaged the girl in conversation. After about ten minutes, he called me over. I introduced myself. My friend said, "You've got to help me translate. My English isn't good enough. I don't know what she's saying."

I took control of the situation and told my friend to get lost, he'd never get anywhere with her.

I was left alone with this very pretty young girl whose name, I discovered, was Martha. We quickly became friends, and more. She was American, a teacher from Washington, where she taught science. She was in Bermuda on vacation. We wrote to each other when she returned to the States, and a few months later she joined me in

Bermuda for good. We were married two years after that, and had our son, George. We lived in a tiny apartment. I remember someone gave me an old wooden cradle before the baby was born. It needed restoring, and I bought a can of blue paint, taking a gamble that we would have a boy. When Martha went into labor, I fetched my Vespa, settled her on the back seat with her little suitcase and took her to the hospital.

Everyone was fairly surprised to see a woman in labor (the technical term is, I believe, "parturient") arriving on the back of a moped. This mode of transport may well have accelerated things, and George arrived very shortly afterwards. I was due to attend a dinner for the island's French community that evening, and George's arrival was celebrated in fine style. Celebrated perhaps a little too much. Two days later, Martha came home with my son. This time, the moped was out of the question. In haste, I bought the first car I owned in Bermuda, a small Simca, for 900 dollars, full of holes because all the cars on the island were devoured by the salty sea spray.

That's the story of the gift I received in Bermuda—without doubt the greatest gift of my life.

~

The Princess was part of an international hotel group owned by Daniel K. Ludwig, one of the richest men in the world, who had made his fortune in shipping, oil, gas, and coal. The hotels were his hobby. I met him on a few occasions at the Princess, where he would come to spend a week with his wife every once in while and carry out a detailed inspection. He would make a point of meeting all the chefs, the head waiters, and almost all of the staff. He was sure to make time to talk to Gurret, the executive chef, Tony Pandin, the maître d', and Roland Mesnier, the head pastry chef. Every time, he would ask if we were being treated well, if we had everything we needed for our work, if there was anything else we required. Often, our requests were provided almost immediately. But he loathed the hotel's directors. One year, we were all gathered with Mr. Ludwig in the chef's office. The hotel's assistant director was there, too. He was terrified of Mr. Ludwig, and followed him everywhere like a poodle. On this day, he expressed the hope that Mr. Ludwig had noticed the reupholstered armchairs and sofas. "Very nice", replied Mr. Ludwig, "but why didn't you do the legs, too? Our sofas are old. Now we have well-dressed sofas with shabby shoes." The assistant director replied that if he was to replace the feet on every sofa, it would cost fifteen dollars per foot. Mr. Ludwig shouted, "What the hell do you care? It's not your freakin' money, it's mine!" We allowed ourselves the smallest of smiles.

After this, the Princess group built the celebrated Acapulco Princess in Mexico—the first hotel in the world shaped like a pyramid, with a glass-roofed atrium overlooked by balconies covered with flowers. It was a superb, immense building with dozens of floors, and 800 rooms overlooking the sea. I was asked to make preparations for the opening of the hotel, and traveled there with the executive chef Edmond Gurret and Bodo Van Alvensleben, President of Princess Hotel International. I was subsequently promoted to executive pastry chef, overseeing the pastry kitchens in each of the group's nine hotels. The Acapulco Princess was equipped with spacious kitchens and a splendid patisserie area. Inconveniently, I spoke no Spanish, and the staff was Mexican. The head pastry chef in Acapulco was German, a grumpy character who was not at all happy that I had been brought in from Bermuda to oversee the opening. The head chef was German, too, a flighty worker, but always ready to show his face on TV. He had no idea how to cook, but specialized in hotel openings. As soon as the management realized the extent of his inabilities, he would leave for another hotel opening somewhere else. It is a crying shame that such people manage to achieve positions of high responsibility.

We began making preparations for the opening of the Acapulco Princess. A grand reception was planned for 3,000 people in a room capable of holding them all for a stand-up buffet, but which was too small for a sit-down meal. We decided on a gargantuan buffet using only Mexican produce. On the next day, a seated dinner was planned for 600 people.

I had agreed to make the sugar sculptures for the main buffet, including a series of giant cacti in vases. Several other pieces had also been planned for the dessert buffet. The head pastry chef, a jealous man who disliked me thoroughly, did nothing at all. A few measly pastries and nothing more.

For the seated dinner, we decided to present the desserts in sombreros made of cookie dough. The crown could be taken off like a lid to reveal the dessert inside. This represented a huge workload: 600 sombreros and 600 desserts to be placed inside the sombreros. Time was running out, but the German pastry chef took not the slightest initiative. Three days before the dinner, he decided to fall ill and took to his bed, leaving all the cupboards in his pastry kitchen locked and no keys. I was furious and told the head chef that if a solution wasn't found within half an hour, I was going back to Bermuda. I explained the situation to Mr. Ludwig, as a result of which the keys were found and delivered minutes later, so that I could open the cupboards and get to work. The executive chef came and helped me make the sombreros in the pastry kitchen—a huge amount of work! We labored for three days and three nights to get everything ready.

Mr. Ludwig had planned a truly grand event. He had invited all the state governors of the United States to spend three days at the Acapulco Princess with their wives and children. On the first evening, the night of the buffet, there was a huge reception in the glass-roofed atrium lobby, lined entirely in marble and decorated with lagoons, rippling streams, and little islands planted with trees. A forty-strong mariachi band played violins, and the only drink served was Dom Pérignon champagne.

Mr. Ludwig did not come in through the same entrance as his guests. He took the back entrance, and made sure to tip over a few garbage cans on the way, checking their contents to see if any food had been wasted. He was the boss, and he was quite right to do so. As it turned out, shortly afterwards, the hotel chef threw out 100 pounds of caviar that had gone moldy in the refrigerators.

Upon his arrival in the dining room, Mr. Ludwig was uninterested in the buffet, which had been a waste of money as far he was concerned. He seated himself at a table with his wife and ordered two grilled fish. The evening went smoothly, but several people were astonished to see that the boss was not happy. He had already spotted a few hitches in the hotel's operations. The next day came the big, sit-down dinner with the sombreros. I oversaw the entire evening, assigning tasks to the staff with Edmond Gurret's help, since the head pastry chef had disappeared. Imagine my revulsion when it was time to serve the dessert and behold! The very same head pastry chef rose from his deathbed, descended to the dining room in full evening dress with his wife on his arm and began passing the desserts out to the waiters, for all the world as if he had made them himself.

My job was done, and I returned to Bermuda, where I learned shortly afterwards that the head pastry chef in Acapulco had been fired together with the German head chef. Once again, justice had been done.

～

Shortly after my return to Bermuda, the Princess group, which had just acquired another hotel in Acapulco, the Pierre Marques, decided to build a new resort on the island, the Southampton Princess. The new hotel boasted 600 rooms, all with a sea view, and a top capacity of 1,200 guests. It was located on a hill directly above the beach, flanked by a superb golf course. One restaurant overlooked the sea and another, known as the Number One Club, was situated on the golf course. A third was located on the other side of the island. As the Princess group's executive pastry chef, I took overall responsibility for the new hotel's patisserie, and designed a spacious, superbly equipped pastry kitchen, which I subsequently used as my headquarters, rather than the smaller installations at the Hamilton Princess. The new pastry kitchen comprised a large workroom where everything was shaped and baked, and where the puff pastry dough and other pastries were prepared. After this came a second, cooler room where the desserts were finished, and cakes assembled and decorated, followed by a third room, used as a storeroom, where we placed the baskets of rolls for large-scale dinners. The fourth room was my office, where I worked on the sugar decorations. The whole kitchen was the ideal place for a dedicated pastry chef to practice his art. We had two large tray ovens, which enabled us to bake large numbers of items at once, such as fillets of beef Wellington wrapped in puff pastry, served once a week. I had ordered a very large table on which to roll out the pastry, and could wrap sixty beef fillets in less than forty-five minutes. And I had a crack staff under my command, pastry chefs from more than twelve different countries, from whom I endeavored to learn as much as possible and get the very best results by encouraging each person to contribute his particular knowledge and skills.

A new head pastry chef was needed at the Hamilton Princess to replace me. I called in Jean-Pierre Glayrousse, who had distinguished himself at the great Battle of Acapulco, to act as sous-chef. Jean-Pierre came from the Savoy and was married to a Scottish woman. He had benefited from the same training as me in London, and I knew I could count on him to build on my achievements at the hotel, over what was now a period of several years.

I moved in to the Southampton Princess to prepare for the hotel's opening. Bodo had left the group, and Walter Sommer had replaced him as the group's president. Sommer was now in charge of all operations. There were staff to be hired and sugar decorations to make. One week ahead of the Southampton Princess's opening gala dinner for 900 people, Sommer came to see me and asked me to create table decorations consisting of sugar baskets decorated with Bermuda's national flower, the hibiscus, all in sugar. With one basket per table, and three blooms per basket, I was to make 90 baskets—and 270 flowers. I have never said no. This was a new challenge and one I would meet like all the others. In addition, I was also working on a sugar model of the new hotel, which was to go on show in the foyer. A crushing amount of work, but the banquet was a huge success.

From time to time, I helped out at the governor's palace in Bermuda. I adored this work—the chef, by the name of Pepino (an Italian, like all the chefs in his team), would prepare superb, hearty meals for us all, which we ate after finishing work, with great camaraderie. I remember one unfortunate incident that befell the head waiter at the Palace. I had helped prepare a dinner for fifteen people in honor of Prince Charles who was, of course, on home territory in Bermuda. The menu included a pale green asparagus soup, served by the maître d'hôtel in white gloves, as is correct. At the end of the meal, the governor's wife called him over and said that she had noticed his thumb trailing in the soup. The waiter swore by all the gods in heaven that he was far too professional to commit such a crime. But unfortunately for him, he had kept his gloves, complete with a green thumb. He was caught green-handed (to coin a phrase). The governor's wife gave him a thorough dressing down, the more so since the prince himself had apparently also noticed the mistake. The waiter was warned that if the same thing happened again, he would be fired on the spot.

After seven years in Bermuda, I felt that it was time to return home to France and open a patisserie of my own. I could get a job while looking for suitable premises. I learned that the Hôtel George V in Paris had been unsuccessfully looking for a new head pastry chef for some time. The hotel was especially keen to find someone who could carve ice sculptures, make chocolates, and create sugar decorations, as well as superb desserts. I contacted the hotel's recruitment team and was proud to be offered the job while still in Bermuda. To be recruited at such a distance by the George V, which had been unable to find anyone in France, made me feel very special indeed.

I began to make preparations for my departure. This was no easy task. My wife Martha and I had made a great many friends. My son George was born in Bermuda, and all his friends were there. He would have to say goodbye to them and to the beautiful beaches where he had such fun playing. It was hard to leave my job, my bosses who had done so much to ensure I was happy in my work, and the sunny island life. But sometimes you simply have to move on.

I went to see my parents, who had now moved to Buthiers, before going up to Paris to find an apartment, and contact the George V. I was given a room in the hotel itself while I looked for a place to live. Martha and George stayed with my parents in Buthiers but hoped to join me as soon as possible. At last, I found an apartment near the Parc des Buttes-Chaumont, not far from the headquarters of the French Communist Party. Martha and George joined me there right away. We all reeled from the culture shock. Paris was dirty and dusty; the streets smelled bad, the metro entrances stank of urine, and the metro itself was full of tramps and drunks. All very depressing when you've just arrived from Bermuda. And the more so given that to reach our home in the 19th arrondissement, we had to traverse Barbès, one of the seediest, most rundown quarters in the city. In Bermuda, everything was clean, pleasant, and smart. We were homesick.

Worst of all, our things had been stolen. From Bermuda, I had sent our most precious belongings ahead, up to Paris: our clothes, treasured ornaments, silver trophies engraved with my name. Winter was coming, and we found ourselves with no warm clothes in a small, uncomfortable apartment in Buttes-Chaumont. One day, I received a note asking me to come to a freight yard—a dark station in a tunnel, dimly lit with neon strips. I was told that my luggage had ended up here. Disaster. The three big trunks that we had brought back from Bermuda had been opened from behind and almost everything of value had disappeared: winter coats, suits, my wife's dresses, and, of course, my silver trophies and platters. Everything was gone, even my son's toys: some plastic fish, a teddy bear that he liked to cuddle in bed, his entire world. This was the worst blow of all. It takes a callous soul to steal toys from a child. All that remained were a few threadbare clothes. The trunks had been left there for weeks; no one had bothered to do anything about them. Our insurance paid a tiny amount in recompense, barely enough to buy some new clothes. It made me desperately sad to think that just days after returning to my home country, we had been robbed of everything we owned. *Bonjour, la France!* I was overcome with bitterness.

CHAPTER 7

A Parisian Interlude

The George V was another fabulous, world-class hotel like the Savoy. The unique wine cellar housed a wealth of fine vintages, laid down to mature in total darkness. The only way to get around the catacomb was to arm yourself with a flashlight or a candle.

The director, Christian Falcucci, promised to review my salary as soon as the outgoing head pastry chef had left. I was to be upgraded, and the raise backdated to the beginning of my contract, covering the whole of the transitional period. After two months in the job, however, my new salary and back pay were still unforthcoming. One morning, I went to see the executive chef to hand in my resignation. He told me to go back to work; he would deal with the problem. One hour later, the hotel presented me with a check covering my new salary and my full back pay. The managing director, Monsieur Saunier, called me into his office. He wanted to know what had happened, and why Christian Falcucci hadn't revised my pay before leaving on vacation.

On his return, Monsieur Falcucci came to see me. He was not happy. Why had I tried to get him thrown out? I replied that we had an agreement, which he had failed to honor, and that I had assumed that this was because he was not satisfied with my work. I had rent to pay and he had gone on vacation, so I had decided to go and see the executive chef.

Our relationship was frosty for a time, but we eventually patched things up. Falcucci was an excellent manager. In his early forties, always impeccably turned out, he had a touch of the Italian playboy about him and enormous energy. He seemed to be everywhere at once in the hotel, knew everything that was going on, kept in close touch with the staff, and was good at resolving disputes. Monsieur Saunier had complete confidence in him.

The management at the George V looked after their staff exceedingly well. At Christmas, anyone with children under seven was invited to meet with the personnel officer and choose a gift from a catalog. One afternoon in December, all the children were invited to a party in the hotel at which Santa Claus himself gave out the presents. It was an afternoon of cakes galore, laughter, and games. Later in the evening, another party for the hotel's male staff culminated in a special show by the girls from the Crazy Horse cabaret—reputedly the most beautiful girls in Paris.

The George V was a fine place to work, and I was sorry to leave, but I wasn't enjoying life in Paris and neither were my wife and son. Little by little, I formed the idea of returning to Bermuda. I knew that I was missed and that I had only to contact my former employers to get my old job back. After a great deal of thought, this was what I decided to do. I had a second job during my years at the George V, just as I had had in Bermuda, at the governor's residence. In Paris, I worked at the Vivarois, an establishment with three Michelin stars on Avenue Victor Hugo, run by Claude Peyrot, a rising young talent in French cuisine who had achieved the Michelin Guide's ultimate accolade seven years after opening his restaurant. Peyrot was hailed as a gastronomic genius. I was full of admiration for everything he did, including the way he ran his kitchen. He worked together with his wife, who was also highly talented. Their restaurant was one of the most famous in Paris.

I went to the Vivarois three or four times each week, at around 3:30 p.m., after my shift at the George V. My job was to train a couple of young chefs to work on the days when I was unable to come. On my days at the Vivarois, I got home at around 10 p.m. and left at 5:30 a.m. next day for the George V.

Once again, these were difficult years with a heavy workload. But I knew that working at a three-star establishment like the Vivarois was essential if I was to progress in my work. I adored working there. Monsieur Peyrot was a very intelligent, very eccentric, and very demanding boss. The work was difficult, and I enjoyed it for that very reason. Peyrot himself was never satisfied, always convinced that he could have done better. Sometimes, overcome with disappointment, he would go home to his apartment in a state of absolute fury and return the following morning, more determined than ever, trying again and again to attain the culinary ne plus ultra he desired. It was rumored among the staff that he would go so far as to disguise himself and wait outside the restaurant, asking the diners coming out what they thought of the food, the service, whether they had met the owner, what the desserts were like, etc.

Peyrot's wife was a very even-tempered woman. Thanks to her, the restaurant ran smoothly with a team of chefs and waiters who had worked with them from the very beginning and knew their jobs thoroughly. The Vivarois opened my eyes to the possibilities of fine cuisine, with food and service of a quality unrivaled even by the Savoy or the George V. I had never seen anyone work like Monsieur Peyrot and his staff. Significantly, the kitchen was kept spotlessly clean. We could, quite literally, have eaten our lunch off the floor. The experience marked a turning point in my career, changed my way of thinking, and taught me that I still had a great deal to learn if I was to scale the heights of which I dreamed.

My time in Paris was coming to an end. Towards the end of my time at the George V and the Vivarois, my friends organized a big party in my honor. We all ate together at a restaurant near Sacré Cœur; it was a delightful evening. I was touched to think that I had made my mark, both professionally and as a friend, in this relatively short time.

And then it was back to Bermuda. I couldn't bear to tell my mother that we were leaving. She had been delighted to have us back in Paris and to be able to see us more often. Before, whenever we came for a vacation, she would start crying three days before we were due to leave. I couldn't bear to see that and decided to leave without a word to anyone.

Back in Bermuda, our arrival was awaited with impatience. Mr. Ludwig, the owner of the Princess Hotel Group, played an important role in my decision to come back. He actually asked me outright to return to the island. And we had so many friends. Seeing them all again—with the blue sea, the pink sandy beaches, the green palm trees, and the flowering tropical shrubs—I felt as if I had returned to paradise.

We had a pretty little house two steps from the sea with a private beach and a pool, all owned by the Southampton Princess, which had created the housing for its staff. We even had a small private garden, entirely surrounded by a hedge. The cottage had two bedrooms, two bathrooms, a living room, dining room, and kitchen, and the aforementioned pool, where George spent so much time diving in, again and again, that his curly blond hair turned green because of the chlorine. He swam like a dolphin. His party trick was to dive down to the bottom of the pool to fetch coins thrown by our visitors, which he would bring up to the surface in his teeth. He took up with his old friends once again, and I was delighted that he had rediscovered his roots in this paradisiacal country.

I returned to my patisserie at the Southampton Princess. A great many new employees had been hired during my absence, and the pastry kitchen had experienced severe difficulties. There was a great deal to be done: the proper running of the pastry kitchen had to be reestablished, the premises needed renovating, and I needed to mold an efficient staff, which meant sorting out the good pâtissiers from the bad. I got to work and succeeded in establishing an excellent team after about six or seven months. Eventually, things worked better than ever with plenty of new ideas, which I had brought back from Paris.

Naturally, we began to exhibit at the trade fair in New York once again. Twenty of us would set off for the event, during which we would organize large, sumptuous buffets, confident that our work was on a par with anything seen in New York. The sugar sculptures that I prepared had to be transported by plane. One year, the piece was very large and took up two seats on its own. Upon arrival in New York, I took the piece in a taxi to my hotel and from the hotel to the exhibition in the morning. Bomb scares were a frequent occurrence on planes at the time, but they were often false alarms or bad jokes. On this particular occasion, an alert was announced while we were waiting to take off in Bermuda. The plane had to be evacuated, but with my heavy package, I had to wait until everyone else had got out before leaving the aircraft myself. Everyone filed past my seat, casting black looks in my direction. With the huge package on the seat beside me, I was convinced everyone thought I was the character with the bomb. I finally managed to leave the plane and waited until the security officials had finished their checks. I felt very downhearted. This was a bad omen. I was sure things would take a turn for the worse. In New York, I told the taxi to drive slowly because my package contained a sugar sculpture. This had the effect of encouraging him to speed through the streets at about 55 miles an hour, in spite of all the potholes. At the hotel, I couldn't believe my eyes. The piece was intact! My little guardian angel Mickaël had definitely been sitting in the taxi. The next day, I took the piece to the exhibition and displayed it alongside the other entries. I won first prize in the sugar sculpture category, and my team of chefs were awarded several other prizes for their buffet display. We returned to Bermuda feeling happy and proud, with a clutch of favorable press reviews to boot.

I started work again at the governor's residence, where I served so many memorable dinners during my time in Bermuda. I remember one in particular, during my first spell at the Hamilton Princess, for the astronaut Frank Borman. I had created an enormous cake with eight tiers, topped by a model of planet Earth orbited by little Sputnik-style satellites. I had just a day or two to prepare the cake, another challenge among many, and another success. Frank Borman came up on stage when we presented the monumental cake. He agreed to have his photograph taken with us, and thanked us all again and again, together with Edmond Gurret, for what we had done.

During my second spell in Bermuda, I took part in an extraordinary event: a dinner to mark the opening of the new corporate headquarters for Bacardi rum. The company's president had requested a model of the new Bacardi building in sugar. The glass building was extremely difficult to reproduce, being completely transparent. From outside, you could see straight into the offices. The building consisted of one enormous floor with an immense foyer featuring a mural, which I also had to reproduce. Every detail was captured in the model, from the furniture to the carpets (in almond paste) and the gardens, all to scale, not forgetting the flags of every country in which Bacardi rum was sold. The structure took weeks to complete, and I was also responsible for creating the desserts for all of the dinners and receptions held to mark the opening.

Around 250 guests had been invited from all over the world. Their arrival marked the start of the festivities. They were filmed stepping down from the plane, after which each personality was followed everywhere by a cameraman, so that they left at the end with their own personal film of their stay in Bermuda. It was a truly magnificent event, and absolutely no expense was spared. The first day featured a barbecue on the Southampton Princess's private beach with a hog baked in the hot sand, Hawaiian-style, and grilled lobster, seafood, and an abundance of fish, filleted on the spot. One savory display featured salamis and cold cuts of every sort, which guests were free to slice as they pleased. Ice-cold beers were dispensed from a cart pulled by two huge brewery horses, who received a great deal of attention. It was the finest barbecue ever; everyone enjoyed themselves, and everyone was in a terrifically good mood, from the waiters to the guests and the executive chef, who had labored to organize this giant party down to the very last detail.

On the following evening, a large buffet was planned in the gardens of the Bacardi building, more or less opposite the Hamilton Princess. This was the event at which I was to unveil the sugar model of the new headquarters. It was a great success, and I duly received the 250 dollars I had requested for the piece (it was 1973). In addition, the wife of the president of Bacardi International, who was staying at the Hamilton Princess, asked me up to her penthouse to present me with an envelope thanking me, she explained, for my splendid work on the sugar build-ing. The envelope contained a 300-dollar tip. I was astonished and happy, but felt quite uncomfortable.

On the second day, we organized a buffet overflowing with fish, shrimp, cold cooked lobster, hams, terrines, and hot dishes. There was Dom Pérignon to drink and music from the same mariachis who had played at the opening of the Acapulco Princess. The band had been brought over to Bermuda for the occasion. They stood on the steps of the Bacardi building, wearing their sombreros and playing their enchanting music against a background of palm trees and fountains. Another splendid, balmy evening.

On the third and last day, we organized a sit-down dinner at the hotel. I created sugar centerpieces for the twenty tables—each one was different. Once again, the Bacardi family showed their recognition of my hard work. Everyone worked hard during the three days. We were thanked with a dinner for thirty people at the Waterlot Inn, one of the finest restaurants in Southampton, operated by the Southampton Prin-cess. The ladies were each presented with a piece of jewelry attached to a stem vase containing a single rose with a ribbon, and the men received gold-plated cufflinks. The superb menu was accompanied by fine, vin-tage wines and still more Dom Pérignon with the dessert.

Daniel Ludwig, the owner of the Princess group, was delighted to welcome me back to the fold, and presented me with generous bonuses. Together with my staff, we continued to take part in trade fairs and exhibitions and carried off numerous awards: first prize in New York, with the compliments of the jury, in 1974; a gold medal from the Con-frérie de Saint-Michel (the professional fraternity of Parisian pâtissiers) in 1975, also with the compliments of the jury; and several times over, a prize in New York for the Southampton Princess. It was 1975, and everything was rosy.

The Southampton Princess planned to open a small pastry shop at the Waterlot Inn, and my boss Walter Sommer, the president chef for the Princess group, promised me a raise to oversee the new operation, plus a percentage share of the turnover. I turned down the offer. I had been in Bermuda for many years now, and I was starting to look around for something new, beyond the confines of the tiny British protectorate. I knew everyone, and everyone knew me. It was impossible to go out for a quiet meal in a restaurant. The Bermudan authorities never granted permission for the opening of the shop, however, and although Walter Sommer offered to compensate me for the nonexistent raise, this did nothing to address the basic problem. Bermuda was a seductive trap—you could live your whole life there, but at the same time life would pass you by. There was nothing much to do besides work. For entertainment and activity you could fly to New York, which was very expensive. And what of the future? I had the best possible job; I had achieved all my ambitions on the island. To do more, I would have to leave and look further afield.

Towards the end of my time in Bermuda, I considered competing for France's national professional awards, the winners of which are subsequently titled Meilleurs Ouvriers de France. This is a prestigious, but highly political competition, to be approached with care. I contacted the president of the Société des Pâtissiers de France, Monsieur Marzet, to find out whether I could enter the preliminary heats without incurring the enormous expense of traveling to Paris. Would he agree to judge my entries via photographs at this stage of the competition? Monsieur Marzet agreed.

Meanwhile, I received several jobs offers from the United States: the Las Vegas Hilton, under the command of a well-known French chef, and others from New York and elsewhere. I would never have left Bermuda for Las Vegas or New York, but a letter from Hermann Rush—a Swiss chef at the Greenbrier Resort in West Virginia, where I had worked for a short time—was more intriguing. Rush told me that the Homestead, another venerable Virginia resort hotel, was looking for a head pastry chef to take over when its current chef retired after forty-five years in the job. The Homestead was about an hour's drive from the Greenbrier, on a vast estate of grassy plains and woodland.

The resort boasted some 500 guest rooms, its own cinema, a bowling alley, three golf courses, and tennis courts. A full-fledged holiday resort! The Homestead seemed exactly what I was looking for, and I contacted the executive chef, another Swiss by the name of Albert Schnarwyler, who had worked there for fifteen years. I visited the hotel in the fall of 1975 and discovered a quite magnificent place. Everything was perfect, except the pay. I told the chef that I couldn't live on what he was offering, and that if he wanted things to move on and progress after the departure of his existing pastry chef, he would have to offer more. Which he did. A few weeks after my return to Bermuda, I received a letter offering me an annual salary of 22,000 dollars, plus overtime. This was more than acceptable, and I accepted. I was to start work at the Homestead on April 1, 1976.

I was not alone in looking further afield for a new life. A number of other employees left Bermuda at the same time, or were planning to do so, for the same reasons. Like me, they wanted to settle in a bigger country.

At the end of March, a few days before starting work at the Homestead, the Southampton Princess hosted a big convention for the American branch of the Young Presidents' Organization. The members of this exclusive club were young indeed: all under thirty-five and all presidents of their respective companies. If any of them had set their sights on another presidential post, at the White House, they had plenty of time to achieve their goal. One thousand delegates attended the event, taking over the entire hotel. This was my last big event at the Southampton Princess, and I wanted to ensure that it was the biggest possible success. The problem was that the club had ordered two large ice sculptures for the closing dinner. I was the only member of staff left who could produce the sculptures, and I was on the verge of leaving myself. The hotel's management was understandably reluctant to refuse the request, when the club's members had spent millions of dollars during their week-long stay. Walter Sommer pleaded with me to stay for two extra days and offered to pay me 500 dollars for my pains—a small fortune. I notified the Homestead that I would like to arrive 48 hours later than planned, provided this was not a problem for them. It was not, and I created two spectacular centerpieces for the dinner, to everyone's great satisfaction.

The time had come to pack our bags once again, and head for the Homestead in Hot Springs, Virginia. I was excited at the prospect of working in a new hotel. As I had seen on my visit, the pastry kitchen was extensive, with a large, exceedingly capable staff—as might be expected of a grand hotel that first opened its doors in 1766.

Our departure from Bermuda was a very sad occasion. Several friends came to see Martha, George, and me off at the airport, and the atmosphere was funereal. I was sad to leave my Bermudian friends, who had been so kind. But I knew that I had to leave if I wanted to advance my career. I felt that I had been called to something bigger, as if someone was leading me by the hand towards greater things. None of which prevented me from crying like a baby when we reached the airport. I knew what I was leaving behind: a perfect job as the sovereign king of my personal pastry kingdom, well-known to everyone, the top of the heap. I had no idea what lay ahead in United States, other than stiff competition in a country that attracted many of the finest pastry chefs in the world. Once again, I would have to prove my worth. I mulled these thoughts over later, but for the moment, I was overcome with grief. My departure from Bermuda was a sad day indeed.

CHAPTER 8

In the Mountains of Virginia

We arrived by plane at the Homestead's own air strip and were greeted by the executive chef's wife. Madame Schnarwyler drove us to the brand new house I had rented, which she had very kindly prepared for our arrival, with pieces of make-do furniture and a stock of essential provisions. The Schnarwylers were kindness itself, and the executive chef even loaned me his own car for a few days before I bought a vehicle of my own.

The Homestead was a majestic building in red brick, its façade decorated with white-painted shingle. In the middle stood a huge brick clock tower—it was impossible to forget the time. The hotel was set in 16,000 acres of countryside. Nothing in the neighboring village of Hot Springs (population 400) suggested that just near by lay a palatial 500-room resort, not to mention three 18-hole golf courses, tennis courts, riding trails through the woods, swimming pools, and more. The Homestead was a place for vacationing, rest, and recreation. On Friday and Saturday nights, the hotel often hosted as many as fifteen different dinners and banquets. Running the pastry kitchen in a place like this was a little like conducting a huge symphony orchestra.

The Homestead had a distinguished history, too. The resort's director, Mr. Thomas Lennon, was then in his seventies and had devoted his entire life to the hotel. He was a distinguished manager with an iron rule. It was said that whenever an employee handed in his or her notice, Lennon would throw them out immediately, stating that if their heart and soul weren't totally devoted to the job and the hotel, they could leave straight away. The staff was afraid of him—he had established a set of rules and regulations that had to be respected to the letter. No exceptions were tolerated.

I met the staff and the hotel's general manager, Dan Reichartz, and the managing director—the top management team. The Homestead was a superbly run place with a highly skilled staff. Everything ran smoothly, without the slightest hitch, even the big dinners and banquets. Everyone knew their place and exactly what was expected of them.

I began my preparations for the competition for the title of Meilleur Ouvrier de France, scheduled for September 1976. I had discussed the idea with my boss and the executive chef, explaining that I had signed up for the event before arriving at the hotel and that this was a highly prestigious award in the world of fine patisserie. Would they allow me to practice for the competition and take time off in September to travel to Paris? They would.

In the meantime, I got to know my staff. My sous-chef was a sixty-year-old Swiss man by the name of Ernest, a great pâtissier but also a dedicated alcoholic. His working day began at noon, perfectly sober, and ended at 10:30 p.m. in a state of advanced inebriation. My own shifts ran from 7 a.m. to noon and from 5 p.m. until the kitchens closed at around 10 or 11 p.m., or later. Every day, when I started my second shift, I would find Ernest completely drunk and the pastry kitchen in a mess. No one was on hand during my break to keep things in order. I was faced with a significant but tricky problem—Ernest had been working at the Homestead for about twenty-five years. He was a highly talented man, but his drinking had doubtless cost him his promotion to the post of head pastry chef.

The other members of my team were all American, many of them born in Hot Springs or the surrounding area. Some were, it seemed to me, rather seedy-looking—unshaven and long-haired—but all of them were warm-hearted and hard-working. I came to like them all enormously during my four years at the Homestead. Many were also volunteer firemen or members of the local mountain rescue service in their spare time and took part in regular rescue operations. I expanded the team with a new chef, Michel Finel, a French colleague from the Southampton Princess, slightly younger than me, a great professional and a thoroughly reliable worker.

We got to work. Managing the pastry kitchen was a tricky job on occasions, requiring a great deal of tact and diplomacy. I quickly realized that the local staff was easily annoyed and completely uninterested in where I had worked and what I had done before coming to the Homestead. Paris and Bermuda were simply not part of their world. I discovered the importance of leading from the front, of setting an example. I demonstrated new ways of doing things, but was careful not to upset the status quo, the day-to-day organization of life in the kitchen. I began by working alongside my staff, in their time-honored way. Then little by little, I introduced new desserts—a delicate operation. This was a tricky process, but essential if I was to retain the cooperation and respect of my staff. After a year in the job, I organized a meeting with all my pastry chefs and asked them if they were aware of just how much the hotel's pastry and dessert menus had changed since my arrival. In fact, all of the old dishes had been replaced.

The chefs were astonished. I had changed their ways of working, and the desserts and pastries they produced, under their very noses, with no fuss or histrionics, so that they had hardly noticed a thing. Working with the locals in the pastry kitchen was a great way to get to know them and gain acceptance. These were hardy country people who grew their own produce and went hunting and fishing. Instead of an office, I worked at a big table where anyone was free to come and talk, and have a bite to eat or a drink. Often, I would find packages of vegetables, game, or fish left for me—the catch or harvest of the day. These were people who delighted in sharing.

September was approaching, and with it the competition for the title of Meilleur Ouvrier de France, for which I was to travel to Vincennes, east of Paris. Just a few days before I was due to leave, I received a telex with the details of that year's theme: springtime. The competitors had to make a cake celebrating this vast topic as well as produce chocolates and a selection of pastries. I took a large array of utensils with me by plane, which was a complicated and costly operation. I received an adequate but far from excessive salary, and I had a family to look after. Altogether, the flight and accommodation in Paris cost me some 5,000 dollars—a small fortune, the price of a decent car. But I was determined to take part in the competition whatever the cost, to demonstrate what I could do, and find out if I was truly worthy of the title.

When the time came, I left for France with Martha and George, who stayed with my family in Buthiers during the competition. I needed to find somewhere to stay in Paris and somewhere where I could practice for the competition. Happily, the George V provided both. I traveled to Besançon to practice with Monsieur Maurivard and prepare sugar accessories for my sculpture, which competitors were allowed to bring to the competition ready-made. Monsieur Maurivard was kind enough to lend me his Renault van; I drove it to Paris, loaded with all my paraphernalia. I was terrified, having hardly ever driven before in France, let alone Paris. The George V was easily reached via the fast route along the banks of the Seine, but not without negotiating the Place de l'Étoile, the giant traffic circle around the Arc de Triomphe. I was panic-stricken.

I felt inclined to shut my eyes and let the Good Lord himself carry me to the George V. I was hopelessly lost, with no idea how to negotiate the traffic. The whole of Paris honked its horn at me that day.

At last, I arrived at the George V, unloaded my van as instructed and put my utensils in the storeroom. I had also been directed to a garage nearby where I could leave the van until I went back to Besançon to fetch my family at Buthiers.

And so here I was, back at the George V, not as the hotel's pastry chef, but as a guest preparing for the competition. I caught up on the news. As I knew from the executive chef, who wrote to me from time to time, the hotel had had a great deal of difficulty finding a replacement for me. I had interviewed several candidates myself before leaving and none of them had proved satisfactory. I had finally appointed the ice cream chef—who had worked at the hotel for a number of years—as an interim chef until a permanent pastry chef was found. A young pastry chef was working at the hotel when I came to prepare for the competition, and things were not going well. But that wasn't my problem.

My former colleagues were good enough to find me a space to work, where I practiced again and again before the competition. On the morning of the great day, a friend from the George V drove me and all my equipment to Vincennes. There were fifteen candidates in all, and we got to work straight away. I arranged my worktable and calculated the time needed to complete each of the tests. Everything went according to plan.

Everything had to be ready and presented on the competitors' tables by midday on the second day. This meant each candidate's pre-prepared sugar sculpture as well as two other presentation pieces, which were to be made on the spot, plus chocolates and petits fours. For these, I had made a pulled-sugar peacock and attached the petits fours to the bird's tail. Several years later, a leading pastry chef in Paris told me that he had once seen an extraordinary piece at a Meilleur Ouvrier de France competition: a sugar peacock whose tail was decorated with petits fours. He thought it had been made by someone from Lenôtre, a well-known Parisian patisserie. I told him that I had created the peacock-feather petits fours. Life can be unfair, sometimes.

On the stroke of noon, our tables were ready for the judges' inspection. All we had to do now was wait. The results were announced in the early afternoon: six candidates were to receive the title of Meilleur Ouvrier de France. Two, including myself, were awarded a silver medal. I remember that, as I put my utensils away in their cardboard box, one of the jury members, a Meilleur Ouvrier de France for whom I have a great deal of respect, came over to congratulate me. He was enormously impressed that I had won the silver medal, working entirely alone and coming from so far away with no knowledge of what the competition really involved.

As I left the high school where the competition had taken place, I encountered the president of the pastry chef association at the bottom of the stairs. I thanked him for allowing me to take part in such a prestigious event and asked if he would be so kind as to send the breakdown of my points to the Homestead in Virginia. This would help me to improve on the mistakes and weak points in my work, which the judges had pointed out.

"Of course," he replied.

That was thirty years ago, I still haven't received my points.

I went back to Besançon, collected my family, and returned to the Homestead. I received my silver medal a few months later at the Palais des Sports in Paris. The awards were to be presented by the French president, Valéry Giscard d'Estaing, and I was determined to receive mine in person. I had spent a great deal of money attending the competition in the first place, so I asked the Homestead's head chef if he would intercede on my behalf and ask the president, Mr. Lennon, if he would agree to pay for me to travel back to France for the occasion. Mr. Lennon readily agreed—it was an honor for the Homestead to receive such a trophy. And so I set off for Paris once again and collected my award. But not from the hands of the president of France. The medals were laid out on a table, where the winners were simply invited to fetch them. The atmosphere was lukewarm to say the least.

Work had got off to a flying start at the Homestead. At the same time, I had taken on a second job, as so often, this time teaching patisserie at a small college in Clifton Forge, near the hotel.

I introduced a number of innovations at the Homestead. At my request, the hotel created a "portable kitchen" on wheels, which could be used for cooking demonstrations for the guests. When the weather precluded a session of golf or a game of tennis, my patisserie classes were a popular attraction. I found that I enjoyed teaching, via demonstrations and professional classes. I also established an apprenticeship system at the hotel, conscious that the best way to ensure a supply of qualified pastry cooks was to recruit local students and train them myself.

For four years, we labored to create sumptuous sugar compositions, working in close collaboration with the executive chef, whom I held in the greatest esteem—he adored his work and, like me, he was always ready to try something different. Our exploits attracted the attention of the newspapers, TV, and radio. I began to appear quite regularly in the media. I was delighted. I was working in a magnificent hotel, leading a lifestyle I enjoyed, and I was far from insensitive to the sweet smell of success surrounding my creations.

I had no desire to work in a big city. I adored the countryside, and country people, and had no intention of working elsewhere although I received plenty of offers, including several from the new casino hotels in Atlantic City. The New Jersey resort had suffered a period of decline in the decades following World War II, but was now enjoying a revival thanks to the legalization of gambling following a New Jersey state referendum in 1976. Often, the packages included salaries well above what I was earning at the time. But I wasn't interested.

I continued to wrestle with one tricky problem—that of the aforementioned Swiss sous-chef and his excessive drinking. I had no idea how he could manage to be so drunk by late afternoon, when I arrived for my second shift, when he had been perfectly sober at midday. I kept all of the wines and spirits in the kitchen under lock and key, and supplied the chefs with the exact measures as required. Despite this, Ernest succeeded in getting drunk on duty, day in, day out, with a dedication worthy of a far nobler cause.

On several occasions, I threw him out, telling him to sober up and take his addiction elsewhere. He would come back two or three days later, smartly turned out in a suit and tie, the perfect gentleman—promising, guaranteeing, swearing that he would never touch another drop, that he would get back to work with a vengeance. He would stay sober for weeks, then get horribly drunk all over again, usually when we needed his services most. I could have fired him, but he was a truly talented chef when he was sober. I wondered what he was drinking. What was he smuggling into the kitchen, that could get him so drunk, so quickly?

Everyone smiled when I broached the subject. The older hands in the kitchen knew exactly what he was up to, but said nothing out of solidarity or a misplaced sense of charity. Until one day, one of my pâtissiers suggested: "Chef, put a mark on the bottle of vanilla extract when you leave at lunchtime."

I was astonished, but did as he recommended. Sure enough, when I returned for my evening shift, Ernest was dead drunk and the bottle of vanilla extract was nearly empty. Vanilla extract has an unpleasant taste, but a very high alcohol content. This is what Ernest had been drinking, day after day. The mystery was solved, but not the problem of what to do with the drunken Swiss pastry chef. I tried very hard to help him and set him back on the right track. He stayed perfectly sober for the whole of my last year at the Homestead. I was proud to have virtually saved his life and restored his self-esteem. I understood that he despised himself for drinking, the more so because he was disgracing himself in the eyes of his colleagues with whom he shared the staff lodgings at the hotel. He had no family. He was entirely alone in life and needed someone to restore his sense of dignity. I believe I succeeded.

I enjoyed life at the Homestead and had no intention of leaving. Until one day, when Madame Schnarwyler, the wife of the executive chef, told me that the First Lady of the United States, Rosalynn Carter, was looking for a pastry chef for the White House. I was skeptical. I had read in the newspapers that the White House had only recently hired a swiss-born pastry chef who had been in America for many years. Why had the post fallen vacant once again, after such a short time? I suspected a joke.

CHAPTER 9

A Meeting with the First Lady

The Homestead often hosted meetings of advisors or staff at the Pentagon or the White House, several of whom confirmed that Mrs. Carter was indeed looking for a pastry chef. They advised me to contact the White House directly. So it was true. But I had no illusions about my suitability for the post. I was working in a tiny, remote village far from the nation's capital and its sphere of influence. Nonetheless, I plucked up the courage to telephone the executive chef at the White House, Henry Haller, and ask if he was looking for someone. Nothing more than that. It was October 1979. In early December, I received a call from the White House asking me to come for interviews with various people. I decided to go, still under no illusion as to the likely outcome. Before going to Washington, I filled in the application form, including a box where candidates were invited to note their salary requirements. Knowing that the previous pastry chef had been paid an annual salary of 26,000 dollars, I asked for 28,000 dollars. This wasn't much, but I didn't want to scare off my potential employer.

I drove to Washington on the day of a state visit by the British prime minister, Margaret Thatcher. I felt quite overwhelmed as I passed through the great gates of the White House in my car. I was a country boy from Bonnay all over again. I couldn't believe that I was about to enter the White House. My heart thumped. I had no idea what to do or what to say. I was completely overwhelmed at the idea of coming to a place where so many great presidents had lived and worked.

I met the White House social secretary, Gretchen Poston, who examined my application, especially the photographs of my sugar sculptures. I was also interviewed by the chief usher, Rex Scouten, whose first words to me were: "I've read your application form. You're asking for a great deal of money. Don't delude yourself: you won't get the job."

This was not, I thought, a particularly auspicious start. I wasn't especially discouraged, however, because I was convinced that I had not the remotest chance of being hired. The chief usher took me to meet the kitchen supervisor, Michael Sandsbury, a young man of about thirty with a background in the hotel industry, who had been hired by the Carter administration to control wastage and pilfering. Sandsbury greeted me warmly, and we sat down to talk. Then he suggested that we head outside to the White House gardens, to watch the ceremony organized in Mrs. Thatcher's honor. It was very cold. I saw the troops on parade, the president, his guest, and all the ceremonial solemnities. It was an extraordinary scene, like something from another world. This was a very far cry from Bonnay or the Maurivard patisserie in Besançon or my early years in Germany or the Savoy or the George V or Bermuda. It was completely different—and alien to me. Was I right to even consider coming here? I had no idea; I felt extremely anxious. After the ceremony, we returned to Sandsbury's office. The executive chef took me on a tour of the kitchens, including the "pastry kitchen"—a simple table at the back of the kitchen area. I was introduced to the pastry chef, who declared that he was too busy to talk to me, which I thought was odd. He was preparing desserts for the dinner for Mrs. Thatcher: Yule logs and small, very uninspiring marzipan decorations. At least I could do better than that, I told myself. About an hour later, he came over, shook my hand and apologized. He was leaving on February 1. He said very little about the job or the White House.

I had no idea as to the outcome of my visit. It was getting late. I began to feel annoyed. I told Sandsbury that I had a four-hour drive ahead of me and would have to leave. They could telephone me with an answer. Sandsbury asked me to stay and sit down. There was roast lamb for lunch—I could stay and eat with the staff.

"No, thank you."

I wasn't hungry. I was too nervous. I told myself that it had been a mistake to come. At about 11:30 p.m., Sandsbury's telephone rang.

"Roland, Mrs. Carter would like to see you. I have to tell you that you are the first candidate she has asked to meet personally. She didn't meet the others, but left them to Mrs. Poston, the social secretary."

This was a better sign. Sandsbury took me to the Ground Floor Corridor. Two ladies were approaching from the far end. One was Gretchen Poston, whom I had already met, and the other was Rosalynn Carter. Mrs. Carter opened her arms in a welcoming gesture and greeted me warmly with the words: "Hello, Roland, welcome to the White House. I hope you enjoyed the ceremony for Mrs. Thatcher. Please come inside."

I was ushered into the so-called Map Room, displaying the campaign maps from World War II showing the positions of the various forces in the worldwide theater of that war. Mrs. Carter took a seat in one of the red velvet armchairs and invited me to sit down. She began with a joke about her hat, which had blown off during the ceremony in a violent gust of wind. I was astonished to find the First Lady of the United States so approachable, so pleasant, and so concerned about making me feel at ease. We talked, and I showed her the photographs of my sugar sculptures, which Mrs. Poston had already seen that morning. I felt that sure that this was what had encouraged her to recommend me to Mrs. Carter. Mrs. Poston pointed out that I was not an American citizen, but only the holder of a green card authorizing me to work in the United States. Mrs. Carter felt that this was not a significant problem. Discussion over. I began to feel that I might have got the job. We talked about patisserie, my personal likes and dislikes, the Homestead, Bermuda, and my past career. Finally, Mrs. Carter, as friendly as ever, asked me: "Roland, if you were to become the head pastry chef at the White House, what sort of desserts would you serve?"

I replied that I would serve simple, low-calorie desserts based on an abundance of fresh fruit, since this was the basis of the finest desserts in the world.

Mrs. Carter thanked me and asked me to return to Michael Sandsbury's office. She called the chief usher, who arrived a few minutes later, confirming that Mrs. Carter would like me start as soon as possible.

"She has also agreed to your requested salary," he added. He turned on his heel and left. I felt like a politician who wants to get elected but doesn't believe he will succeed and finds himself swept to power against all expectations, then thinks better of it, realizing that he has absolutely no policies. I had made up my answer to Mrs. Carter's question, on the spot—my guardian angel must have whispered in my ear. In truth, I felt quite unprepared for the White House.

I thanked Sandsbury for his kindness and said goodbye to Henry Haller and his assistant chef, Hans Raffert. I was very impressed by the spotless cleanliness of their kitchens and their uniforms.

I began the drive back to the Homestead, and home, and stopped on the way to try and eat something. I was overjoyed. The job at the White House was the crowning achievement of my career. I hurried to tell Martha the news, although she was less than enthusiastic at first. She adored life at the Homestead, too: the countryside, the people, the woodlands. She had begun teaching classes to small children at the church next to the great hotel, deeply rewarding work that drew on her natural vocation and experience as a schoolteacher. George loved the Homestead, too, his school, and all his friends. We would all have to leave so much behind, and get used to a new way of life, in a new place, a completely different world.

The time came to announce my decision. I told the head chef and confirmed that I was happy to work a month's notice, as was the norm. He reminded me that the hotel's president, Mr. Lennon, was in the habit of booting out anyone on the spot who dared to resign.

"Be ready!" he warned.

This was an unpleasant prospect. I had never been fired from anywhere, and would have taken it as a cruel blow. I gave my resignation and notice in writing to the head chef and Mr. Lennon on January 1, 1980.

Our next task was to travel to Washington and look for a house. We made appointments with various real estate agents, and although Martha was not looking forward to the search, we were lucky to find a pleasant little house to rent, since we had no money to buy a home. The house was in Burke, Virginia, a small town about twenty miles from the center of Washington.

The move demanded a great deal of organization. Everything had to be packed and made ready for transfer to our new home. It was hard, too, to say goodbye to my colleagues and friends in the pastry kitchen at the Homestead. It was not the first time. My career had been marked with separations and goodbyes, and they were always difficult.

The days went by at the Homestead. At noon, when I headed for the dining room to inspect the buffets and talk to the waiters, I often met Mr. Lennon, who would shake my hand and exchange a few friendly words. Since January 1, however, he had taken to looking the other way and swearing under his breath whenever he saw me. He refused to speak to me, but at least he hadn't thrown me out. I was reassured, although I missed our friendly chats. One day, however, about two weeks after I had handed in my notice, I was inspecting one of the dining rooms before a big lunch party when Mr. Lennon came over to talk.

"My compliments to the chef. I haven't slept in two weeks. I'm mad that you're leaving because I like what you do, but you can't pass up on a job at the White House. If you had left for another hotel, I would never have forgiven you. But you're leaving to work at the White House, so that's OK by me."

I felt as if a great weight had been lifted from my shoulders. Mr. Lennon continued to talk to me after that, every day. He was still deeply unhappy about my departure. Someone had looked at the list of menus since my arrival at the hotel, and calculated the number of different desserts I had created in the space of four years: 510 in total.

The time came to say goodbye. One morning, I said farewell to the staff in the pastry kitchen. Everyone had signed a huge card and contributed to my going-away present: an extremely sophisticated travel trunk. I still have it today, more than thirty years later. It's a treasured souvenir. Whenever I have left a job, I have always received a card signed by everyone and a splendid gift. And every time I have felt deeply touched.

The moving truck arrived in early February, in freezing cold and heavy snow. George was very sad. I was keenly aware of the unhappiness I was causing him by pursuing what I wanted to do in life. It was a difficult time for everyone. I remember looking out of a window that opened onto the golf course while the truck was being loaded, contemplating the icy landscape and wondering if I had made the right decision. Would Washington smile on us? Would working at the White House be a positive move or a hellish experience that I would regret for the rest of my life? I turned the possibilities over and over in my mind. It was a huge step, but I couldn't be sure that it was the right one.

We left with our cats—cats have always been a tradition in our household—and we spent the night in a Washington hotel, waiting for the moving truck to arrive the next day, when we would receive the keys to our new house. Normally, animals were not allowed in the hotel, but we had managed to smuggle in food and a litter tray for a discreet feline overnight stay. The truck arrived on schedule and unloaded our furniture. Now it was up to us to organize our lives all over again. Not an easy task. We were no longer deep in the countryside. Our lifestyle would have to change and there would be new constraints. Some things would be easier, too, but we would have to adapt to a completely different environment.

I went to work at the White House the next day. The Swiss executive chef, the German assistant chef, a *commis* chef, an American dishwasher, and I all worked in the same room. The kitchen was not huge, but it was very well-equipped and spotlessly clean, as were everyone's dazzling white uniforms. I was reminded of the Vivarois, where Claude Peyrot worked every day in full chef's regalia, including the toque, a practice that has, sadly, been abandoned in many kitchens since then. A cook or pastry chef should be proud of his or her work and the uniform that goes with it. Like its military counterpart, it is a badge of honor. We are ready to do battle, too. The White House kitchen was air conditioned and fitted with ultramodern equipment. I had the use of a wooden worktable, about forty square feet, and a slightly bigger marble table, measuring about fifty square feet. There were very few storage cupboards. In addition to this, on the third floor, I shared a small office with the executive chef and the assistant chef, next to a bedroom furnished with a bed and a sofa, in case we needed to sleep at the White House in the event of bad winter weather, or problems in town. Here, I would spend hours thinking up new desserts and finding solutions to the many problems that lay ahead.

The White House was also equipped with a second, smaller kitchen where meals were prepared for the kitchen staff, waiters, chambermaids, cleaners, and maintenance workers. Meals were not provided for the other staff members and professionals at the White House: the florists, carpenters, mechanics, engineers, gardeners, horticulturists, even one or two people assigned to look after the presidential pets (when there were any), not forgetting a full-time doctor and professional nursing staff. Altogether, the permanent staff at the White House numbered approximately ninety people, sometimes more, sometimes less, from one presidency to the next. The presidential "palace" operated as autonomously as possible: security considerations prevented the use of external suppliers. The building also housed offices used by the secret services.

The kitchen staff had the use of a storeroom stocked with everything we needed. New supplies were collected from town in a nondescript truck driven by a secret service agent. The suppliers never knew that they were supplying the White House. No one outside the kitchen ever knew what was being prepared and served for the president, his family, and their guests.

Life at the White House was highly theatrical with its public face and all the goings-on backstage. The "front of house" comprised the drawing rooms, banquet and dining rooms, and offices, and the private apartments of the presidential family on the second floor. Behind the scenes were the people whose job it was to ensure the smooth running of the entire operation. And, as always, the effectiveness of the back-stage operation depended to a large extent on the personalities of the people in charge. The maître d'hôtel had spent his entire working life at the White House, working his way up to his present position. With a team of six or eight waiters and stewards, he exercised exceptional authority.

The Carters had four children. The eldest, Jack, was born in 1947. He had a wife, Judy, and a son, Jason. Their second son, Chip, born in 1950, was divorced from his wife Caron and was living at the White House when I arrived. A third son, Jeff, born in 1952, was married to a beautiful lady by the name of Annette. The two of them often stayed at the White House. The Carters' fourth child was Amy, born in 1967 and aged about twelve when I first came to the White House. Amy's nanny was another essential member of the family, who had accompanied them from Georgia, their home state, to look after the girl. A trusted, highly respected woman and a close confidante of the Carters, she lived at the White House and took almost all her meals with the First Family.

Annette and Jeff were a delightful couple who often came down to the kitchen to watch the meals being prepared—a show they never tired of. They far preferred to eat sandwiches in the kitchen rather than take their meals in fine style in the presidential dining room on the second floor. That said, the Carters were sticklers for discipline and expected their children to take family meals at set times, properly dressed.

The Carters owned a family property on their celebrated peanut farm in Plains, Georgia, but they spent most weekends at Camp David, the official presidential retreat about seventy miles from Washington in the mountainous state of Maryland. The first president to use Camp David (in 1942) was Franklin D. Roosevelt, who originally named it Shangri-La after the Tibetan paradise in James Hilton's novel *Lost Horizon*. The property was renamed Camp David by Dwight Eisenhower, after his grandson. It's a fine place with a number of lodges built from local timber and painted dark green, each with a different name. The president's lodge is called Aspen. It boasts fine views of the surrounding landscape through vast picture windows and has its own swimming pool and putting range. The camp has a bowling alley and a movie theater for the presidential family. One of the other lodges, Laurel, is the size of a large house, with spacious meeting rooms, a dining room, a drawing room, and a vast, professional kitchen capable of catering for banquets for a hundred people or more. Visiting heads of state take their meals here, and the lodge is also the venue for the First Family's private parties on the evening of Christmas Day and New Year's Day. The camp is surrounded by a high-security fence with massive gates. It is guarded by military personnel and members of the secret services—more so than the White House, understandably enough, given its remote mountain location. There's a landing pad for the presidential helicopter and a presidential car waits nearby to drive the president to his lodge in bad weather. Camp David is, then, a place of pilgrimage in a magical setting—a place where the First Family comes to spend time together, reflect, and recharge batteries.

The Carters had simple tastes. They preferred Southern-style dishes, such as fried chicken or fish. The president adored fishing. Whenever the opportunity presented itself, he would fish for trout in a superb river in the mountains near Camp David. And he always returned with a splendid catch. His own guardian angels, the ever-resourceful secret service agents, would release hundreds of fish into the river before his arrival. Mrs. Carter would often accompany him. She adored fishing, too. Camp David was their private paradise, a place where they could truly relax. All the presidents I have known enjoyed Camp David.

The president of the United States always travels with a large entourage. In town, he travels by limousine and is accompanied everywhere in the world by the presidential motorcade of vehicles, which are sent on ahead by plane. The president leaves or arrives at the White House on one of the ultramodern HMX-1 helicopters of Marine Helicopter Squadron One. It's an unforgettable scene. The great machine touches down gently on the White House lawn, the rotor blades decelerate and stop, the doors open, and the president steps down, greets the guard of honor and waves to the crowd of waiting journalists while (most often) avoiding their barrage of questions. I have watched the spectacle many times in the past twenty-five years, and it has lost none of its thrill—a forcible reminder that the president of the United States is indeed the most powerful man in the world.

The president's other main mode of transport is his "fleet" of two private jets, which I have never had the honor of visiting. I'm told that the interiors are fitted out like a flying apartment, with an office where the president can function exactly as if he was installed in the Oval Office at the White House, keeping in constant touch by video link and telephone. Currently, the fleet consists of two specially-configured Boeing 747-200B series aircraft. The call sign "Air Force One" is used whenever the president flies on board one of these or any other US Air Force aircraft.

The White House is a supremely comfortable residence with 132 rooms, including bathrooms, archives, and storerooms. There are three floors above ground level and a basement. The First Family's private quarters are on the second and third floors, where they sleep, take their meals, and receive private guests and family. Public occasions, ceremonies, and banquets are held on the State Floor. The state dining room is capable of accommodating seated dinners for 200 people or standing receptions for 300 to 400 guests. The Green Room, the Blue Room, and the Red Room can hold 40 people apiece, while a second dining room holds around 140. The main hall is used for receptions, and the entire floor can be given over to events hosting some 1,200 people. In summer, the garden barbecues are attended by up to 3,000 guests.

Contrary to popular belief, the president's famous Oval Office is not in the White House itself (many people assume it is located behind the building's southern façade) but in the West Wing.

So much for the working life of the White House. Leisure facilities include a bowling alley installed in 1973 and a movie theater built under

Roosevelt in 1942 and often used by the First Family. The White House is also blessed with extensive grounds tended by an army of gardeners. Part-time staff swells the ranks of the ninety full-time employees, so that several hundred people may be employed at the White House at any given time. And every day, the building also welcomes up to 6,000 visitors from the general public: it is symbolically "open" to every American citizen. The president occupies the White House during his term of office, but the building belongs to the nation as a whole.

And so I began my first day at the White House, proud but terrified that I would not be up to the enormous task ahead. My predecessor had left no provisions beyond some eggs, flour, and butter. There was a great deal to do—and fast. Throughout the whole of my first year at the White House, I scarcely spoke; I was so afraid of failing to complete what I had been asked to do. I have already mentioned the lofty, all-powerful maître d'hôtel, who lorded over the kitchens and the domestic staff in general. The kitchen staff, many of whom had worked at the White House for years, treated me as the new boy, ready to pounce at my first mistake. There was no question of enjoying the job. I just had to knuckle down to the task in hand and avoid making the slightest mistake.

After a few weeks, someone came to tell me that a car was waiting for me outside: a big, sleek black limousine of the sort seen in TV shows, carrying important officials or mafia types. I was to come straight away, no time to change. I was taken to an office near the train station in Washington. An official behind a desk asked me a series of questions about U.S. institutions: the Supreme Court, the government, its structure and workings. Naturally enough, I had no idea. My questioner became quite annoyed. He asked me if I was at least aware of the name of the president of the United States.

"Of course I know. I cook for him every day. It's Jimmy Carter."

"Well done," he congratulated me. "You've passed. Just one more thing. Write this down in English: 'Today is Thursday, and it is a beautiful day.'"

I did as he asked.

"Very good. You've passed the examination. Now go back to the car. You'll be driven to an office in Alexandria, for an administrative tribunal. They're expecting you."

I still had no idea what was happening. I arrived and found myself in the presence of a court official who asked me to place my hand on a copy of the Bible, and repeat a number of oaths and phrases, which I did, very meekly and obediently. After which, he announced: "Congratulations, you're an American citizen."

Mrs. Carter had kept her promise and put me on the fast track. I returned to the White House as a U.S. citizen and a French citizen, too, since I had not given up my nationality of origin. I was now fully cleared to serve the president of the United States.

As is well known, one of the greatest challenges of Jimmy Carter's presidency was the need to secure the release of the 52 U.S. hostages held by a group of Iranian students for 444 days at the American embassy in Teheran. President Carter devoted almost all of his time to efforts to bring the hostages home, efforts which caused him enormous anguish. We were not party to everything that was going on: such things are not and should not be revealed to the domestic staff. But one day, we gathered that something was afoot; the president spent longer than usual in the Oval Office. As a rule, he worked from 6 a.m. to around 6 or 7 p.m. He worked a great deal and was often criticized in the press as being unable to delegate. Now, he broke all the records and ordered plates of sandwiches to be delivered to the office every evening. The president held meeting after meeting, late into the night. Was the long-awaited freeing of the hostages finally about to take place? We learned that a small dinner was to be held in the private apartments for the evangelist Billy Graham. Something important was clearly about to happen. Graham was invited to every special occasion. That evening, the guests all held hands around the table and prayed that the hostages would be returned home. They prayed that the forthcoming rescue mission, which Carter had been so busy planning, would be a success. It was not, of course: the men who were sent to mount a raid on Tehran and bring the hostages back died in a helicopter and plane crash in the desert near the Iranian town of Tabas. The incident came as an appalling shock for President Carter and his family and Mrs. Carter in particular, who played an active role in state affairs. We knew that the mood in the White House would be grim indeed the next day and redoubled our efforts in support of the First Family.

Amy Carter was a ray of sunshine at the White House. Twelve years old and full of joie de vivre, she was a playful character who adored having fun and joking with her classmates. She attended a public school, like everyone else, and received no special favors. When she came home from school, she often would ask us to send up the ingredients for her favorite treat, sugar cookies, so that she could make them herself. I still have her handwritten recipe. She would make the dough for these, cut them out, pop them in the oven, set off for a spot of roller-skating while they were cooking, and forget all about them. After about fifteen or twenty minutes, smoke would be seen rising above the White House, while an acrid smell of burning filled the corridors, setting off the alarms, which in turn sent the secret service agents scurrying to my pastry kitchen, thinking that I was the culprit. Not so. The problem was up on the second floor in the presidential apartment. The secret service agents would then rush up the stairs four at a time, take the sugar cookies out of the oven, open the windows, and try to get rid of the smoke. No more cookies. Poor Amy! I knew what to do and prepared a secret stock of the same cookies, which I kept in the kitchen. The following morning, as often as not, Amy would appear in the kitchen, sleepy-eyed, explaining that she was supposed to take a batch of cookies to school, but had none to take. I asked what had happened to the flour, sugar, and butter I had sent up the previous afternoon.

"There was a small accident."

I confided that I had smelled the accident. Everyone in the White House had smelled the accident. Amy would give her small half-smile, as much as to say "OK, it won't happen again." I would give her a fine bag of cookies, whereupon she would thank me warmly and run off to school. Often enough, exactly the same thing would happen all over again the very next day. Amy was a keen roller skater and was criticized in the press for practicing her art on the precious hardwood floors of the White House. She was a young girl of twelve! She needed to have fun and felt perfectly at home at the White House, not in the slightest bit over-awed. She had a little tree house where she would spend hours in one of the big pine trees in the grounds. She was a talented child and learned to the play the piano and the violin. She liked to think of herself as a good cook, despite the somewhat blackened sugar cookies, and liked to make colored eggs for Easter. That year, her last at the White House, I helped her make little chocolate houses and ducks and we took photographs of them. The president and Mrs. Carter—like parents the world over—were anxious that Amy should not be spoiled. One day, Amy's father invited her to attend a state dinner for the Mexican president José López Portillo. A dinner with a tableful of important dignitaries talking politics is no fun for a young girl. I remember that Amy took a book along with her and read it between courses. Apart from this, she was impeccably behaved and chatted politely with the guests of honor.

The White House hosted numerous events for children. When a circus came to Washington, the elephants paid us a visit. In celebration of the release of the hit film *The Black Stallion*, its twin stars (the child actor Kelly Reno and a magnificent ebony horse by the name of Cass Ole) visited the White House gardens, and I was able to bring George along to meet them. This was the first time that George and Amy met. They didn't become close friends, but George was enormously proud of having chatted to the president's daughter.

The Carters certainly enjoyed a party. Family reunions and birthdays provided some relief from the crushing burden of the hostage crisis shouldered by President Carter and the First Lady. During my year as their pastry chef, I was honored to prepare Amy Carter's birthday cake: she had asked for a square cake decorated with all of her favorite things: a violin, a piano, her cat, and, of course, a pair of roller skates.

The same year, I was also called upon to make a birthday cake for President Carter himself. The date coincided with the Democratic National Convention, which would be nominating its presidential candidate for the forthcoming elections. We celebrated President Carter's birthday just before his departure for the convention. I created a round cake for about a dozen people decorated with a two-wheeled cart pulled by a donkey, the Democratic Party's mascot. The donkey was made of blown sugar and the cart (also of sugar) was filled with white carnations, the president's favorite flower. The cake was inscribed with the words "Happy Birthday, Mr. President." A few days later, Mrs. Carter came down to the kitchen to present her compliments for the splendid cake. The "leftover" cake, together with the sugar donkey and cart, were taken to the convention, where each one of the president's collaborators was presented with a piece.

The press was not kind to the Carters and took particular pleasure in sneering at the state dinners held during their mandate. This was quite unfair. The Carters' dinners were every bit as successful as those given by other presidents, if not more so. The food was very well prepared, the menus carefully chosen. But the fact remained that the president was a Southerner, and the press had pigeonholed him as a hick peanut farmer who knew nothing about fine food and appreciated it even less. This was completely untrue, as I knew very well.

During my year with the Carters, we prepared one of the finest lunches I have ever witnessed as part of a private visit to the president by King Baudouin I of Belgium. The lunch took place in the East Room, the largest reception room in the White House, which was set with long tables arrayed with dogwood blossom—a traditional sign of spring in the northeastern US—arranged in garlands. The flowers, the vermillion tableware, the crystal glasses, and the dazzling white table linen were all superb. The menu began with cold lobster served with phyllo pastry and Gruyère wafers, followed by medallions of veal accompanied by a jardiniere of vegetables, salad, and cheese, and the dessert as the final flourish. The latter was a hibiscus flower, the Hawaiian state flower, served on individual plates and filled with freshly made coconut ice cream drizzled with a dash of coconut liqueur and decorated with fresh fruit.

On April 8, 1980, we received an official visit from President Anwar Sadat of Egypt, who had signed the Camp David accords—in which President Carter had played a key role—with Prime Minister Menachem Begin of Israel two years earlier. This time, the main course was a fillet of beef Wellington. The fillets and foie gras stuffing were prepared in advance by the chefs, and it was up to me to prepare the finished pastry cases. This was followed by a salad served with Brie cheese and a dessert of strawberry soufflé with glazed strawberries accompanied by a platter of petits fours.

Shortly afterwards, we received an official visit from the Israeli Prime Minister, Mr. Begin—a quite different affair, since everything had to be kosher. Preparations for the meal were overseen by a rabbi in the White House kitchen, while other rabbis arrived with gas torches, which were passed over the pastry table, the interior of the ovens, the burners, and cake molds—anything that was likely to come into contact with the food. The tableware was plunged into boiling water, all of the tables were covered with sheets of tin foil, and we were advised to take the greatest care with our preparations, under the watchful eye of the rabbi. The menu featured salmon served with a green herb sauce, duck breast with peaches, wild rice, and asparagus, and a dessert consisting of an iced gateau filled with orange sorbet. The White House was not equipped with an ice-cream maker, and so I made the sorbet in the kitchens of a well-known Washington hotel, the Watergate. The Watergate's chef took the opportunity to inform the press that he had created the dessert, when in fact he simply let me use his sorbet machine.

The gateau was a sponge cake made without butter, filled with orange sorbet and decorated with non-dairy whipped topping—kosher rules excluded the use of fresh dairy cream—and orange segments dipped in red and yellow sugar, all served with a Grand Marnier and apricot jam sauce, floating with pieces of diced orange. Prime Minister Begin declared that it was the finest kosher cake he had ever tasted. My first year at the White House was marked by some successes, after all.

The months went by, and the presidential election approached. The hostage crisis continued to weigh heavily upon President Carter, and there were further difficulties at home. We had no idea how things would turn out, but we hoped that the president would be reelected. Everyone at the White House adored the Carter family. The older chambermaids were especially close to Rosalynn Carter and embraced her affectionately whenever they met. Mrs. Carter was respected by all her staff. She supported her husband to the hilt and played an active role in state affairs to the very best of her abilities. She was a passionate advocate of humanitarian causes, a hard worker, and a real fighter.

As a newcomer to the White House, I had no desire to experience the upheaval of a new president and shared the general mood of growing anxiety as election day approached. At last, however, the guillotine fell and on November 4, 1980, Ronald Reagan was elected with fifty percent of the vote. President Carter polled just forty-one percent. The experts all agreed that the hostage crisis had been a decisive factor in the outcome. Naturally, President Carter was deeply affected by the result. Christmas at the White House was not an especially happy celebration that year, although the Carters, with their characteristic kindness and consideration, did their very best to ensure that everything went well.

President Carter had lost the election, but in the meantime it was business as usual, with receptions, lunches, and dinners to be hosted. There were hands to shake and official photo calls, smiles, and civilities. President and Mrs. Carter handled everything with genuine grace and aplomb. And all the while, they continued to fight for the release of the hostages.

Just after Christmas, the cooks, pastry chefs, chambermaids, and waiters were invited to lunch with the first family at Camp David, which none of us had visited before.

We were collected from the White House in a fleet of buses and taken straight to the Laurel Lodge, where the lunch was to take place. We were surprised to find a well-stocked bar laid on for us—at the

White House, the Carters served only wine or mineral water to their guests. At their request, whisky and other spirits were forbidden. At Camp David, the staff was offered every imaginable type of strong liquor. Mrs. Carter arrived, all smiles, and announced that the president would be with us shortly—he was busy with his second favorite pastime after fishing, namely woodwork, in a specially installed workshop at the camp. Fifteen minutes later, President Carter arrived, smiling cheerfully, wearing corduroy trousers and a sweater speckled with sawdust. He welcomed us and chatted for almost an hour before inviting us all to take our seats for lunch at four tables each set for ten people. We enjoyed a hearty menu of soups, quiches, salad, and dessert. Throughout the meal, President and Mrs. Carter circulated from group to group, ensuring that no one was forgotten.

After dessert, Mrs. Carter asked to be excused and left for the Aspen bungalow while the president took us on a personal tour of Camp David and its various lodges. He strode on ahead, telling us all about the events of two years earlier, when Messrs Begin and Sadat had stayed at Camp David for a week, at his invitation, to discuss the possibility of an Israeli-Egyptian peace accord. It had taken him three days to persuade Prime Minister Begin to come out of his bungalow, greet President Sadat, and shake hands with him. Three days to negotiate a handshake! We moved on to the Aspen lodge, entering through the kitchens, which were old and dilapidated. The Carters refused to spend public money renovating them—a frivolous expense in their eyes. Finally, the president showed us his fishing tackle and how he tied his own flies with horsehair, wrapped around the hook. I enjoy trout fishing, too, and couldn't resist asking him: "Mr. President, why do you take such trouble to tie flies when everyone knows that trout love cheese?"

He replied that "with cheese, it wasn't sport, but organized suicide." He didn't know at the time that the secret services regularly released hundreds of trout into the river for his pleasure.

At Christmas, the Carters left for their home in Plains, Georgia. They returned for the New Year, and spent the first days of January making preparations for their departure, scheduled for January 20, the traditional date of the presidential handover. Everyone approached the date with a heavy heart. As the days went by, we saw less and less of President Carter, who was fighting desperately for the hostages. He held endless meetings and spent long hours on the telephone, doing everything in his power to secure their release before the end of his mandate. But time moved on inexorably. The day came for the Carters' last dinner at the White House. I can still remember the menu: simple, Southern cooking, as so often. The guest of honor was Willy Nelson, the country singer, with twelve others, mostly family. The dinner was held in the president's private dining room. It was not a happy occasion, but between each course, everyone got up and danced: Willy Nelson had brought his guitar and sang nostalgic songs about Georgia. There were tears, and everyone tried to comfort everyone else. It was a very sad evening for me, too.

The following morning, on the eve of the Carters' departure, it was time to say goodbye. A difficult day, particularly because rumors had, of course, begun circulating about the Reagans: they painted a worrying portrait of a hard-nosed, highly demanding family with a particularly tough taskmistress in the person of Nancy Reagan, the new First Lady. We were very worried.

That morning, I was working alone in the kitchen. I felt angry that the Carters were leaving, angry at what I saw as the unjust outcome of the election, angry at everything. I threw some saucepans into the sink with a great clatter, but regained my composure when I saw Mrs. Carter approaching out of the corner of my eye. I didn't want her to find me in a temper. She shook my hand, then hugged me warmly, said goodbye, and thanked me for everything I had done for the family since my arrival at the White House. She added that the president also sent his best wishes, but that he was very busy and unable to say goodbye in person. We were both on the brink of tears. Rosalynn Carter was an enormously courageous woman. Before leaving, she made a point of speaking personally to every member of staff to thank them.

In the meantime, the president continued to work ceaselessly for the release of the hostages.

On the day of their departure, the Carters left their private apartment at 9:30 a.m. and went down to the Blue Room, where they were to meet President and Mrs. Reagan before leaving with them in a shared limousine for the Capitol and the handover of power. We served coffee. The two presidents and their First Ladies were accompanied by the vice presidents and their wives and other members of the Cabinet. We had prepared a platter of breakfast pastries, but it was left untouched. The tension between the guests was palpable.

We hovered behind the doors, hoping for a glimpse of the new president. It felt to me as if he was taking the White House by force, that this was President and Mrs. Carter's rightful home. This day was even worse than the last. In the kitchens we set about preparing meals, pastries and desserts for the new president, who would soon be arriving at the White House with the First Lady and their guests. We had no idea of their likes and dislikes, however—or which dining room they would choose for the meal or how many people were expected. We had been told nothing, other than that the Reagans would be touring around Washington a great deal later in the day—ten gala balls had been organized to celebrate the Republican victory, and the new president would be attending all of them with the First Lady, as was traditional. The Reagans were in for a busy evening, but they would certainly need to pause for something to eat, in the midst of all the to-ing and fro-ing. We were all on duty in the kitchen, working hard to produce enough food and a wide range of dishes to suit all tastes.

Meanwhile, the Carters' personal belongings were being moved out of the White House: furniture, clothes, carpets, rugs, and paintings. The new president's furniture and belongings were moved in during the morning. Everything had to be present and correct when he returned to the White House in the afternoon, after inspecting the troops. This quick-fire change of décor was difficult and painful, too, adding to my impression of a wholesale invasion.

Even during the morning coffee reception, President Carter continued to make calls to further the cause of the hostages' release. And when the two presidents arrived at the Capitol, he started all over again; as a result, there was hardly any conversation between the two men. Ronald Reagan was left waiting around for the ceremonies to begin, when an aide came to tell Jimmy Carter that the long-awaited release was imminent. President Reagan generously stated that if confirmation came through during his inaugural address, he would interrupt the ceremony and invite Jimmy Carter to take the podium and announce the hostages' release himself. In the end, this is not what happened. The announcement of the hostages' release came twenty minutes after the new president had taken power.

President Carter had missed his appointment with destiny by just twenty minutes. The timing, we can imagine, was cruelly calculated by the hostage takers—whose actions had also cost him the presidency—to deprive him further of the public acclaim he deserved after so much effort and so many days devoted to bringing the hostages home.

CHAPTER 10

Ronald Reagan's Sweet Tooth

I had arrived at the White House in 1979, on a very low salary, which I now decided to supplement. I called François Dionot, the director of a well-known Washington cooking school known as L'Académie de Cuisine, whom I had met at the Homestead. I suggested that I could give classes at L'Académie, as I had done for guests at the Homestead. He agreed, and I began teaching. At the same time, I was receiving calls from a great many restaurateurs and hoteliers around Washington looking for pastry chefs. There were none to be found. I called François Diniot, asking if we could join forces to try and solve the problem. He asked me to draw up a proposal.

I went up to my fourth-floor office at the White House and came up with a plan for a 200-hour pastry course, to be held in four-hour sessions on Monday evenings and Saturday afternoons. I included a schedule and an estimate of the optimum number of pupils. François liked the idea. The school included a small pastry shop in the foyer, which could be adapted to receive a series of small worktops and sinks. An oven was installed in the window area and a refrigerator in the corridor. We started with thirteen students, who all completed the fast-track course, and pronounced themselves highly satisfied. Some found jobs in Washington right away. But if the course were to continue, we needed bigger premises. François was able to rent a room on the upper floor of the building, where we installed a professional pastry classroom capable of holding classes of up to twenty-one people, with a worktable and tools for each pupil. With a fee of 2,500 dollars for the full course, this gave us a turnover of 52,500 dollars for the year. The course proved profitable. With high-quality, professional teaching, we had no difficulty placing our graduates, often straight out of the school. I taught at L'Académie for ten years, until 1990. The classes still operate today, twenty-five years after they were set up, under the tutelage of one of my former students, Mark Ramsdell. An achievement of which I'm proud.

President Reagan, the fortieth president of the United States, had two children from his first marriage—Mike and Maureen—and two more from his second marriage: a daughter, Patti, and a son, Ron. There was also the family dog, Lucky, and a faithful friend in the person of Ted Graber, a Hollywood interior designer who was to become the White House's new decorator. Each new president traditionally brought in his own decorator to refurbish the private apartments as required.

On the afternoon of the day on which the Reagans were due to take over the White House, the day of the handover of power, I was preparing desserts in the kitchen when a blob of raspberry purée splashed onto my jacket. I decided to go up to my office to change. When I arrived at the staff elevator and pushed the button for the fourth floor, I found myself eyeballing a man I had never seen before, who took one look at me and said: "Oh! I can see there are going to have to be a few changes around the White House."

I was panic-stricken. Scared shitless, as the saying goes, and trembling in my shoes. I got changed, and went back down to the kitchens, where I told my colleagues what had happened. Everyone was as worried as I was. Yes, the Reagans were coming, and no one knew what to expect!

The first day passed without incident. The Reagans were busy with the many social niceties following the handover and had very little time to eat. Things began in earnest the next day. We had decided to produce a weekly schedule of menus for the presidential family meals for Mrs. Reagan's approval. All of the provisions ordered for the White House are carefully recorded, and distinction is made between the food ordered for official events and food for the private consumption of the president and his family. The cost of the former was reimbursed by the State Department, while the latter was at the personal expense of the president—needless to say, great care was taken with these orders, with an eye to the resulting bill.

We got to know Mrs. Reagan and the president day by day: their personal tastes, the type of food they liked to serve at receptions and dinners, and what they liked to eat themselves. They had arrived from their ranch with frozen bags of their favorite "hamburger soup," so called because it featured (along with beans and noodles), a few miniature hamburgers floating in the broth. The soup was delicious, and fun. We started out by serving it to the president and his family as a welcome taste of home.

One day, in the kitchen, I was practicing a dessert for an official dinner. I had split some coconuts down the middle, scooped out most of the flesh, provided each one with a pretty rim of sugar, and decorated the whole thing with exotic flowers and a sugar ribbon tied in a bow to one side. The resulting baskets were filled with coconut ice cream, drizzled with coconut liqueur, and garnished with fresh fruit. Nancy Reagan was passing by the kitchens—a few days after her arrival at the White House—and saw what I was doing. She was delighted by the results. She felt that it would be a good idea from now on to present her with samples of proposed desserts before serving them to the guests. And so a new White House tradition was born: the "dessert dinners" at which the president's family would taste and test the new desserts, ensuring that everything was to the satisfaction of the First Lady and her guests.

Little by little, the Reagans took possession of their new home, the White House. They were, however, reluctant to visit Camp David, where Mrs. Reagan had decided to renovate the kitchens and change a great many other things that she didn't like. While work was in progress, the Reagans preferred to relax at their ranch in California, the rather grandly named Rancho del Cielo. The "ranch" was, in fact, a quite modest house in the middle of nowhere or, to be more precise, in the empty desert country around Santa Barbara. It was the perfect property for riding, which the Reagans both loved. Above all, it gave them privacy and time alone together. The president loved chopping wood or climbing up on the roof to replace a shingle, doing odd repairs around the place. He had a Jeep, which he loved to run over the rough surrounding country—Mrs. Reagan lived in constant fear of an accident. The president was always watched over by a posse of secret service agents. He was heedless of accidents and danger, particularly when wielding a chainsaw or circular saw.

Lucky, the dog that Mrs. Reagan had brought with her to the White House was a black, female Bouvier des Flandres—a large, shaggy breed not at all suited to the place. She was quickly sent back to Rancho del Cielo, and we acquired a new presidential pet in Washington—a cocker spaniel named Rex after Rex Scouten, the long-serving White House chief usher, whom Mrs. Reagan held in great esteem.

Some time after the episode of the coconut baskets, I received an order from Mrs. Reagan. Some friends would be coming to lunch in a few days, and she wanted to serve them raspberry mousse garnished with spun sugar—she was always very clear about exactly what she wanted. I prepared a sample for her inspection that afternoon, taking care to follow her instructions as closely as possible. The raspberry mousse was as light as could be and enriched with fresh raspberries. The net of spun sugar was made using pink sugar and featured little green leaves. All around this, Mrs. Reagan had asked for an assortment of fresh fruit—kiwis, pineapple, and raspberries—so that the result was as colorful as possible. At around 5 p.m. I took the dessert up to the kitchen of the private presidential apartment for Mrs. Reagan to inspect. Quite characteristically, the first lady took the trouble to rearrange the fruit on the plate herself with her bare hands. Just then Ronald Reagan arrived in the kitchen, back from the office, wearing jeans and a plaid shirt. He saw the dessert, declared that it was very beautiful, and wanted to try some.

We hunted for a spoon, but the kitchen was in disarray following the handover. No one knew where to find one. The president took the big kitchen spatula that I had used to arrange the fruit around the raspberry mouse and dug in. Unfortunately, everything fell off the spatula and slopped down the front of his shirt before it reached his mouth. Mrs. Reagan was clearly infuriated by this display, after which President Reagan proceeded to use the spatula to scrape the mousse off his shirt. The First Lady was more furious still, but the president went on to taste the dessert and take some more, completely unabashed.

"Hey, Honey, this is terrific! It's great."

He was plainly delighted. From that moment on, I understood that Ronald Reagan had a very sweet tooth. Whenever he tasted a dessert, there was a look of utter glee on his face.

Shortly after this, we celebrated the president's seventieth birthday in February 1981, just a month after his arrival at the White House. The event was marked by an unforgettable dinner attended by le tout Hollywood: Elizabeth Taylor, Frank Sinatra, Cary Grant, Gregory Peck, Charlton Heston, Jimmy Stewart, and a host of other stars for whom Ronald Reagan was not only their president, but also a former colleague and friend "on the set." A truly magical evening.

The birthday cake was immense: a truncated sugar pyramid, standing about five feet high, supported the platter for the cake itself, on which I had placed a bucking white horse—all in sugar—like the horse presented to Ronald Reagan by the Mexican president, José López Portillo. Around this was a "coronet" of ten further sugar plates, each one supporting a cake, inscribed with "Happy Birthday, Mr. President" and ten pyramids made of carved ice, decorated with balls of ice cream and sorbets of every imaginable flavor: lime, orange, raspberry, coconut, chocolate, vanilla, pistachio. Inside each pyramid was a battery-operated light. When these were switched on, the effect of the ice sculptures, softly lit from within, was magnificent. Each cake was also surrounded by seven candles, representing the president's seven decades.

But while Ronald Reagan made his birthday speech, I found it hard to think of him as "our" president. I saw Jimmy Carter in his place, in the magnificent East Room. President Carter was still, I felt, the rightful president. I couldn't accept the idea that Reagan had replaced him.

Everyone remembers March 30, 1981—the day when President Reagan was due to address a union convention at the Washington Hilton hotel. A day like any other. Towards the end of the afternoon, I had finished work and gone upstairs to my office to change and get ready to go home. Everyone at the White House was issued with a pass, which we wore around our necks on the end of a small chain. I never wore it while I was at work, in case it got caught in one of the mixing machines. I preferred to leave it in my changing room, but made sure to wear the pass whenever I entered or left the building, wearing my normal clothes.

On the day in question, I went upstairs to change as usual and emerged from the bedroom on the fourth floor onto the corridor leading to the elevator. Suddenly, I found myself surrounded by a squad of men in black, armed with machine guns, who slammed me against the wall and yelled, wanting to know what I was doing, where the hell was I going, why had they never seen me before, and what my name was.

"Hold on! I'm the White House pastry chef, and I'm on my way home."

"Where's your pass? Get that pass around your neck, so we can see who you are. You should never walk around the White House like that!"

They carried on shouting at me, and I still had no idea why. I took the elevator down, thinking they had all gone crazy. There were more men like them posted all over the White House, scurrying about like a colony of frenzied ants. I got into my car, turned on the radio, and heard immediately what was going on. I couldn't believe my ears. The president had been shot outside the Hilton by a deranged young man by the name of John Hinckley. President Reagan was in hospital, and doctors were not yet able to pronounce on his condition. I was deeply shocked and full of foreboding. This was why the White House was full of armed officers. Someone high up had clearly decided that the attack on the president was part of wider plan—a diversion to draw attention away from a subsequent attack on the White House itself. In the early 1980s, America's sworn enemies were the Russians and President Qadafi of Libya. Everyone dreaded what they might be capable of.

The next day brought better news. When I returned to work at the White House, I met the president's private physician, Dr. Daniel Ruge, who gave us instructions for President Reagan's meals. He was able to eat, which indicated that his injuries were not as bad as feared. Dr. Ruge suggested I prepare two of the president's favorite desserts, which Mrs. Reagan would take to him in hospital. These were fruit jellies prepared with white wine, an excellent Gewürztraminer from Alsace. The delicate preparations were placed in small glass dishes with an assortment of fruit and the now famous coconut ice cream. The president returned to the White House after several weeks' convalescence to a rapturous reception. The entire staff, several hundred people, stood on the west steps leading to the executive office building to welcome him back.

In May 1981, the White House received a visit from the Prince of Wales. A grand dinner was organized in his honor, and Ted Graber, the interior decorator, asked me to create sorbets and ice creams using the red, white, and blue of the British and American flags. Coconut, raspberry, and blueberry sorbets were to be placed in a special mold resembling a crown. In the center stood the Prince of Wales's emblem: three curved feathers, each about twelve inches high. I had planned to surround this with fresh raspberries, blueberries, and blackberries, a sauce, and a selection of petits fours. The dessert was named the "Prince of Wales Crown of Sorbets." The feathers were particularly difficult. I made some examples out of sugar in advance. When Ted Graber saw them, he thought they were pretty, but not exactly what he was looking for. He brought me a photograph, to show me exactly how they were structured. They are, in fact, extremely fine and delicate. It would be impossible to reproduce them in blown sugar. I had the idea of carving the design on two blocks of wood. I could press the hot sugar between these two molds, lined with a thin film to prevent the mixture from sticking. This would give the desired shape and design. After this, I could warm each piece slightly, to bend it into the required curve, with a sharp point at the bottom. The bottom tips of the three feathers could then be inserted into a sugar straw, which would emerge from the center of the crown. I was pleased and proud of my new invention. It worked!

The dinner was held in the private dining room at four tables of ten guests apiece. Each table would have its own dessert, with the sorbets, the feathers, and the petits fours. When the time came to serve the desserts, we took them up to the dining room with our hearts in our mouths. They arrived safely, the dessert was served, and everyone was delighted. But when the waiters brought the centerpieces back down to the kitchens and placed them on the table, there was a sickening crack. All of the feathers fell over onto the floor. I shuddered to think of the consequences if this had happened while the dessert was being served upstairs. Mrs. Reagan would have been unhappy, to say the least. But the honor of the White House was intact.

A funny thing happened the next day. Prince Charles was being entertained in the Oval Office. Asked if he would like something to drink, he replied naturally enough that a cup of tea would be lovely. The White House butler contacted the butler at the Navy mess, a small in-house restaurant installed beneath the Oval Office. The butler duly brought up a tray with a pot of hot water, slices of lemon, and a cup in which they had placed a teabag. The Prince of Wales looked at the cup rather anxiously, but made no attempt to help himself to the tea.

The president could see there was a problem, but feeling rather embarrassed himself and not wishing to embarrass the prince further, did nothing.

After dinner, tongues were a little looser. Host and guest felt more relaxed in each other's company, perhaps after sharing a glass or two of wine. The president plucked up courage to ask the prince why he hadn't served himself a cup of tea. Had there been a problem? The prince replied: "The problem was, I didn't know what to do with the little bag."

It seems that no one was aware that in England, "real" loose-leaf tea is infused in a teapot, which has been warmed in advance, before being poured into the cup through a little silver strainer. Apparently, the prince had never seen a teabag in his life.

Luckily, everyone saw the funny side.

The same year, in October 1981, we learned of the assassination of President Sadat. A tragedy for the entire world and particularly the White House, which had collaborated closely with him and where his efforts to achieve peace in the Middle East had been greatly appreciated. Presidents Nixon, Ford, Carter, and Reagan gathered at the White House before flying to Egypt for the state funeral. We served coffee. It was a fascinating scene: four great American presidents drinking coffee together, united in sorrow with the entire nation, over which the news had fallen like a sheet of ice. The four men greeted each other warmly: each of them knew what it was like to occupy the most powerful post in the world. At this moment, I realized more than ever that the White House is a nerve center, where the shocks of the world are felt more keenly than anywhere else.

During the first year of the Reagan administration, we also played host to Jacques Cousteau, who took lunch with the president and three or four others on one of the terraces near the Oval Office. I served a dessert inspired by the sea: a large seashell made of multicolored chocolate, filled with fish and sea creatures of various sizes, made from sorbets or ice creams shaped in molds, which I had bought specially. The shell was placed in front of a "backdrop" of sugar seaweed, and the fronds were dotted with little multicolored chocolate fish. Cousteau was extremely touched and thanked President Reagan very warmly.

At the same time, I was faced with an increasingly difficult situation. I was coping with more and more work, with very little help and very little sympathy or understanding from the executive chef, who was a highly accomplished professional, but with little real knowledge of patisserie. I felt very isolated, to the extent that I seriously considered handing in my notice and concentrating on my classes at L'Académie. I was unsure what to do, and help was not forthcoming from the White House, despite the high expectations and demands of the first family. I could see that my colleagues were unsympathetic to the difficulties I faced, taking the attitude that if I left, there would always be someone ready to step into my shoes. I was deeply worried.

Part of the problem was the fact that the executive chef planned all the menus himself without consultation. I knew that Mrs. Reagan did not like to see the same desserts appearing too often. The Reagans loved sorbets, but these would feature on the menu two, three, or four times per week. You can enjoy a dessert without having to eat it almost every day. And my own repertoire extended, as we have seen, to more than 500 different desserts, catalogued and listed at the end of my time at the Homestead. I would have loved to serve these at the White House, but this was out of the question under the régime of a head chef who repeated the same menus time and again. Until the day when, following a great many acid remarks from Mrs. Reagan, I decided to take the bull by the horns and told him that if he would let me plan the dessert menus, I would be sure to include plenty of interesting dishes, and we would have no more problems with Mrs. Reagan.

I was also encountering staff problems of my own. When I arrived at the White House, an assistant pastry cook was already in place, a person of decidedly limited skills. A woman was appointed to replace this incompetent cook, but her professional skills and training were those of a home helper rather than a professional pastry chef. She was replaced after a year by a girl who had worked as a pastry chef in Belgium. She possessed some skills, but it quickly became apparent that she had not come to the White House to advance her professional career, but rather to find herself a husband. She hung around the secret service agents and was never there when I needed her. She, too, was replaced after a year.

The executive chef, aware that I was dissatisfied with the staff he hired for me, decided to give me carte blanche to recruit my own assistant. And so, in 1982, I hired one of my own students from L'Académie. Things improved, but my new recruit proved less devoted to her task than I had hoped. Her passion was dance, and after a year she left to join a ballet company. When she left, I took on an "external" replacement, who was not a full-time member of the White House staff.

Despite these difficulties I was learning the ropes, and my confidence and autonomy increased. The White House operated on a very tight budget at the time, and we were not allowed to incur unnecessary or excessive expenses. I took to trawling the antique shops and flea markets for ice cream and sorbet molds, usually from defunct hotels where they were used by the hundred. The molds came in every size and shape, and some were made from an iron alloy designed to keep their contents perfectly cool for as long as possible. I bought them at my own expense, since the White House was not able to advance funds to that end. Over the years, I amassed a fine collection. The molds came home with me when I retired, but their originality and beauty were a precious asset during my years at the White House. I was the only pastry chef in Washington with such a collection at my disposal.

Little by little, my status with the first family began to rise. My creations were greatly appreciated. I was untouchable! I had succeeded in freeing myself from the constraints imposed by the executive chef through consistent, top-quality work. An object lesson in the best way to set about achieving your goals.

When I began working at the White House, the ice creams, sorbets, and a large proportion of the pastries were bought in from outside. I was very unhappy with this and dreamed of the day when everything would be produced in the White House's own kitchens. For this reason, in 1981, I bought a little machine imported from Italy, at a cost of 700 dollars, and received the dubious honor of an article in a Washington newspaper (inevitably, someone had informed the press), declaring that the White House's pastry chef was squandering public funds on a pointless gadget. I was furious. The accusation was unjust—and the machine is still being used today. A little later, I bought another, identical machine. The little "gadgets" allowed me to make all my own sorbets and ice creams at the White House for 25 years. They were infinitely preferable to the "professional," industrial versions, which cost a great deal more and produced greatly inferior results.

On April 19, 1982, the White House played host to Queen Beatrix of the Netherlands, accompanied by Prince Claus—another important visit and dinner that demanded a spectacular dessert. The event was scheduled for a Tuesday evening, and I had presented four successive ideas to Mrs. Reagan in the course of the preceding week. Characteristically, all of them were rejected without explanation. Whenever Mrs. Reagan needed to discuss a serious matter or was unhappy with something, she would tilt her head slightly to the right—a sure sign of the storm that was about to break over the head of the unfortunate person stood in front of her.

When I presented the fourth dessert, on Saturday, Mrs. Reagan was lunching with the president in the Solarium on the third floor, a conservatory-style room with huge windows overlooking the South Lawn, and a panoramic view of the Washington Monument and the Thomas Jefferson Memorial. Mrs. Reagan loved to take lunch in this sunny, cheerful room. I entered carrying my dessert and placed it beside her on the table. Sitting opposite the First Lady, the president eyed the plate greedily, but Mrs. Reagan tipped her head to the right and said: "No, Roland, this won't do at all. It isn't 'fine' enough. It needs to be more impressive. We'll have to think of something else."

The president intervened: "Leave the chef alone, Honey. It's a superb dessert. Everything will be great."

Mrs. Reagan tipped her head still further to the right and suggested that he mind his own business and leave her to take care of the food and hospitality at the White House. The president didn't insist. I returned to the kitchen in a black mood, as may be imagined. Had this tirade sounded the end of my career? Could I really continue like this? It was becoming harder and harder to cope. Mrs. Reagan was a hard taskmistress, and I had limited working space and an inadequate staff. I had no idea what to do. I was ready to give up and admit defeat—I was unable to fathom exactly what Mrs. Reagan was after. At that moment, the telephone rang. It was the head usher. Mrs. Reagan wanted to see me and was waiting in the Solarium. I went up and found the First Lady sitting alone. The president had left, presumably minding his own business. Mrs. Reagan said: "Roland, I know what I want to serve Queen Beatrix. You can make sugar baskets and in each basket there are to be at least three sugar tulips. We'll serve orange sorbet and fresh fruit in the baskets with petits fours to follow."

I stared at Mrs. Reagan: "Madam, there are just two days left, and I'm alone in the kitchen."

Naturally enough, Mrs. Reagan tipped her head to one side. I thought, "Oh my God, what's going to happen now?"

She said: "Roland, you have two days *and two nights*."

I answered, "Yes, ma'am," turned on my heel, headed back to the kitchens, and got straight to work.

Fourteen sugar baskets, plus fourteen times three sugar tulips: a total of forty-two flowers. This was a truly enormous task, and I was not sure I would be able to finish it in time. I did, as it turned out, and everything was a great success. I felt greatly reassured and encouraged, but apprehensive as to what further trials the First Lady could have in store.

In November 1983, President and Mrs. Reagan went to Camp Lejeune in North Carolina to take part in a ceremony honoring the Marines killed in Lebanon and those who had lost their lives in the attack on Grenada. A long, intense day. Both were in a bleak mood on their return, the more so because their itinerary had been changed several times due to terrorist threats. The CIA confirmed that Islamic terrorists were indeed planning to fire a rocket at the presidential helicopter. As a precaution, several helicopters from the Marine One fleet took to the skies at the same time, so that it was impossible to know in which one the president was traveling. We also learned that the president's daughter, Maureen, was the object of a terrorist assassination plot; she was then placed under the constant protection of the secret services.

There were occasional respites from the presidential round of state occasions, official ceremonies, problems, and dangers. When the Reagans ate alone, without guests; they preferred very plain food. Nancy Reagan enjoyed calf's liver, which the president detested, and so this was often served for the First Lady when he was away or with an alternative dish for the president. The president's own favorite menu consisted of a fine steak served with macaroni and cheese, followed by chocolate mousse. This was served whenever Nancy was away from the White House—we would have been shot if ever she found out! The president, for his part, was overjoyed to forget his stringent dietary obligations for one meal at least.

Ronald Reagan took an interest in the art of sugar sculpture. Over the years, he learned the technique of pulled and blown sugar and the ingredients of my desserts, becoming quite an expert. At small lunches or dinners, he would often impress his fellow diners by analyzing the dessert. One such occasion was a pre-expedition lunch for a crew of astronauts, including the first woman in space, Sally Ride. I created a very realistic bottle of Dom Pérignon made from pineapple and champagne sorbet, with a chocolate cork and a label bearing an inscription wishing the astronauts luck in their mission. The bottle lay in a pouring basket and was surrounded by roses. The president detailed the sugar-work that had gone into the piece, so that his guests could appreciate its full complexity. It was a highly informed, thoroughly well received speech, delivered by a true connoisseur.

During the early years of the Reagan administration, Mrs. Reagan's personal staff asked me to prepare an attractive cake for her birthday. The First Lady would be the guest of honor at a party in the Navy mess, directly beneath the Oval Office, and I was to create a dessert for about twenty people. The result was an iced cake made with Grand Marnier and raspberries. On the sugar icing, I painted Mrs. Reagan's portrait. She was extraordinarily touched by the time and trouble I had taken.

From that moment on, our relationship was more relaxed. Whenever the presidential family left for Camp David on Friday evening, I would prepare a box of petits fours—*cigarettes russes* (Russian cigarettes) or *langues de chat* (cat's tongues)—and slices of fruit cake. Mrs. Reagan adored this assortment, provided everything was absolutely fresh. When the occasion demanded, a birthday cake would be sent up, too.

CHAPTER II

An Iron First Lady

Christmas at the White House was a grandiose affair. I had to produce 120,000 petits fours as well as cakes, truffles, and chocolates. Receptions took place throughout the month of December, and these were very tiring events for all concerned, not least the First Family, who often had to greet up to 1,200 people waiting in line in front of the Christmas tree to shake hands with the president and Mrs. Reagan and have their photograph taken. Twelve hundred hands to shake, twelve hundred niceties to exchange! The toughest challenge was the tea party for military personnel, secret service agents, and members of the administration: 6,000 guests, from noon to 10 p.m., who collectively consumed around 30,000 petit fours and slices of cake, some five or six items each. The forces of order and the defenders of the Union had hearty appetites. This was the day we dreaded, but I was comforted each time by the president's compliments, reassuring me that I was doing an excellent job.

The year 1983 saw a particularly busy schedule of banquets, state dinners, and receptions of all kinds. On April 12, we welcomed the sultan of Oman, for whom I created a mango and raspberry *vacherin* topped with a spun-sugar turban—a great success. On October 1, it was the turn of Princess Margaret: jellied lobster, chicken and orange supreme, sorbets and petits fours. I created a series of near life-size blown-sugar peacocks, their tails dotted with a variety of sorbets. The president's private dining room was set with four tables for ten: the arrival of the butlers carrying these majestic birds on trays was a great success.

On December 7, we hosted the king of Nepal, for whom I created sugar swans cradling a selection of sorbets between their folded wings.

A bed of fresh fruit was arranged around the birds, each of which held an iris in its beak.

The year 1983 also saw the United States invade the Caribbean island state of Grenada, whose government was strongly influenced by Fidel Castro's Cuba. I was, of course, unaware of events—state secrets were always closely guarded at the White House, and neither I nor anyone else knew anything about the invasion. I first heard the news on my car radio while driving to work one morning, and stepped on the gas to hurry in to the kitchen, knowing that this would be a day filled with meetings, with a great deal of food to prepare. Everyone was very worried about what would happen next, but the operation was very quickly over. After anxiety came pride in the president's action and the way the intervention had been conducted.

On January 10, 1984, we welcomed an unusual guest to the White House: Mr. Li Xiannian, the president of China. This was the occasion for an exceptional state dinner, the success of which was a diplomatic necessity, with a great deal at stake. The event called for a performance of some pomp and circumstance, given the delicate state of Sino-American relations. It behooved us to show a fitting degree of deference to the representative of the People's Republic. The Reagans' decorator took especial care over this reception for 150 guests and even tried to tell me how I should go about creating a stupendous dessert. The menu featured poached turbot, stuffed *boeuf en croûte* with truffle sauce, dauphine potatoes, and a carrot soufflé. The name of the dessert, as so often, did little justice to its taste and complexity or to the work that had gone into it. To create the "pomegranate sorbet with fresh fruit and petit fours," I needed to extract the juice from the pomegranates and remove the tiny seeds: delicate, exacting, and unpleasant work. We succeeded nonetheless in creating a truly extraordinary piece: a traditional Chinese junk loaded with vegetables, fruit, or fish. The back of the boat was raised up and supported a sugar shrub, at least sixteen inches high, in which sat a phoenix, the legendary bird of Chinese mythology, similar in appearance to a peacock, but with a different neck. Its tail swept down and around the back of the junk, and the branches of the bush were hung with blue and white flowers, and elaborately shaped, typically Chinese foliage. In the bottom of the junk was the pomegranate sorbet, with fresh raspberries and litchis. The dessert was a resounding success, and a photo of it was printed in the magazine *US News & World Report*. It took a great deal of work to produce, particularly with so little assistance. The mold for the junk was constructed from pieces of wood, which I cut myself in the White House workshop. This was then covered with strips of sugar to obtain the shape of the boat.

March 22, 1984 was an important day for me. The White House was to host a state dinner for President François Mitterrand of France and his wife Danielle. I felt doubly honored, as a Frenchman and as the White House pastry chef. Everyone knows that the French are discerning gourmets. Everyone in the kitchen knew it, too, especially me. We pulled out all the stops. The menu featured salmon, fillets of veal *en croûte* with a truffle and asparagus sauce, Brie cheese with salad, and a dessert of red-wine sorbets known in the United States as "springtime sorbets." The sorbets were prepared in a savarin mold and surrounded with freshly poached peaches. These were placed in front of sugar decorations: a branch of blossom with a cardinal, the state bird of Virginia, perched on each one. The top of each sorbet was decorated with lacy swirls of white chocolate contrasting prettily with the purplish red of the sorbet. Mrs. Reagan was delighted.

The visit was marked by a number of amusing, and less agreeable, incidents. Upon entering the dining room, the president, who had naturally placed the French "First Lady" on his right, indicated that she should walk in front of him and take her seat. Madame Mitterrand didn't move. She murmured a few words in French in the president's ear, which he, of course, failed to understand. The president insisted, showing his guest her seat with a gallant gesture. Madame Mitterrand continued to stand her ground, and Ronald Reagan's surprise was plain to see. Happily, the interpreter had seen everything: he approached the president and pointed out to him in English that he was standing on the trailing hemline of Madame Mitterrand's dress.

The rest of the visit was less pleasant for me. On the morning before the dinner, the French president and several French army officers were greeted at a welcoming ceremony in the White House garden. Two or three times, I tried to speak to the presidential party. I hoped to be able to greet them, as would any Frenchman proud to see his country honored at the White House. Above all, I hoped I might be able to speak to President Mitterrand himself. I walked along the corridors of the White House—something I seldom did—telling myself that I had to find a way to speak to someone from President Mitterrand's entourage. Yet every time I said *bonjour* to one of the officers, I was completely ignored. The military gentlemen were exceedingly aloof. They might at least have answered me—my Franche-Comté accent was clear proof of my origins. They might at least have smiled or raised a hand in greeting. Instead, there was nothing. The officers didn't bat an eyelid. I was ignored, regarded with suspicion. I felt deeply sorry. I felt as if France itself was turning its back on me.

A little later, in the afternoon, the kitchen doors opened and two young men in civilian dress entered the room. Without a word of introduction, they began opening the doors of the refrigerators. I asked them if I could be of any help. Were they looking for something? They replied that they were members of President Mitterrand's entourage and that they wanted to know what he would be served that evening. They were there to check the food. This was the proverbial bridge too far. I told them that in the first place they had no right to wander around the White House without an American secret service escort and, in the second place, the menu planned for President Mitterrand was no concern of theirs. The menus were the personal preserve of the First Lady herself. Thirdly, they had no right to search my refrigerators. If they wanted to see something, they could at least ask me to open the doors for them. They were not, I reminded them, members of the White House staff, but guests. They should, at the very least, have introduced themselves and told me their names and business. They left, red with fury and swearing in French. For my part, I felt deeply angered that my home country—which these men were, after all, here to represent—behaved so badly at the White House.

I could have reported the men to the secret service agents and had them detained for half an hour or so. They had infringed the White House security rules, which forbid anyone from a visiting delegation to wander around the building unaccompanied. Looking back, I wish I had done so. Later, I discovered the identity of one of my prying visitors: he was one of President Mitterrand's cooks, his so-called private chef, who took it upon himself to check the president's food when traveling. At the White House, no one checked the food apart from the First Lady and, after her, the chefs. The French visitors had committed a terrible faux pas. There are days when everything seems doomed from the start. This one was far from over, and neither were its troubles and travails. It was not my finest hour. Mrs. Reagan had invited Julia Child, the doyenne of American cooks, to dinner. Mrs. Child had worked in France for many years in her younger days and decided to specialize in French cuisine on her return to the States. She had starred in a successful TV cooking show, written a number of books, and became a noted authority on all matters gastronomical, particularly among the young. She was a woman for whom I had a great deal of respect. She certainly deserved the honor of dinner at the White House after her long years in France.

But the event was a disaster. The White House employed just two pastry chefs at the time, and faced with a huge number of dishes and plates to prepare for dessert, we needed help from the other chefs. We gave them a helping hand in return. When the time came, they cleared their worktables to make space for us. The desserts were sent upstairs in the dumb waiters, to the first floor, where they were lined up on a table with their cutlery, ready to serve. There were fourteen dessert plates, fourteen platters of petit fours, and fourteen sauce boats—a total of forty-two items to serve, which was a difficult task. The chefs were in the habit of taking photographs of our desserts, and they were kind enough to give me prints of them afterwards. On the day in question, Hans the sous-chef kept back one of the desserts to take a photograph. I took no notice until all of the desserts had been taken into the dining room, after which one of the waiters came to warn me that one was missing. I realized, quite angrily, that Hans had forgotten to send up the plate he had photographed. I telephoned the kitchen for him to send it up as soon as possible. This he did, but instead of waiting for the lift, he decided to take the spiral stairs and save time. Inevitably, he tripped and fell, taking the dessert with him. The plate wasn't broken, but the sugar decoration was shattered. I patched everything up as best I could, in haste because the plate had to be taken to the dining room without further ado. I was furious. I told Hans that in future he was not to keep desserts in the kitchen in order to take photographs of them. No more photos! I returned home highly dissatisfied with my day, and with a deep sense of foreboding. Given my luck, I told myself, the broken dessert was bound to have ended up in front of Julia Child herself.

The next morning, I discovered with horror that this was indeed the case. Mrs. Reagan hadn't noticed, but I knew it wouldn't be long before she discovered the truth and that Julia Child would probably have told her anyway.

Things turned out even worse than that. Two days later, Julia Child wrote about her impressions of the meal in a Washington magazine. She didn't like the veal fillet, which she found tough. As for the dessert, she described it as a pile of broken multicolored bits of sugar, adding that it was neither beautiful to look at nor good to eat. I felt terrible. Mrs. Reagan was not happy. I knew I would have to work even harder to avoid a catastrophe.

Upon her return from a presidential visit to the United Kingdom, Mrs. Reagan called me into her private apartment and told me that she had eaten a truly extraordinary dessert at Winfield House, the London residence of the American ambassador. She would like, she said, to re-create it for a state dinner at the White House. She gave me the recipe on a sheet of paper, but the explanations were inadequate and she was unable to give me any further hints herself. Mrs. Reagan telephoned London for the full recipe, which I read. It began with a cup of egg whites—four whites in total, according to the Winfield House pastry chef. But four egg whites only amount to half a cup. You need eight egg whites for a cup. I told Mrs. Reagan that the recipe was wrong—or perhaps Winfield House was using ostrich eggs? She laughed. The recipe, I told her, was for nougat glacé. I asked to be allowed to prepare it using my own recipe. Mrs. Reagan was delighted with the result.

In July 1985, President Reagan was found to be suffering from colon cancer, necessitating surgery. The White House and the entire nation waited anxiously for news. After the operation, we were given explicit instructions by the president's doctor with detailed lists of forbidden foods. No more peanut brittle, which Ronald Reagan adored and which we often prepared for him. And no more popcorn during showings of his favorite films—often at Camp David—starring Humphrey Bogart, Burt Lancaster, or John Wayne, actors he knew well. As a general rule, the president was to be allowed no more cereals and grains, which could lodge in his intestine and cause an infection. In place of peanuts and popcorn, he was allowed small, homemade "White House" chocolates and the simplest kinds of petits fours with no hazelnuts or walnuts.

Mrs. Reagan faced up to the ordeal with great determination, as always. Her natural authority often earned her the criticism of the press, who nicknamed her "Queen Nancy" and criticized her for being aloof and cold. She was particularly criticized for having bought a new dinner service for the White House, in red and gold, decorated with the presidential crest. In fact, the service was paid for with funds donated from large private companies or friends and cost the American taxpayer nothing. The same donations paid for the construction of a private chapel at Camp David, where Mrs. Reagan liked to reflect and pray. The chapel was also used for the baptism of her grandchildren and family weddings.

Many people thought that Nancy Reagan was a difficult woman to work for. I didn't think this was the case, but she was an undoubted perfectionist in matters of decorum. This included the flowers decorating the tables at state dinners. Mrs. Reagan would insist that the florist present a selection of arrangements to help her choose, and the table settings were always rehearsed in advance, from the tablecloth, flowers, and plates right down to the napkins, knives, forks, and food.

The same rule applied in the private apartments, where splendid decorations of fresh flowers were the norm. One day, a cricket found its way into the presidential apartment in an abundant delivery of flowers and foliage. The creature struck up its habitual serenade and Mrs. Reagan was not amused (perhaps it was a Democratic cricket?). Orders were issued for the offending insect to be found and caught as soon as possible. There was, however, seemingly no way of telling in which decoration it was lurking. It had probably jumped free and was creeping around under the carpets. An army of cricket hunters was mobilized throughout the apartment, and no one was allowed to leave until the prey had been presented to Mrs. Reagan.

Ronald Reagan, for his part, was a man of simple tastes. His diet presented just one small problem: he hated tomatoes and hadn't eaten one in seventy years as a result of an innocent prank in his earliest childhood, the kind that often marks one for life. Someone had given him a bag of tomatoes and told him they were apples. He took the biggest one and bit into it with relish. Imagine his shock at the unexpected taste. On the other hand, as I have already mentioned, he adored desserts and preferred them to just about anything else on the menu. At dinners where he was scheduled to speak, the president was always afraid that he would be called to do so during the dessert. At the White House, he would always take a generous portion of the dessert, and then call the waiter back for another helping. He also adored squirrels: not to eat, but to feed. At Camp David, he never walked out without pocketfuls of acorns, so that the squirrels quickly came to recognize him and accompanied him in droves around the gardens.

As it happens, the squirrels were the cause of an embarrassing mishap for me. President Reagan was giving a state dinner for the president of the Federal Republic of Germany in October 1983. It was autumn, and I decided to create hazelnut logs covered in chocolate, decorated with marzipan squirrels and mushrooms. The president's daughter Maureen, who was on excellent terms with her father and stepmother, attended the trial dinner, which was organized, as always, prior to the official banquet itself. I introduced the dessert and explained its inspiration: "Here, on the hazelnut log, we see a squirrel eating his nuts." I had no idea that in English the word "nuts" is also a slang term for "testicles." My words were greeted with gales of laughter, and Maureen—a delightful, warm person—was quick to join in.

CHAPTER 12

A Second Term for the Reagans

The 1984 elections were approaching. President Reagan was standing for a second term of office. We all knew that he would be reelected, which he duly was, and with a huge majority. His second inauguration ceremony took place in January 1985. As usual, the program featured grand parades before the presidential tribune, where the First Family occupied the place of honor. That year, however, it was so cold and the snow so heavy that all of the outdoor parades were canceled. The president performed his swearing-in ceremony for the next four years at the Capitol and returned to the White House, where he hosted a reception for around 200 invited guests for whom we had prepared a selection of buffets.

A few months later, on November 9, 1985, we hosted the Prince and Princess of Wales at an official dinner for which the strictest instructions had been handed down so that nothing could go wrong. Nothing short of absolute perfection would do for a state visit from the heir to the British throne. In fact, all eyes were on Diana rather than Charles and the princess was very much the guest of honor and star of the show. I was told to prepare a distinctively feminine dessert. We created white chocolate baskets, framed by a kind of trellis punctuated by diamond-shaped panels decorated with small pale roses and a single rose leaf—hundreds and hundreds of sugar flowers, each one made by hand. The baskets were filled with peach-shaped sorbets, made using molds from my collection. Fourteen baskets each contained around fifteen peaches. I had very few molds, so the sorbets had to be shaped and turned out in successive batches—an enormous amount of work. Inside each sorbet peach was a chocolate "pit," more delicious than the real thing, and considerably easier to bite into. The sorbets were arranged in pyramids inside each basket, and the Prince of Wales's feathers were placed above each one (they held this time, remaining in place well beyond the end of the dinner). The dessert was served with champagne sauce and petits fours. The tables were decorated with huge vases filled with hundreds and hundreds of pale, peach-colored roses. I remember that these were the subject of knowing looks and speculation about what they must have cost. But no one minded, since the object of the evening was to serve the finest dinner anyone had ever seen. It was.

In the same month of November 1985, Mikhail Gorbachev visited the United States as general secretary of the Communist Party of the Soviet Union. I was sent to Camp David to help prepare his meals. I was the first member of the White House kitchen staff to work at Camp David in this way: President and Mrs. Reagan were perfectly satisfied with the work of the local chefs, but they were not happy with the desserts. Mrs. Reagan had already asked me to go to Camp David on a number of previous occasions to sort out problems. I traveled there in a White House car with all my utensils, equipment, and ingredients, and installed myself in the kitchen of the presidential lodge.

In later years, I often had the opportunity to visit Camp David. As I was leaving the kitchen this time, I had the privilege of seeing Mr. Gorbachev walking towards me with President Reagan. They stopped a few yards from me to talk with the help of an interpreter. I dearly wanted to shake the hand of Mr. Gorbachev who was, of course, a hugely popular figure in America—it was the height of what became known as "Gorbymania." Protocol forbade White House employees to approach official guests, though, so I held back. I could see that Mr. Gorbachev was looking in my direction, perhaps curious to know what I was doing. But it was not my place to speak to him, and I regretfully stepped back into the kitchen.

Two years after this first visit, on December 8, 1987, the White House gave a grand dinner for Mr. Gorbachev and his wife Raisa. The Soviet

Union and the United States were embarking on the opening stages of glasnost. On the following day, they signed a major nuclear disarmament treaty. There was a great deal at stake, and the evening was heavily symbolic. I decided to serve a dessert likely to please the Russian palate. I knew that the Russians were enthusiastic tea drinkers and that they adored honey and fresh raspberries. The dessert was served on a large oval platter in the middle of which stood a series of chocolate domes. The dinner was a great success, but the press reported an apparent tiff between Mrs. Reagan and Mrs. Gorbachev. Incidents—or rumors—such as this need to be handled with extreme care, particularly when one was not present. Which is why I have nothing to add on the subject.

What is certain is that Presidents Reagan and Gorbachev got on extraordinarily well and shared a great many jokes and anecdotes.

One of these was published in a Washington newspaper. Strict orders had been given to the Moscow road police: speeding drivers were to be given a verbal warning, regardless of who was in the vehicle. One day Secretary General Gorbachev was returning to Moscow from his *datcha* for a meeting at the Kremlin. Realizing he was late, he asked his driver to trade places and ride in the back—Gorbachev would drive the car himself. He set off at top speed, and the speeding car was spotted by two policemen on motorcycles who immediately gave chase. Eventually, one of the bikes was outstripped and admitted defeat. The other held on and finally caught up with the car. When he rejoined his colleague, he explained that he hadn't given the verbal warning. The other policeman wanted to know why not? Their instructions were to caution all speeding drivers, regardless of how important they were. But in this case, the reckless driver was none other than Gorby himself, so you can imagine how important the guy in the backseat must have been.

Looking back over my notebooks, it seems as if the entire world passed through the White House—or at least its highest representatives. And each time, it fell to me to devise an appropriate, pleasant greeting. Because desserts, like cooking itself, are a universal language to which the different cultures of the world bring their particular accents. Like music, food has the power to soothe and relax: good food, at least. This was true to such an extent that the dishes and desserts served at state dinners truly played their part in the political process. Guests spoke to each other, most often through interpreters, about high matters of state and world affairs, but no interpreter was necessary for them to share the enjoyment of a fine dessert. Which is why, for official guests, I always tried to prepare desserts that would speak to them of their own country, as a way of showing that they were understood and honored.

Hence, on April 30, 1987, when the White House hosted the Japanese prime minister, Nakasone Yasuhiro, I chose to prepare a dessert reflecting his county's national passion for oranges. The result was a series of blown-sugar oranges the size of balloons covered with chocolate specially treated to resemble orange peel, each filled with *gianduja* mousse covered with orange sorbet. Each piece was finished with sugar orange blossoms and accompanied by fresh fruit. When this magnificent dessert was brought into the dining room, Mr. Nakasone asked Mrs. Reagan where we were able to buy such huge oranges. It was a well-known fact that everything was bigger in the United States, he said. Perhaps the oranges came from Texas? Mrs. Reagan explained that these were in fact sugar oranges made by the White House's own pastry chef. I took it as a terrific compliment.

Nancy Reagan was a tough character who never hesitated to say exactly what was on her mind—as during a second visit from President Mitterrand of France in 1988, a visit marked by a small, happily not "diplomatic," incident. The visit was classed as "official," but the dinner was a private affair in the presidential dining room on the second floor. For dessert, we served pears in an almond-milk mousse with sabayon sauce and petits fours. After dinner, the forty guests were to take coffee in the Yellow Oval Room, and Mrs. Reagan asked for a fire to be lit, as it was rather cold. The job fell to a rather incompetent butler who succeeded in lighting the fire, but forgot to open the draught. When it was time for coffee, the entire apartment was wreathed in smoke. Mrs.

Reagan was extremely angry and made her feelings abundantly clear to the butler responsible. The same person was in charge of Rex, the presidential dog, who for obvious reasons was never allowed into the kitchens of the private apartments. Often, the butler would doze off on a chair and find himself shaken awake by Mrs. Reagan, promising that it would never happen again. But it always did.

One day, I had a problem with Mrs. Reagan. The first lady had stipulated that state dinners should finish with a dessert based on fresh fruit rather than chocolate, which she felt would be too calorific. However, we were about to receive a visit from the Italian prime minister, a chocoholic, I had heard, who always carried a few pieces in his pockets. I decided, for once, to include chocolate in the dessert and to explain my reasons to Nancy Reagan. I took the dessert up to the private apartments at 10 a.m., placed it on a small table next to the door, and explained to Mrs. Reagan that after reading the service notes, which referred expressly to the prime minister's love of chocolate, I had decided to incorporate it in the dessert. I hoped she would find the results satisfactory.

Mrs. Reagan exploded with anger. "I am the only person who decides what is to be served at White House dinners, Roland. Not you or anyone else. If I say that the dessert should contain chocolate, it will contain chocolate. But if I say that there is to be no chocolate, then there will be no chocolate. I hope I am making myself quite clear." I was at a loss to know what to say. I wanted to do a good job and was now being penalized for it. I wanted to help, not overstep my responsibilities. I was literally shaking in my shoes. Mrs. Reagan saw how badly I was affected by her words. With her head in her hands, she excused herself. "Forgive me, Roland, I should never have spoken to you like that. This is a very difficult time, I hardly no which way to turn. You are right. Chocolate is a very good idea. I know it is. I'm so sorry—but still: no chocolate!" I thanked Mrs. Reagan and headed back to the kitchens to work on a different dessert.

The year 1986 was marked by a host of significant events. On January 28, we witnessed the explosion of the space shuttle Challenger at Cape

Canaveral, ninety seconds after takeoff. The shuttle's crew of seven all died in the inferno, including a woman, Christa McAuliffe, a schoolteacher who would have been only the second woman in space. The United States entered a period of national mourning, and the disaster was a major personal setback for President Reagan.

On February 7, we celebrated President Reagan's seventy-fifth birthday. Ted Graber suggested a quite unique dessert: a Western-style corral surrounded by a wooden fence made of cake with a sign hanging over the gate bearing the words "Happy Birthday, Mr. President." Inside the corral were "snowballs," a crunchy dessert with all manner of delicious fillings, rolled in grated coconut, which the president adored. On each of the snowballs, Ted Graber wanted a ranch-style "brand" of the president's personal cipher, two "Rs" back-to-back. I had the brand cut specially by the White House's plumber and metalworker, and heated it over a gas ring in the kitchen before branding each of the snowballs. This was a quite extraordinary, highly imaginative dessert, and the president loved it.

In April of the same year, the President took the decision to bomb Libya as a warning to Colonel Qadafi, who had threatened a number of terrorist strikes. It seemed that France was refusing to let the U.S. Air Force planes fly through its airspace, which soured relations between the two countries—my two countries. France and the United States experienced a difficult relationship throughout these years, although I knew they remained allies at heart.

As a sign of this, President Mitterrand and his wife visited the White House on July 4, 1986, as part of celebrations marking the centenary of the Statue of Liberty, that symbol of democracy recognized the world over, standing on Governor's Island at the entrance to New York's harbor. The statue is, of course, the work of a French sculptor, Auguste Bartholdi, with an internal steel structure built by none other than Gustave Eiffel. Over 3,000 diplomats, journalists, and guests of honor from all over the world gathered on the island. More than a million spectators crowded the Manhattan shoreline to watch the fifteen-mile procession of sailing boats of all sizes and warships. Over thirty nations were represented. The day before the event, we were told that we were to be present on the island to oversee lunch for the president. As it happened, for some reason, I had had an intuition of what lay head. Without knowing that we would be called to Ellis Island for the big day, I had already made an entire series of miniature Statues of Liberty in chocolate, each about sixteen inches high. Naturally, when the order came to leave for New York, I took them with me in a picnic basket. We were transferred in military helicopters, deafened by their appalling din and clambered out numb and disorientated by the experience, which was not unlike being churned around in a washing machine. I had also created a three-tiered cake with chocolate icing, filled with three different-colored ice creams: blue (blackberry), white (coconut), and red (redcurrant). The Statue of Liberty took pride of place on the top, surrounded by green leaves and raspberries. The lunch was to be held in several different places: two private houses and a third venue, where we could use the kitchens. This complicated matters, and we had to devise an elaborately choreographed system to ensure that everything left the kitchens and reached the various tables at the same time. The menu featured beet with caviar, crab mousse with artichokes, and my dessert with petits fours. Everything went smoothly. We had left the White House at 3 a.m. and returned very late that evening.

In 1986 I took part once again in the Meilleur Ouvrier de France competition. I had decided to pull out all the stops this time. I took three weeks off work at my own expense, and made my preparations at the patisserie school in Vincennes, east of Paris, which had invited me along for the occasion. The competition took place near the city of Lyon, and the theme was "springtime." I created my personal masterpiece: a life-size peacock in blown sugar decorated with every type of early spring flower. I would be competing with no less than twenty-three other candidates. A tough prospect. In Vincennes, I chatted to the teachers as I worked. One of them confided that I had been the victim of an unpleasant slight back in 1976. He had been among the organizers of the competition that year and saw the points obtained by each candidate. I had scored enough points to secure the gold medal, but the committee had decided that because no one knew me, because I was young, and because I worked abroad, the top prize should go to a candidate who had already competed several times. I was saddened to learn the truth, ten years later.

I traveled to the competition at Yssingeaux, the home of a noted patisserie school near Lyons in the French *département* of Haute-Loire. The building was reached by a staircase that divided halfway up, the two flights of stairs leading to separate workshops. Two of the competition's organizers were standing talking on the landing. Suddenly, I overheard one of these two gentlemen say to his companion: "Him again?"

To which his colleague replied: "Don't worry, he won't make it."

This was my third attempt at the competition. I knew that the jury members were distinguished, accomplished professionals, people for whom I had the greatest respect. But there were other parties involved, too. People who nursed a violent, jealous grudge against me, bordering on what I can only call hatred. Because I had come from the United States, because I was working at the White House, because I was doing a job which they could never aspire to themselves. I worked harder than ever for the competition, putting my very heart and soul into the task, so that by the end of it I was in a state of near collapse, both physically and emotionally. Our creations were displayed in a tent, and we waited impatiently for the announcement of the results.

After several hours, the jury began to call up the winners. There were no silver medals awarded this year. I was the last person to have been granted that particular honor in 1976. But this time, my name wasn't even mentioned. I left for the United States without another word and returned to work at the White House. A few years later, the "mystery" was solved. I was attending a professional gathering in New York organized by a body known as the Philanthropic Initiative, when a delegate came up to me and introduced himself as one of the organizers of the competition at Yssingeaux.

"It was really bad luck," he said, and right away I could feel my hackles rising. I would have preferred to be told that I had failed to score enough points. But no! When the jury began its deliberations, the members fell immediately into two distinct camps: the French pastry chefs, who insisted that I should be the winner, and a second group, headed by the organizer whose comments I had overheard, who insisted that I should not. The two sides argued angrily about me for a good thirty minutes, and we know the result.

I had my revenge nonetheless in late 1987. I was named French Pastry Chef of the Year by the Société des Pâtissiers Français, the French patisserie professional body, and traveled to Paris for the presentation of the trophy at the InterContinental hotel. I was very proud to have been nominated by my fellow pâtissiers rather than the members of a manipulated jury. President Reagan sent a personal letter to the Société des Pâtissiers Français on February 9, 1988, congratulating them on their decision:

> For the past eight years, it has been our privilege to be served by Roland Mesnier, who has distinguished himself continually by producing superb, highly creative desserts, and an unrivaled array of fine pastries. Before coming to the White House, Roland Mesnier was the winner of numerous highly prestigious culinary competitions. This prestigious award is another cherished accolade. Mrs. Reagan joins me in presenting our warmest compliments and best wishes. May you enjoy a memorable award ceremony and may God bless you all.
>
> Ronald Reagan

I have recorded my experiences and thoughts about the Meilleurs Ouvriers des France for the benefit of young pastry chefs just starting out. No, life is not always kind. No, fortune doesn't always smile on you. But the obstacles you encounter are no reason to give up. Yes, you should carry on and strive for higher things, without bitterness or hard feelings. Yes, there will be people who try to sabotage your success, but they are there to be overcome. For me, the competitions were an opportunity to go forward, to push myself to the limit. Being a "best pastry chef" is something I strive for every day as a professional and as a private person—not simply for the span of a short-lived competition. I discovered that many of the people who received the title were far from exemplary characters. Many others were, however, and I salute their achievement. A Meilleur Ouvrier de France should not only excel at patisserie in all its forms, but should also demonstrate absolute personal integrity.

That said, I would never discourage young people from entering the competition. Competitions are always valuable. They are the ideal way to learn, hone your skills, and explore new techniques that you might otherwise never use. The prize itself is incidental. Everyone recognizes a truly accomplished professional, whether or not you're wearing a medal around your neck. But I would also encourage today's young professionals to do away with a system that encourages flagrant nepotism at the expense of true merit. Political chicanery of this kind undermines the reputation of certain professional competitions and discourages young people from entering. Young chefs should forge ahead and uphold their integrity; established professionals should look beyond the glittering prizes to lead from the front and set the best possible example.

There was more in store in 1986, a hectic year by any standards. On October 14, we received our last visit from Prince Rainier of Monaco, who was deeply respected by the Reagans. I served a soufflé of dried apricots with an almond and Amaretto sauce, and a side dish of whipped cream. Mrs. Reagan was amazed by the combination of flavors—this dessert, served warm, was one of my greatest triumphs at the White House. Sadly, the end of the year was a dark time for the president's family: the scandal of arms sales to Iran broke just before Christmas and cast a long shadow over the festive season.

The Reagans spent every Christmas at the White House, and each year I created a series of spectacular desserts, which Mrs. Reagan particularly enjoyed. One year, I conjured up an enchanted forest of pine trees in green sugar, in front of which stood a guard of little snowmen made from coconut ice cream with hidden fillings of chocolate, caramel, or strawberry cream. President Reagan took great delight in the surprise each time. On another occasion, I made "Christmas-Tree" ice cream flavored with a liqueur made from pine extract. That same year, the pine-tree forest was made of ice: the hand-sculpted trees stood around fourteen inches high, each topped with a white chocolate angel; there was a scattering of pine cones around their base, made from pomegranate sorbet and chocolate scales molded on (what else?) artificial fingernails. The melted chocolate was poured onto the plastic nails, which were removed once it had cooled and hardened. The resulting scales, which were remarkably lifelike, were then stuck onto the sorbet cones, giving them the shape and outward appearance of a pine cone. Finally, everything was coated with liquid milk chocolate to obtain the distinctive pine-cone color. All this was for a dinner for twenty guests. We made plenty of extra pine cones, so that the final platter was as spectacular as possible. Mrs. Reagan was delighted.

The following Christmas, however, was catastrophic. No fault of the pastry chef: the White House kitchens had a new executive chef, who had taken over when his predecessor retired. The new recruit was a young chef from Florida with scant knowledge and skills, who made mistake after mistake, so that it was a wonder to all of us how on earth he had managed to secure the job in the first place. Perhaps he was panic-stricken by the high responsibilities of the job. At Christmas, Mrs. Reagan was horrified by the standard of the food served. The turkey looked as if it had been blown up—it was served in pieces on a platter and quite unrecognizable. The same chef surpassed even this during the festivities leading up to Christmas. Traditionally, several turkeys were roasted for the permanent staff, and I was surprised to see the sous-chef arrive in a fury, fling open the oven door, remove all of the turkeys, and then put them back in again later. Our chef had forgotten to take out the giblets. The birds had been roasting in the oven with their innards still perfectly intact and unrinsed. Naturally enough, Mrs. Reagan invited the chef to take his talents elsewhere and the sous-chef, Hans Raffert, took over the direction of the White House kitchens. He had worked with us for several years already, and things quickly got back to normal.

The year 1987 was a difficult one for Mrs. Reagan, during which she was diagnosed with breast cancer and underwent essential surgery with enormous courage. Her personal physician, Dr. Hutton, did a remarkable job, but her morale remained very low. This did not, however, prevent her from carrying on her duties as first lady.

When she returned home from the hospital everyone at the White House felt deeply sorry, and we didn't know what we could do to help. To make matters worse, shortly afterwards, on October 26, 1987, Mrs. Reagan learned of the death of her mother. What could we say? It was very difficult to make known how sorry we felt: the staff is sometimes kept further away from the first family than we would like. Everyone was demoralized, but little by little Mrs. Reagan regained her strength and returned to her old, redoubtable self. We were delighted to have her back.

Mrs. Reagan never made effusive compliments. It was high praise indeed to hear her say that everything was fine. I was warmly congratulated once or twice in the eight years during which I worked for her, but that was all. She enjoyed unusual desserts and often broke with established White House traditions. One recipe which we often prepared specially for her was "monkey bread." I have no idea where the name comes from, but the "bread" is a Christmas tradition consisting of lightly sugared balls of soft bread soaked in melted butter and stuffed into a hollow ring mold, baked, turned out and served to guests. Mrs. Reagan also enjoyed pita bread, which she ate in thin slices, toasted, with a little goat cheese, Brie, or Gruyère cut into little triangles.

At the end of President Reagan's eight years in office, the cumulative effect of the staff problems we had experienced in the kitchen, the lack of space, and the enormously hard work and high standards demanded by Mrs. Reagan had taken their toll on me. Nancy Reagan always expected us to do that little bit better and "go the extra mile" every time. Now, with hindsight, I am grateful. Thanks to her high expectations, I became the pastry chef I am today.

Nonetheless, I had reached a crossroads in my career, and I had no idea where to go or what to do. I was very tired. My classes at L'Académie de Cuisine clashed with my work schedule at the White House. I would get home after midnight after the class on Monday nights, often with a state dinner to prepare for the following evening, so that I was had to get up at around 5 a.m. Saturday was my day off, but half of this was spent at L'Académie. I was on excellent terms with the school's director, François Dionnot, who was a native of Besançon and hence from the same neck of the woods as me. On his mother's side, he was related to a well-known family in the French *département* of Doubs, the L'Héritiers, who owned a transport company. In the old days, when I was a boy, their trucks often rolled up at my mother's grade-crossing barrier, next to our tiny house beside the railroad. For a time, I considered concentrating on teaching full-time and giving up my work at the White House, particularly in light of repeated, lucrative offers from the Johnson & Wales University's College of Culinary Arts.

But working at the White House entitled me to an excellent government pension, which I had no intention of losing. Any decision needed careful thought. I decided to start by asking the White House for a raise and finding out whether space could be found on the premises for a dedicated pastry kitchen, away from the main kitchens. The decision to stay or go would depend on the White House's response. The Reagans' chief usher, Gary Walters, agreed to everything. I would have my own pastry kitchen, and we began to look for a suitable location. Problem solved. The year was 1987.

A few weeks later, in the same year, I received a telephone call from Guy Legay, the chef of the Paris Ritz, asking if I would be interested in returning to work in France. The Ritz was opening a school of fine cuisine and patisserie, and he hoped that I would teach there as the hotel's pastry chef. I was honored and arranged to meet Monsieur Legay in Paris in 1988, during the trip to receive my Pastry Chef of the Year award. I took along photographs of my work, which he admired, but I asked for time to think before taking my decision—a difficult and important one for me, particularly given that the White House had agreed to my requests. Guy Legay hired a temporary chef while he waited to hear from me, and I returned to Washington. After a great deal of thought, I decided not to accept his offer. Guy was greatly disappointed and resigned himself to finding someone else for the post.

On March 31, 1987, we were surprised to find ourselves hosting a state dinner for the French prime minister, Jacques Chirac. I was puzzled. State dinners are usually reserved for presidents and heads of state. The menu featured lobster mousse and medallions of veal in a Périgueux sauce. The cheeses (Coulommiers and Saint-Paulin) were accompanied by a chicory and endive salad. Dessert was a gin and honey parfait with grapefruit, a complex, unusual combination of flavors. The parfaits were decorated with branches of lily-of-the-valley made from sugar, surrounded by triangles of *nougatine*.

At around the same time I also set to work minting gold: mint pastilles wrapped in gold paper, resembling large coins, and stamped with the emblem of the president of the United States. The mold was specially made at my request by a laser-cutting company. We made six or seven thousand of these coins each year, and they were a considerable improvement on those distributed by the White House when I first arrived. The coins were placed on tables at the White House for the guests, and Maureen always had some in her pocket to give to colleagues. I even made some for Air Force One, so that the president would have them to hand when he was traveling.

President Regan was nearing the end of his second term of office, after which he would be leaving the White House. A few days beforehand, I went up to the presidential apartment to present a dessert to Mrs. Reagan. She was eating on the Truman Balcony, named for the president for whom it was built, where she liked to eat her meals, weather permitting. Suddenly the telephone rang, and Mrs. Reagan got up to answer it and saw me standing nearby, dessert plate in hand.

"What are you doing there?"

I explained that I was waiting for her to inspect the dessert.

"Why are you standing in just your socks?"

I explained that I had taken my shoes off on the landing, so as not to dirty the carpet when I crossed the room. Mrs. Reagan took me by the hand and led me over to the telephone while she took her call, then back to the room where she had found me, still holding me by the hand. I had no idea what to make of this curious display—perhaps it was her way of expressing her affection and gratitude. I had certainly worked extraordinarily hard for her. I remember one winter's day when I had begun preparations for the next day's lunch dessert for a party of thirty. When I left in the evening, the work was half finished. The next morning, I woke to find that some three feet of snow had fallen overnight. Taking the car was out of the question. The White House always refused requests for special favors on principle, but this time I got lucky. I telephoned one of the house managers to ask for a car to come and pick me up. Impossible. I told him that he would have to explain to the first lady why the lunchtime dessert was not ready. I also pointed out that a limousine was useless—nothing short of a truck would get me out of my snowbound house. Half an hour later, a truck duly appeared. The administrator didn't want to risk the wrath of Nancy Reagan. She succeeded in getting the White House back on its feet, with a fitting sense of glory and grandeur. And despite their repeated health problems, the presidential couple had spent eight truly remarkable years in office.

We knew that Vice President George Bush was a candidate to succeed Ronald Reagan, and we hoped he would win, which he did. The Reagans' last Christmas at the White House was truly nostalgic.

We made a special effort to prepare a superb series of meals; one of the final menus was entirely based around caviar and champagne. The Reagans were sorry to leave, but they would be returning to their beloved California. It was early 1989, just five years before Ronald

Reagan announced that he was suffering from Alzheimer's disease. At the time, no one had the slightest inkling that the illness was perhaps already taking hold. He continued working as normal, and represented the United States like no other president before him, with tremendous personal authority. He was very tall, very well-built, with chiseled features, and the constitution of one of those early pioneers who conquered the West. He was an extraordinarily charismatic presence, particularly in the eyes of a small peasant boy from the Franche-Comté fascinated by the giant with his immaculate, movie-star wardrobe emerging from meetings wreathed in an aura of power and success.

I have one small regret with regard to President Reagan. On one of our trips to France, my wife and I traveled to Arbois to visit a fellow chef and friend, Christian Paccard, and his wife Yvette, with whom we set out on an excursion to Château-Chinon. The cellar was a treasure trove of exceptional wines, including some very old vintages, looked after by an amiable eccentric whose underground fiefdom was equipped with a coffin fitted with a telephone. He wanted to keep in touch after he had died. We were shown bottles dating from Napoleonic times, with the emperor's seal engraved in the glass. Our guide asked me the year of President Reagan's birth. I hazarded a guess at 1905 (in fact, it was 1911). A bottle of 1905 cognac was produced from the cellar to be presented to the president upon my return to the United States. I was speechless: the bottle was worth a great deal of money. I didn't presume to present it to Ronald Reagan in person, but this was a mistake. I discovered later that he never received the precious bottle. It was a mystery, and one that I regretted. He would have loved the cognac and the gesture.

I often thought of the Reagans in later years, especially when the president was suffering with Alzheimer's disease, which also afflicted my mother. I knew what was coming. Alzheimer's is a terrible disease whose victims lose their memories, ability to listen, personality and dignity. In short, they lose everything and are reduced to a truly wretched condition. I was deeply saddened to think of this giant of a man, whom I had served for so long, in such a distressing state. I felt strongly, too, for his carers and, above all, Nancy Reagan herself. I knew that she faced difficult times ahead and would need enormous courage: physically, the president was as strong as an ox, with years of life ahead of him.

One final, bittersweet anecdote about the Reagans. When Ronald Reagan's funeral was held in Washington National Cathedral, in 2004, his son Mike came to see me at the White House. He recalled a host of small details that I had completely forgotten, including the time when, during a football game on TV, I had served cookies and cakes, including one topped with a blown-sugar football. This was in the early 1980s, but he had never forgotten the gesture, which had greatly touched his father and himself. I was enormously pleased to think that he had held on to so many memories of things I had done for the family and was able to recall them years later.

On January 20, 1989, the Reagans moved out of the White House. Their personal furniture was taken out, and the Bushes' belongings moved in. The new president was not an unknown quantity for us: we had often met him at the White House as vice president. Very early in the morning, President Reagan entered his office for the last time and took a final look around at the furniture and familiar objects—his working environment for the past eight years, the works of art that had sustained him in his task. Everyone was there to say goodbye—about eighty members of the White House staff were gathered in the dining room. We all applauded the Reagans for the eight fabulous years we had shared with them.

With his characteristic sense of humor, President Reagan told us that it would feel strange to wake up the following morning with no one to switch on the light, open his curtains, and serve breakfast. He wasn't sure he would be able to work the light switches any more—he had hardly touched one in eight years.

At 11 a.m. the Reagans set off for the Capitol to watch the swearing-in of President George Bush, our next boss at the White House.

CHAPTER 13

The Day George Bush Cried

The forty-first president of the United States was due to arrive at the White House on January 21, 1989. The hotels, apartments, and office blocks along Pennsylvania Avenue were decorated with the Stars and Stripes for the occasion, and a succession of parades passed through the city center throughout the day. A large, heated, glazed grandstand had been set up outside the White House. After the swearing-in ceremony at the Capitol, the new president, his family, and their guests took their seats to watch the military procession. Then the president saluted the officers, and everyone headed for the White House.

After a tough régime over the past eight years, we were once again expecting some changes. Would I be strong enough to survive another four or eight years with this president? Would he appreciate my work? The same old worries.

In fact, my professional status was riding high. Work was underway on my new pastry kitchen, I had obtained a raise, and I was satisfied with my new salary. But I couldn't hold down two jobs any longer. I decided to leave my teaching post at L'Académie de Cuisine and sent a letter of resignation to François, who quickly found a replacement. Unfortunately, the new recruit, a Frenchman from the InterContinental hotel in Paris, was entirely motivated by money and completely uninterested in his students. The impact was quickly felt. When I left L'Académie, there were 140 students waiting to sign up for my classes. With twenty to twenty-two pupils per class, we had a seven-year waiting list. After two years, the new teacher had succeeded in running it down to zero. François asked for my advice. We decided to hire three new patisserie teachers to turn things around. But in vain. Matters failed to improve, until one of the three, Mark Ramsdell, put himself forward for the job and set out his conditions. He was forty-five years old, a former student who had scored the highest possible marks, and who had subsequently worked on a number of courses at L'Académie as an assistant, so that he was thoroughly familiar with the curriculum. He was asking to be appointed as the college's sole patisserie teacher, or he would leave altogether. We hired him and, fifteen years later, he's still teaching. Mark is a talented pastry chef and a superb teacher who is adored by his pupils. It has been a huge pleasure for me to see the continuing success of my pastry course and of one of its former pupils. A pleasure, too, to see L'Académie flourishing under the directorship of François and his wife Patrice from New Jersey. I was proud to see someone else from Franche-Comté putting down roots in the United States. At around the same time, during the filming of a television report, I met a second native of my home region: Christian Malard, an expert on American politics, a familiar and respected figure at the White House, and my great friend. Malard has interviewed all the presidents in office since Jimmy Carter, as well as many politicians in Washington, and has earned great respect from them and their staff. He was the third in the powerful triumvirate of Franche-Comté natives in Washington!

I already knew some members of the Bushes' staff, especially one of the president's valets, Ariel, whom the family had more or less adopted as their son, and Laurie Firestone, who was to become their social secretary. A great many changes were made, in a very short space of time. Under the Reagans, the White House was an oasis of calm, a place of quiet, serious duty—almost a museum rather than a home. Now, within the space of just twenty-four hours, the corridors were ringing with children's laughter and excited barks from the Bushes' dog, Millie, who arrived with Mrs. Bush's personal affairs. Millie was a very presidential pooch, well versed in matters of protocol, who always trotted six feet behind the first lady, never barked during meals, and was thoroughly well-behaved at all times.

The Bushes were a big family, with four sons, George, Jeb, Neil, and Marvin, and one daughter, Dorothy (known as "Doro"), and a happy band of grandchildren. The family owned a holiday compound at Kennebunkport, Maine. They also had the use of Camp David, of course, which they renamed Camp Marvin.

Mrs. Bush's first orders at the White House were to empty the refrigerators. The children should have no opportunity to snack between meals. Processed, artificial foods were out. Everything should be one hundred percent natural, and meals were to be balanced and healthy.

President Bush, for his part, had quite distinctive tastes, unlike those of the presidents we had served. We prepared dishes based on eggs, oysters, and fish roe. He adored fish and Chinese food. From time to time, before a meal, he would sip a martini, and he enjoyed a glass of wine with his food. He was a true gourmet and liked nothing better than a fine plate of meat and friends to share it.

In the earliest days of the new presidency, I was walking along the corridor behind the kitchens, heading for one of the cold storerooms to fetch provisions, when I saw President Bush coming towards me, flanked by his secret service bodyguards. I stood well back against the wall to let him pass, but he did the same, which perplexed me. Finally, we came face to face, and he shook my hand:

"Hello, Roland. How are you? Everything OK? There's a lot of work, huh? Thanks again for the desserts. I love what you do, it's fantastic!"

At the same time, he turned to his bodyguards and pointed towards me: "You see this guy? He's the one trying to assassinate me with calories. So please, keep an eye on him."

I blushed tomato red. I was speechless. I didn't like to hear the word "assassinate" in the presence of a president of the United States, even if the joke was his. This was undoubtedly one of those times when the truth of the old adage "If you can't think of anything nice to say, don't say anything at all" was painfully clear. I said nothing.

A few days later, in the same corridor, Mrs. Bush appeared with her dog Millie, trotting along the requisite six feet behind. The First Lady greeted me warmly and asked: "Roland, come here so that we can have our photograph taken together."

The photograph was taken there on the spot, with beaming smiles all round. I was delighted that my relations with Mrs. Bush had gotten off to such a good start. I felt truly at home in the White House.

Mrs. Bush never stood on ceremony. She was always utterly straight-forward, a highly intelligent woman with a great sense of humor, who always knew how to put people at their ease. She began each day with a swim in the White House pool, generally sporting a mask, snorkel, and flippers. One day, the president, who was nearby, had decided to take a break for a game of horseshoes (one of his favorite pastimes) with a friend. Mrs. Bush was enjoying a quiet swim in the pool when suddenly a rat swam into view in front of her mask. Mrs. Bush leapt out of the water and ran screaming into the White House. President Bush, fearing some sort of attack, rushed to the pool, where he and his friend dealt with the unfortunate rodent.

I often met Mrs. Bush on her way back from the pool, wearing a tracksuit, her hair in disarray, Millie trotting along behind. She would always tease me, joking: "Roland, what are you doing hanging around here? Haven't you got any cakes to bake? You're not here to mess around, you know."

Mrs. Bush was never afraid to show us exactly what we were to prepare for her. The Bush family had a special way of preparing certain dishes, and these culinary traditions often dated back several generations. I remember one visit in particular to Camp Marvin by the Prince of Wales. Mrs. Bush asked me to prepare the dessert, while Ariel the valet, who was also a skilled and knowledgeable chef, prepared the rest of the meal. I devised a dessert of lime sorbet and honey-and-vanilla ice cream molded in the shape of asparagus spears (the vanilla ice cream formed the tips). The "asparagus" was served with raspberries and blackberries and a sabayon sauce on kitchen platters, surrounded by sugar pansies—a cheerful, rustic dessert. For the main course, Mrs. Bush had chosen to serve swordfish. However, Ariel was unsure how to set about cooking it in accordance with Bush family tradition. Mrs. Bush came into the kitchens to show him. Armed with a large knife, she seized hold of the huge fish, skinned it, cut the flesh into chunks, and explained how to slice and season it before cooking it thoroughly on a hot barbecue grill. A true professional. Like many families, the Bushes had their pet words and sayings. They detested what they called "a wet fish," one that was insufficiently cooked in the middle. The fish was served with ordinary, mass-produced mayonnaise, lemon juice, salt, and pepper.

Later on the same day, the president was to greet Prince Charles when he landed at Camp Marvin by helicopter. He decided to go to the landing pad on foot. The weather was extremely cold, with snow and ice, and a cutting wind. President Bush hunted for his scarf, but couldn't find it anywhere. Ariel was making frequent trips outside to the barbecues and had donned a scarf for the purpose. President Bush stepped up behind him and deftly swiped the scarf, declaring that he would have no need of it while slaving over a hot grill.

It was an affectionate, fatherly prank. I was very touched to see the Bushes treat all of their staff with the same humanity and simplicity.

During the month of May, we learned that Millie was expecting puppies. This was extraordinary news, and the press soon got wind of it, publishing regular updates on Millie's health and progress. The White House carpenter was asked to make a special "nursery" kennel lined with a warm layer of shredded newspaper. The kennel was placed in Mrs. Bush's office, which also served as her hairdressing parlor.

On March 17, the Bushes decided to watch a film before a family dinner, and asked Paula, their long-serving Mexican maid, to look after Millie, who was due to produce her litter at any moment. Paula had looked after all of the Bushes' children and was very much one of the family. At 9:45 p.m., Millie gave birth to six adorable puppies. More than once, I sneaked up to Mrs. Bush's office in her absence to pet them and give them a cuddle. Everyone was delighted, not least Millie, who had the air of a queen surrounded by her offspring and heirs. One of the most delightful photographs of President George Bush shows him stretched out on the White House lawn, surrounded by all his dogs, totally relaxed, and smiling broadly.

Mrs. Bush liked to see her family gathered together for meals. One day, her grand-daughters Jenna and Barbara failed to show up. Mrs. Bush asked their mother Laura where the girls had gone. Laura had no idea, but one of the butlers explained that they had asked the kitchen staff to prepare them some sandwiches and have them sent along to the White House bowling alley. Barbara Bush was furious. This was the first and last time that such a thing happened during her years at the White House. There was no question of anyone disappearing off to have fun elsewhere, while the rest of the family was sitting down to eat.

Whenever a problem arose concerning one of the Bush children, the entire clan would rally round to set them back on the right track. The Bushes set great store by traditional family values. This is the environment that George W. Bush has known and appreciated since child-hood—something that I am sure is not always fully understood in my home country.

In May 1989, President Mitterrand traveled to the United States for a meeting with President Bush. He was not received at the White House, however. President Bush chose instead to invite his French counterpart to his private property at Kennebunkport. The property consisted of the main house and a smaller, very simple house that had been a wedding gift to the president's mother, ninety years earlier. The Mitterrands were to stay there, in the Bush family cradle, so to speak. A few days before their arrival, Mrs. Bush asked her daughter Dorothy to take care of preparations at Kennebunkport. The house needed a thorough spring clean. When the French secret service agents arrived before the presidential couple to inspect this rather basic lodging, they were less than happy. "Doro" had assured them that everything would be ready and that suitable, comfortable furniture would be hired for the Mitterrands' stay. The French asked for the toilet seats to be replaced, and Mrs. Bush and her staff saw to the task themselves. A magnificent, old-fashioned, wrought-iron bed was installed. Everyone arrived on Friday evening, and Presidents Bush and Mitterrand began their talks, during which Mrs. Bush took Madame Mitterrand on a tour of the Maine coast.

Dinner was served in the big house, at two tables of ten guests each. The two presidential couples spent their evenings here, in front of a roaring fire, enjoying the simplest food, Bush-style: quiches, pasta, thoroughly grilled fish. Typical American fare, which President Mitterrand greatly enjoyed. This rural "homestay" marked the beginning of a great friendship between the two statesmen, which lasted until President Mitterrand's death. From then on, the Bushes often invited other heads of state to their Maine residence, rather than the White House, which they found somewhat austere. The British prime minister, John Major, the prime ministers of Saudi Arabia and Denmark, King Hussein of Jordan and many others enjoyed the Bushes' hospitality in Maine.

We hosted a great many state dinners during the Bushes' four years at the White House. One in particular stands out in my memory, a dinner for the governors of each state in the Union, held in Charlottesville, Virginia, at Monticello, the historic home of Thomas Jefferson, the third president of the United States and the chief architect of the Declaration of Independence. Monticello is a magnificent building, and Jefferson was a keen gardener who cultivated fruit trees and enjoyed a reputation as a gourmet and connoisseur. He spent twenty-five years of his life in the service of the United States, notably as governor of the state of Virginia, a Congressman, and America's ambassador to France, where he acquired a taste for French cuisine, grand receptions, and dinners *à la française*. Jefferson's menus featured such dishes as *boeuf à la mode*, *boeuf Bourgignon*, galantines, roast chicken, vegetable *chartreuses* (a kind of terrine), and veal with olives. His presidency marked a turning point in the history of American cuisine, with the advent of typical, homegrown ingredients such as sweet potatoes, Virginia ham, crab, and corn, which he grew in his embassy garden in Paris. It was Jefferson, too, who introduced a hitherto unknown delicacy to the United States:

ice cream. And it was he who, in 1803, bought the state of Louisiana from Napoleon Bonaparte.

As one of the first occupants of the White House, Jefferson established many of the rules of protocol that are still practiced to this day: every guest is greeted personally with a handshake. More recently, every handshake has been recorded by a photographer. Guests each receive a copy of their photograph, one week after the dinner or reception in question. Jefferson was a widower, and Dolley Madison acted as chatelaine of the White House during his presidency. Jefferson also established the sizable White House staff, including his European-trained chef, Étienne Lemaire, a second French chef, and fourteen serving women.

At Monticello, Jefferson created a superb garden, which I was able to visit on the occasion of the governors' dinner. The kitchen garden, designed by Jefferson himself and executed by a leading gardener of the day, features every imaginable variety of fruit and vegetables. I discovered one of the president's menus, using many of his homegrown vegetables: *boeuf à la mode* with fennel, mushrooms, green beans, onion, and carrots, spiked with bacon, and served with a wine sauce. The dessert was a red-wine jelly with an English-style pudding, all washed down with the finest French wine.

On the day of the governors' dinner, a huge tent was erected in the grounds at Monticello. The walls of the tent had windows and were hung with paintings. I had never seen anything like it. With a hardwood floor, plants, flowers, and chandeliers, the whole setting resembled a splendid château. I witnessed my share of "tent disasters" at the White House, including—on a later occasion—a downpour that left the guests ankle-deep in mud. But there were no such problems here. Huge, diesel-fired ovens had been installed by the army—great furnaces that left us "red-skinned" in the truest sense of the term. The menu was suitably elaborate: seafood "turbans" with lobster sauce, medallions of lamb with mint sauce, mushroom croustade, Parisienne potatoes, and a side dish of assorted vegetables, followed by Brie cheese, and my dessert—a pistachio *marquise* and a six-sided cake surrounded by a chocolate fence, resembling that around the Monticello estate, and a chocolate bust of Jefferson, served with raspberry sauce and petits fours.

Charlottesville is about ninety-five miles from Washington, necessitating a major expedition from the White House kitchens. We left at around 6 a.m. and returned at midnight. In the afternoon, at about 3 p.m., we found a moment to visit Jefferson's plantation, still beautifully maintained, from where the president would distribute fruit and vegetables to the local people. We were stepping back into history. It was rumored that Jefferson had fathered a child by a local black woman, a servant at Monticello.

A dinner held at the White House on October 1989 for President and Señora Salinas de Gortari of Mexico was, for me, the occasion of an extremely unpleasant incident. The menu featured fillet of sole in a champagne sauce, stuffed saddle of veal with sauce Périgourdine and vegetables, a cheese platter, and a dessert entitled "Mexican Fantasia": two or three typically Mexican houses, of differing heights, with red tiled roofs and brightly colored shutters, all made from coconut ice cream with a creamy filling and crispy pieces of "crunch." Leaning against one of the walls, we had placed a seated, marzipan figure of a Mexican man, taking a siesta beneath his sombrero. The whole piece was finished with fresh raspberries and sauce. Just as the composition was about to be served, the Bushes' social secretary, Laurie Firestone, stared at it in surprise and declared that the marzipan figure snoozing against the wall was a bad idea and might cause offense by implying that Mexican people spend their time taking siestas and doing nothing much else. I hadn't meant to imply anything of the kind. The sleeping figure featured on travel posters and photographs of Mexico; he had become something of a national symbol. Laurie Firestone was unconvinced. She consulted a Mexican guest, who thought it was a charming idea and not at all offensive. In spite of this, just as the dessert was about to be brought into the dining room, Laurie Firestone removed the figure—an incident that caused a major stir in the newspapers and is still talked about today, fifteen years later. When I saw what had happened, I have to admit that I left immediately, slamming the door behind me and speaking to no one until I reached home. I was on the point of handing in my resignation there and then. I was deeply humiliated by Laurie Firestone's gesture. To have removed the figure in front of everyone, just as the dessert was being brought into the dining room was inexcusable. Had she come to see me in private beforehand, I would have happily complied and accepted her decision without question. Back at work the next day, I didn't know what to do. Things had gone too far. Laurie Firestone had behaved scandalously towards me, as I made quite clear when she came to present her apologies. I wasn't in the least bothered that she wanted to change part of one of my desserts, provided that she consulted me and asked me to do it myself, with enough notice to allow me to make the required changes and propose an alternative. She could even come to see me three, four, or five days in advance and ask what I had in mind. But she was in no way entitled to make a fool of me in front of everyone, almost inside the presidential dining room itself. The affair was an insult to me. If it happened again, I made it quite clear that I would resign. She accepted my position, and we remained friends in spite of everything.

In August 1990, history came knocking at the door of the White House. It was, you may say, a frequent visitor, if not a permanent resident. But this time, the pretext was the outbreak of war. Saddam Hussein had invaded Kuwait and was universally condemned for this act, especially in the United States. There was a great deal at stake: Kuwait was one of the world's biggest exporters of oil. If Saddam laid hands on the black gold, the economic and political stability of the entire planet would be threatened. Political leaders from the Middle East and all over the world gathered for meetings at the White House, and we redoubled our efforts to serve them all in appropriate style. On January 13, 1991, Congress gave President Bush its approval for the liberation of Kuwait. If Saddam failed to withdraw his troops by January 15, the president had the green light to attack if he felt it necessary. For my part, I was due in Lyon on January 20, as part of the American team competing for the World Pastry Cup. My wife Martha was extremely worried about the prospect of me flying to Europe when the nation was at war.

The hostilities began a few days later, and missiles were launched throughout the region. At the White House, we knew that the situation would take a turn for the worse when we heard that the Bushes had invited Reverend Billy Graham. His last visit to the White House, under the Reagans, had marked the start of America's war with Grenada. Reverend Graham was always called on the eve of a major decision of this sort to lead prayers or officiate at a religious ceremony.

In Lyon, the World Pastry Cup took a back seat. Everyone was glued to their television screens, and the atmosphere was tense and anxious—the more so when Saddam decided to turn his missiles on Israel. If Israel was drawn into the war, this would surely herald the start of a new global conflict. The thought was on everyone's mind. Everyone feared it. I returned to Washington after the World Pastry Cup, worried that I had been wrong to travel to France at such a critical time. In the White House kitchens, everything had gone smoothly during my absence, and I returned to work as usual. The president was working night and day to tackle the immense problems he faced. The war was over by February 28, when the Iraqi forces capitulated: a great victory for George Bush and United States.

Life is seldom a bed of roses for the White House pastry chef. Take the mishap that could so easily have turned into a professional catastrophe during the visit of Queen Margrethe II and Prince Henrik of Denmark. The menu for the state dinner featured lobster, a crown roast of lamb, salad, and cheese. For dessert, I had planned a raspberry soufflé, served warm with vanilla sauce and petits fours. As everyone knows, soufflés wait for no man. At the White House, the president and his guests should never be kept waiting either. When it's time to serve dessert, everything has to be ready: not a moment sooner or later. Serving soufflé was a risky decision on my part.

I tested the recipe several times, refining it as I did so. On the eve of the presidential dinner, I prepared my raspberry purée and all my molds, well buttered. I intended to make a series of large soufflés, each one serving ten people. They would need to cook for over an hour. I would put them in the oven when the guests moved into the dining room, taking into account the time it would take for everyone to be seated, listen to the speeches, and eat the rest of their meal. A complex calculation. But I had set myself a challenge, and I intended to pull it off. The recipe itself is relatively simple: egg whites beaten until they are stiff, as for a meringue, over which is poured a specially prepared, boiling sugar syrup. This is then mixed with the raspberry purée, and that's it. The preparation is poured into the molds, these are placed in the oven, and you pray to God that everything turns out all right.

As the guests began to arrive, I started making the soufflés, beginning with the egg whites and sugar. The egg whites refused to stiffen. I measured out a second batch from my emergency reserves. Still they refused to stiffen. And the minutes were ticking by. I had to wash the mixing bowls, break and separate a whole new set of eggs, measure out the sugar once again, boil it up. The dining room was full of dignitaries, gathered to honor the queen, and the dessert was a disaster! I started again, a third time. Failure yet again. There was no time left to boil up another batch of sugar, it would take too long, the soufflé would never be ready. We opened another box of eggs to make sure they were fresh, and I decided instead to make the meringue mixture that was the basis of the soufflé without boiling a fresh load of sugar. We would pour the sugar on to the egg whites as it was, mix it up, and let the Good Lord do the rest. My career was in His hands. I saw myself entering the dining room, announcing to the first lady, her guests, and the queen of Denmark that tonight's dessert was off due to technical problems in the pastry kitchen. My chef's hat was wringing wet with sweat. My career was headed for an early grave. There was nothing for it but to carry on and hope for the best.

We placed the soufflés directly on the bottom of the oven, which was extremely hot, rather than on a rack and poured a little water around the dishes. Meanwhile, the savory dishes came and went. The lobster had been served; the crown roast of lamb was on its way up to the dining room, leaving just the cheese and salad before it was time to serve the dessert. I stared through the glass door of the ovens, wondering what would happen. The soufflés rose impeccably: they looked all right. In any event, I was fated to serve whatever came out of the oven, whether or not it was any good. Too bad if my endeavors failed. I had taken a chance and would have to pay the price.

Off went the salad. The moment of truth. The soufflés would be placed in a heated, covered cart ready to be taken upstairs to the dining room. We took them out of the oven. They didn't look too bad at all. But would they collapse before reaching their final destination? I was increasingly worried. I had never made soufflés using this method, and for good reason. It was entirely possible for them all to collapse at once, just as they were being taken into the dining room. And even if they didn't collapse, it was anybody's guess what lay hidden at the bottom of each one. Water, perhaps? The egg whites hadn't been prepared using boiling sugar; perhaps they hadn't "taken"? There was no time to speculate now. The butlers were ready to go. We dusted the soufflés with a little icing sugar, having taken them out of the oven one by one. Each one was placed on its serving dish, decorated with a folded napkin. Off they went to the dining room. I waited.

I had no idea what to expect, expect perhaps a furious reproach regarding the inedible slush served for dessert. But none came. Or rather, several butlers came down to ask if it was possible to have more soufflés? Then another group of butlers asked for the same thing, and then another. Whenever a warm soufflé is served at the White House, it's advisable to make more than you need, in case of unforeseen circumstances. In this case, the unforeseen circumstance was the enormous success of my dessert. Everyone was asking for more. It was more than a success. It was a triumph.

I tasted a little to see for myself. I was surprised and delighted: the soufflé was light, airy, moist, and delicious, with an incredible taste of fresh raspberries.

What had happened? A drop of something—probably cooking oil, certainly some sort of fat—may have got mixed up with the egg whites when I prepared them on the evening before the dinner. This is all it takes to stop the whites from rising. But I had saved the day in extremis, and I was proud of myself. Proof yet again that one should always persevere to the bitter end. The dinner brought us nothing but compliments.

May 14, 1991, brought another incident, this time mildly comical, but for which I could in no way be held responsible. The White House was hosting a visit from Queen Elizabeth II and Prince Philip. Lobster with cucumber mousse, crown roast of lamb with dauphine potatoes, salad, and cheese. And dessert. This time, we planned a pistachio *marquise* with a truly extraordinary presentation, in the finest White House tradition. The *marquise*—a kind of mousse—would be served in a reproduction of the queen's own state carriage, accurate down to the last detail, but minus the royal arms, which Ms. Firestone had decided would be inappropriate, when I consulted her on the subject. I complied with her wishes, of course, although I was inclined to disagree. We began by making a wooden model of the carriage, which was subsequently cast in silicon. The difficulty consisted in making the carriage wheels strong enough to withstand the weight of the dessert. I succeeded. The result was truly magnificent. The *marquise* was topped with fresh raspberries so that the carriage looked as if it was transporting a cargo of fruit. The platter upon which it was presented was covered with marzipan modeled to resemble a cobbled street in Old London Town. A little bush of wild roses was placed on the front of the carriage.

And the comic incident? The queen was due to make a speech at a ceremony as part of her visit. Sadly, no one had thought to raise the height of the podium for the occasion. The queen is a diminutive lady, as is well known. The audience heard her words very clearly, but all that could be seen of the royal personage was her hat, which appeared to be delivering the speech all by itself. The press had a great deal of fun with the incident. I have no idea who was finally held responsible, but the cascade of angry words may well be imagined.

In 1991 President and Mrs. Bush made an official visit to the U.S.S.R., where they were entertained by President Gorbachev and, in return, organized a grand dinner in his honor at the U.S. embassy in Moscow. Mrs. Bush asked the White House executive chef, Hans Raffert, to travel to Moscow to oversee the preparations. The menu featured watercress soup with cheese *feuilletés*, fillet of beef with a truffle sauce, roast potatoes, and green beans, salad, and a selection of cheeses. The dessert was a lime sorbet enriched with vodka mousse, served with a half-frozen raspberry compote and petits fours. Everything was sent out on Air Force One in a hermetically sealed container capable of withstanding extremely high temperatures. The sorbets were placed in rectangular molds, and I made sure to take photographs of every stage of their final decoration and presentation. In Moscow, this would be handled by the Navy mess chefs, who were usually highly expert. I indicated that the sorbets should be dotted with half-frozen raspberries just before they were taken into the dining room. I was proud to see my desserts transported all the way to Russia, where they were received with great enthusiasm. I had created a combination of flavors entirely to their taste. The dessert has since become a firm favorite at the White House, particularly when Russian guests are being entertained. Unfortunately, the molds never made it back from Russia. They had been very difficult to find, and I missed them throughout the rest of my time at the White House.

Naturally, the quality and style of life at the White House depends very much on the personality of the First Lady. I have served five first ladies in succession and if I had to award a gold medal for the best of the bunch, it would undoubtedly go to Barbara Bush. It would be no bad thing if the spouses of presidential candidates were all required to pass a "Barbara Bush test" to assess their aptitude for the post of First Lady. Mrs. Bush had a great sense of humor, was at ease in any situation, and carried out all her tasks with enormous enjoyment. She was extraordinarily well versed in politics and economics, and could hold her own in conversation with any member of Congress. Just a few hours later, she might be found in her private apartments, telling her dog or her grandchildren to quiet down a little or in the kitchen demonstrating the preparation of a recipe to her taste or swimming in the White House pool. She often wore several different outfits during the course of a day and as many hats, always of the utmost elegance. She was truly a woman for all seasons, with a brilliant, sparkling personality.

When the Bushes were at the White House, or traveling privately as they often did, Millie the dog was always at their side. On official visits, however, Millie was not allowed to join the delegation and was left in the care of the White House engineers, whose offices were located in the basement of the building. In particular, the engineers were responsible for walking Millie, and each one would leave a note for his successor on the bulletin board, reminding him to take her out. One day, when the Bushes had left for an official visit to Japan, one of the engineers left a terse note for the next person on duty, to the effect that he should remember to "walk the stinking dog." Alas, the first person to see the note was Mrs. Bush herself, who had returned from the visit earlier than expected and hurried down to the basement to fetch her beloved Millie. No one was in the room. Mrs. Bush said nothing, took Millie, and made sure to find out who had been on duty at the time from the White House administrator. The next day, the author of the message was summoned to her apartment, where he was thanked for looking after Millie in the first lady's absence and presented with a box of chocolates tied with a big ribbon, to which a small card was attached. The engineer hurried back to his office and quickly opened the envelope containing the card. It read: "Enjoy the chocolates. From the stinking dog." You might say that he looked stinking annoyed. He was extremely angry, but the lesson was deserved and delivered with a great deal of tact and humor.

Millie's puppies grew up and were given to friends. "Presidential puppies, free to good homes." The Bushes had no trouble at all finding adoptive parents for the dogs. One of the litter, Ranger, a male, found himself living with the Bushes' son Marvin, who lived near Washington and often came to the White House with his wife Margaret, a keen swimmer and tennis player. Margaret was always escorted by Ranger, a naturally lively and somewhat naughty dog who adored running all over the place and chasing squirrels. President Bush had a sign made by the White House carpenters: "Squirrels, beware of Ranger." Millie was a supremely presidential pet, as we have seen, but Ranger had no sense of protocol whatsoever—to President Bush's frequent annoyance during official visits. Ranger had to be shut in on such occasions to prevent him from doing any diplomatic damage.

On one occasion, we had planned a barbecue in the White House grounds. A long table had been set out with salads, quantities of vegetables, cheese, and desserts. Further away, the chefs were busy around the barbecue, grilling hot dogs, steaks, and hamburgers. People helped themselves and took a seat at one of the tables. I had decided to stroll over and say hello to the cooks, when I saw an elderly lady coming towards me with a plate. Armed with her bun, mustard, and ketchup, she asked the chef for a hamburger, who prepared it in the traditional way, with a slice of tomato and lettuce, all the trimmings. I was greeted with a friendly "Good day, chef, and how are you?" The lady was delighted to be there, at the White House, on such a fine day.

Leaving her plate on the corner of the buffet table, she went off to fetch a drink. At the same moment, Ranger came bounding up, saw the hamburger, slid to a halt, rounded the table, took a running leap, jumped up onto the table, picked up the hamburger in his mouth and disappeared. When the old lady returned with her Coca-Cola, she looked at her empty plate and laughed, thinking that I had hidden the hamburger: "Now where's my hamburger? What have you done with it?"

I explained that I hadn't touched it. A little further away, Ranger had settled down in the grass to enjoy his treat, which was by now quite unrecognizable. I indicated that it was Ranger who had stolen the hamburger.

President Bush, who had watched the entire scene from a distance, strode over to make amends. Seizing Ranger by the collar, he shut him in a nearby car, with the window left slightly ajar. There Ranger stayed for the rest of the party, quietly digesting his hamburger.

The Bushes were great animal lovers. In the early years of George Bush's presidency, a party of ducks settled around the two White House fountains on the South Lawn. They nested in the flower beds and a few days later, the gardeners found a clutch of duck eggs. Mrs. Bush took a close interest in the matter. When the ducklings were hatched, she asked the White House carpenter to make a special cage for them, fearing that they might be attacked by Ranger, Millie, or other animals on the grounds. The cage was placed over the nest, with an opening leading to the pond, just big enough for the parent ducks, but impassable for any other animals. Mrs. Bush made frequent visits to the baby ducks, making sure they had enough to eat. She took her grandchildren along to watch the ducklings learning to swim. When the ducklings were big enough to fly, the cage was removed, and they left for new lives elsewhere.

Mrs. Bush did not enjoy birthdays—certainly not her own, at least. For her sixty-fourth birthday, I made a cake in the form of a wrapped present with a pretty sugar ribbon tied in a bow around a red rose. Instead of writing the words "Happy Birthday" on the cake, I drew the musical notes of the song "Happy Birthday to You" in chocolate. Mrs. Bush was delighted and touched by the thought. She had arranged to take lunch alone, with a favorite book, but we couldn't let the day pass unnoticed.

On the other hand, Mrs. Bush was always full of plans for celebrations in honor of the birthday of her best friend and tennis partner Andie Stewart, whom she had known and adored for many years. One year, Mrs. Bush asked me to make a birthday cake evoking their favorite sport. I made a full-sized tennis racquet in chocolate, standing up straight on top of the cake, with slightly slack strings, entwined with roses. Game, set, and match! Everyone was delighted. The only other birthday cakes I made during George Bush's presidency were for the children, but there were a great many of these, including their personal favorite, a peanut-flavored cake with redcurrant jam.

Once again, history was a guest at the White House table, and it fell to us to devise a suitably imposing menu. On June 16, 1992, Boris Yeltsin, the newly elected president of Russia, visited Washington for the first time. Yeltsin had played a decisive role in the dissolution of the U.S.S.R in 1991, and his visit was eagerly awaited by the American people. The menu began with sturgeon *à la sauce diplomate* (appropriately enough), followed by veal served with wild mushrooms, duchesse potatoes, and carrots. Dessert was a duo of mousses made with caramel and crystallized pears, decorated with pieces of orange and arranged in alternate layers in an oval mold, served with vanilla sauce and petits fours. The result was wonderfully attractive, and amazingly delicious. I decided to decorate the dish with seasonal flowers made of sugar: black-eyed Susans arranged in bouquets above each dessert. These were also scattered with fine slivers of chocolate. President Yeltsin was greatly pleased. Like every head of state on his or her first visit to the White House, he was somewhat overwhelmed and unsure exactly how to behave with regard to his host. The two presidents exchanged few words during the visit, which provided them with an initial opportunity to get to know one another. The meal went without a hitch, and the atmosphere was extremely cordial.

The year was drawing near, and with it the date of the presidential elections. George Bush was riding high in the polls on the strength of his success in the first Gulf War. No one in the Republican camp doubted his chances of reelection. None of the Democratic candidates demonstrated comparable stature or statesmanship, it seemed. People were talking about a certain Bill Clinton, but he was a relative unknown to most people, and no one rated his chances. President Bush continued to work hard, as always, and life went on peacefully enough at the White House.

But life always has a few surprises in store, and sometimes of an unpleasant nature: 1992 was also the year when news broke of a scandal apparently involving Neil Bush, the president's third son, who held a seat on the board of directors of a Colorado bank. Neil Bush was accused by the U.S. Office of Thrift Supervision of "numerous breaches of his fiduciary duties involving multiple conflicts of interest." The affair was greeted with shock and sorrow by the Bush family, which had always upheld a strict code of absolute rectitude in all aspects of life. Everyone knew Neil to be a person of the utmost honesty. But it is not always easy being a child of the president of the United States. Presidential offspring are inevitably dogged by the press everywhere they go, ready to pounce on the slightest hint of a rumor. Neil decided to resign and rebuild his life elsewhere. For him, the only way out was to give up everything and start from scratch. But the wound still smarted. His reputation, and that of his family, had taken a severe blow.

A happier event took place in June 1992: Doro Bush was married for the second time, following her earlier divorce. I had hoped that the wedding would take place at the White House, with a splendid party. But this was a second marriage, and Doro—who disliked pomp and circumstance—opted for a simpler celebration at Camp Marvin. We began baking cakes three weeks before the ceremony to find the perfect flavor, and submitted them to Mrs. Bush and Laurie Firestone for tasting. Their final choice was a passion-fruit cake. The cake was all white, topped with a white sugar vase from which white sugar roses tumbled all the way to the base. The result was extremely pretty, simple, elegant, and delicious. The cake itself was nearly six feet tall and had to be transported from the White House with extreme care. I was in charge of cutting it, together with my assistants and Pierre Chambrin, the White House's new executive chef. The cake was to be served on around 150 plates, decorated with little molded peach sorbets filled with chocolate and coated with raspberry sauce. The wedding day was drawing nearer, and there were a thousand small details to attend to.

On the morning of the big day, we loaded the truck ready for the drive to Camp Marvin. It was quite an undertaking: the truck contained the various elements of the cake, the utensils we would need to assemble it at Camp Marvin, the chefs' equipment, and the food for the wedding buffet, including a batch of fresh salmon sent from Alaska by the Bushes' great friends, the Stevens, which had been cooked at the White House. Camp Marvin was reached by a winding road, and I was terrified that the dessert would arrive broken in pieces. Once the truck reached Camp Marvin, it had to pass the various military controls and security checks, which was another major undertaking. Finally, at 11 a.m., we were ready to unload.

Everything was to be installed in the big conference room at Camp Marvin. My assistant helped me to assemble the cake, which looked fine but was nonetheless quite fragile, like all spectacular cakes. We hoped it would stay standing until the beginning of the evening.

It was an exceptionally fine day. Up in the mountains, at Camp Marvin, we enjoyed a superb view. At midday, Mrs. Bush came to see us while we were preparing the dinner, and we persuaded her to take a light lunch of tuna and tomato salad. After an active afternoon of horseshoes, cycling, and swimming, it was time for the ceremony. Evergreen, Camp Marvin's little chapel with its green wooden walls, was filled with flowers and music. Everything had been meticulously prepared. The only person not actively involved had been President Bush himself, who had busied himself with a host of sporting activities and had even forgotten his suit, so that he attended the ceremony in "smart weekend" attire: a navy blue blazer, pale slacks, white shirt, and a tie doubtless borrowed from Ariel the butler. It was a moving ceremony. Doro was adored by everyone in the family and everyone at the White House. Her young groom, Robert P. "Bobby" Koch, was handsome and well-dressed, had perfect manners, and was plainly very much in love. A supremely happy moment.

Dinner was served around the pool, and the guests enjoyed aperitifs while the band played a succession of jolly tunes. After the buffet came the dessert, which had stood its ground. After the dessert, there was dancing. It was a splendid evening. We were all tired but happy and conscious that we had shared a very special moment: a genuine love match. Doro and her husband had insisted on absolute discretion. No information about the ceremony was to be given to the press.

During the week of November 11, 1992, the White House hosted a visit from Lech Walesa, who was to be presented with the Presidential Medal of Freedom, the highest honor an American president can bestow on a foreign national. A great many personalities were invited for the occasion: tea for 250 people. The ceremony went on for a long time, which suited us perfectly—all the better to repair a catastrophe in the dining room. A table loaded with food had collapsed under the weight of a guest, who had made the mistake of leaning against it rather heavily. We never discovered the identity of the man in question, but he must have weighed around 330 pounds. A government figure? He would have been identified straight away. He looked more like a lawyer. Everything was scattered across the carpet, just minutes before the reception was due to begin. It was imperative that no one should suspect anything was amiss. The entire team got to work, like furious ants, to evacuate the mess, cover the stains on the carpet, put the leg back on the table, and restock it with food once again.

After Lech Walesa's visit, tension mounted as the presidential elections approached. We all hoped that President Bush would be reelected and felt sure that this would be the outcome. But as time went on, our conviction crumbled. The other candidate, Bill Clinton, had evidently succeeded in convincing many Americans that he would make a better president than George Bush. Clinton's wife, Hillary, was a major strength in his campaign. Quite unlike Mrs. Bush, she was less family-oriented and closely involved in political life, a force to be reckoned with. Together they formed a remarkable, highly individual couple. Election day drew closer, and everyone at the White House went to vote, myself included. I was extremely worried, and spent the day with fingers crossed. I wasn't at all sure that I would be able to carry on working under another president. The job was highly stressful, and I didn't feel able to learn "new tricks." Who was Bill Clinton? I knew nothing about the man and even less about his tastes and expectations. The arrival of a new president is always a tough challenge. I wasn't getting any younger, and I felt less and less able to spring into action under a new boss.

On the afternoon of election day, George Bush's eldest son, George W., came to tell his father that he had lost. The entire family, all of whom adored George and Barbara Bush, were overcome with sorrow. The failure was hard to bear, even for the White House staff. We knew the Bushes by heart: their close friends, their pets, their habits, and their smallest likes and dislikes. I felt their departure as a veritable disaster, a great personal loss. Within the space of two months the White House would have a new occupant. The important thing was to carry on to the end of the mandate, with dignity and our heads held high.

On a personal level, even before the elections, I had given a great deal of thought to my future. Should I stay on the White House? I thought back over my life. Professionally, everything was going well. I had finally moved into my new pastry kitchen, which was small but very well equipped, and which still offered slightly more space than I had had at my disposal beforehand. So far so good. My son, then aged twenty-three and living in Florida, was a little more problematic—like every son, no doubt. He had chosen a career in hotel catering, like me, but found that it was not at all to his liking. He had always had a deep love of music; he was a genuine artist, who lived and breathed music. He had formed a series of small bands with friends and played in clubs around Florida. He played bass guitar and enjoyed his lifestyle in Florida, so reminiscent of the tropical climate of his childhood in Bermuda. He came to see us every now and then, especially at Christmas. Each of us was enjoying a busy, fulfilling career. On the whole, things looked good. I was encouraged to carry on. But I had hoped that President Bush would be reelected, enabling me to carry on working for a few years more for a family for whom I felt a great deal of affection. But you can't always get what you want.

With heavy hearts, we served the final family Christmas at the White House for the Bushes and their guests. What would next Christmas have in store? We had no idea, but we carried on doing the best job possible in the meantime. The Bushes celebrated Christmas in style: their style, with a host of decorations collected during their travels.

Hundreds of professionals were called in to help decorate the White House. Often, the president would come down to shake hands with them. Mrs. Bush invited parties of schoolchildren, usually with their teachers, to come for hour-long storytelling sessions, for which I made cookies in the shape of Christmas trees and Santa Clauses, presented to the children in little bags, with a photograph of the first family. I would be on hand to give them out and wish everyone a Merry Christmas, dressed in my pastry chef's uniform. The White House also always displayed a gingerbread house, which we constructed from gingerbread baked by a noted German chef. For the Bushes' last Christmas, the chef had retired, and the task of baking the gingerbread and constructing the house fell to me. Traditionally, the house was quite simple, but prettily decorated, with a roof in the shape of a capital "A." I decided to try something different and created a Christmas village with houses of many different colors and shapes. We peopled the village with children sledding, also made from gingerbread, and pastry animals, together with a marzipan figure of a lady not unlike Barbara Bush carrying a tray of cookies for the children. Further along stood a figure of George Bush, with the dogs Millie and Ranger, together with all the Bush children. The whole village was dusted with icing sugar to look like snow. Mrs. Bush was delighted with the new-look gingerbread house.

The Bushes' last Christmas at the White House featured a grand dinner in the president's private dining room, for which I created a large sugar sculpture: a sleigh full of presents, pulled across the snow by reindeer, driven by Millie dressed as Santa Claus. When the piece was placed on the table, Mrs. Bush cried out: "George! Come and see what the chef has made for us. It's absolutely magnificent!"

The president shook me by the hand and told me how much he liked the piece, especially the figure of Millie.

That year, at the end of the festive season, Mrs. Bush decided to host a last dinner for the children, plus a few friends: twenty people in all, including Neil Diamond and Julie Andrews. The dinner went very well, and everyone was in high spirits, except me. I had just served my last big dinner for the Bush family, and I felt profoundly sad. I left at the end of the meal, at around 9:30 p.m., sunk in a black mood. While I was getting changed in my little office before heading for home, someone knocked at the door. One of the butlers asked me to get dressed again—Mrs. Bush was waiting for me downstairs with her guests. I went back downstairs with my heart thumping, unsure what to expect, or how to behave. Why was Mrs. Bush asking for me and no one else?

Back in the dining room, Mrs. Bush introduced me to her guests. I greeted everyone, but was unsure of what to do. Next, Mrs. Bush took me over to the gingerbread village, which was all lit up, and began to tell everyone about my work, showering me with compliments, particularly with regard to the village: the first one ever made at the White House and specially for the Bush family. I felt extremely proud and not a little uncomfortable surrounded by such a fine group of people. After this, Neil Diamond and Julie Andrews took turns at the piano, leading a sing along. Mrs. Bush invited me to do the same. Unfortunately, I'm a very bad singer. I stood in my corner and wished the floor would swallow me up. Then, Neil Diamond was asked if he would sing one of his own songs with Julie. He declared that he couldn't, because he didn't have his sheet music with him. I suspect that he might have noticed how ill at ease I was and decided to put me out of my misery. The plan worked; I seized my opportunity, asked to be excused, and fled. Martha laughed out loud when I told her about my adventure.

There were no more grand receptions after this, and everyone helped to take down the Christmas decorations at the White House. These included about twenty Christmas trees, a Nativity scene, and a whole host of baubles and ornaments. The "operations" department oversaw the replacement of the furniture, and the carpenters, painters, and curator's office worked to put everything back to normal by January 1. The gingerbread village was broken up and thrown away: after over a month on display in the dining room, it was, of course, no longer edible.

The Bushes left to celebrate the New Year together with a private family party, after which they returned to the White House once more, before leaving for a final weekend at Camp Marvin on January 9. The family was not present for this final weekend, but the president's guests included the Canadian prime minister, Brian Mulroney, and members of the National Security Council. President Bush took the opportunity to speak to François Mitterrand about the situation in Iraq one last time. This was an emotional and difficult weekend for the Bushes. Before boarding the helicopter to return to Washington and the end of his mandate, President Bush received a tribute from all of the staff at Camp Marvin.

On January 13, just before his departure from the White House, President Bush presented the Presidential Medal of Freedom to former President Ronald Reagan. This was to be Ronald Reagan's last public appearance. The former president had lost none of his charisma. We all gathered in the Diplomatic Reception Room, and everyone had a kind word for the Reagans.

The next day, January 14, 1993, President Bush, as commander in chief of the Armed Forces, attended a review of troops for the last time at Fort Myers, Virginia. George Bush was very popular among U.S. servicemen, who saw in him a true leader. It was a day of farewells. Colin Powell, as commander of the Armed Forces and chairman of the Joint Chiefs of Staff, gave a remarkable speech in which he stated that he considered his commander in chief to be the greatest leader in the world.

It was time to pack and send the Bushes' personal belongings to their home in Houston. Mrs. Bush took advantage of these last weeks to organize a tea party for her private staff. A difficult moment, for we had all shared so much, and all of us considered Mrs. Bush a friend. Many tears were shed.

World affairs continued apace, and Saddam Hussein flouted the conditions imposed upon him by the United Nations, provoking the resumption of the bombing campaign in Iraq.

The departure day drew near. The White House was empty and cold. No more children's voices, no more barking dogs. The atmosphere was even gloomier than that surrounding the Reagans' departure. It was as though the White House was losing something of its soul, as the boxes and crates were carried away.

For their last meal at the White House, the Bushes invited the president's older brother, together with a couple of friends, the Grahams, and Doro. This was their last evening at the White House.

The following morning was more somber still. George Bush was leaving as a result of a disaster at the polls. Before leaving for the Capitol and Bill Clinton's swearing-in ceremony, he joined the White House staff to say his farewells. Seeing us all gathered around, the president broke down in tears. He was quite overcome, unable to speak. Mrs. Bush spoke his few words of thanks in his place.

CHAPTER 14

Miniskirts in the White House

And so the Clintons arrived at the White House, from Arkansas, where Bill Clinton had been elected governor at the age of thirty-two—the youngest state governor in American history. He was now forty-six—a fine age for a president. Ahead of the inauguration, the Clintons stayed at Blair House, directly opposite the White House, a modest-looking row of buildings occupying almost the entire length of the street, but which is in fact the U.S. president's guest house—a luxury hotel with a sizable staff of its own. Visiting heads of state stay at Blair House when they are not staying at their own embassies.

Now, Clinton was at the Capitol, swearing the presidential oath on a Bible held, touchingly, by his daughter Chelsea. After this, he would watch the various parades and marches that took up a large part of the day. Washington was in a celebratory mood, and security was tight. After this, Bill Clinton would make his official entrance at the White House as the tenant—for the next four, or possibly eight years—of its 132 rooms, 32 bathrooms, 412 doors, 147 windows, 28 chimneys, 7 staircases, and 3 elevators. Not forgetting the magnificent gardens, tennis courts, swimming pool, jogging track, sixty-seat movie theater, and billiard room. After all these years, there are still plenty of corners left for me to explore. The building was originally known as the "President's Palace," but was renamed the White House by Theodore Roosevelt in 1901. It is indeed the president's private house, but it is also the people's house, and its doors are always open to visits from the American public (uniquely for the residence of a head of state), completely free of charge. The building receives an average of 6,000 visitors every day, and some

30,000 or 40,000 people pass through the grounds at Easter. On this day, 2,000 members of the public were present for the inauguration of President Bill Clinton, their names having been selected at random in a draw. The weather was superb. A miniature White House had been installed in the grounds for the occasion, where family and friends could wait before entering the main building itself.

The Clintons arrived with their own habits and ways of doing things, to which we would have to adapt. Once again, I reflected on the peculiar situation we faced, each time a new president arrived with his entourage at the White House. We served the first family to the best of our abilities, taking account of their lifestyle, tastes, pet peeves, and passions, so that we always came to feel as if we were part of the family itself. And then the electoral sword would fall once more after four years, or at the end of two successive mandates, bringing the party to a sudden end. The event felt almost as a period of mourning for the presidential family and for us, the staff, too. And each time it fell to us to start over from scratch. For those of us who were getting older, like myself, the task seemed increasingly difficult.

The Clintons brought an immediate change of tone, from their very first day. Early on their first afternoon, everyone was busy making preparations to welcome the family and arrange things to their satisfaction. I had prepared a great many chocolate figures, including one of the presidential seal. Suddenly, the door separating the kitchens from the Downstairs Corridor swung ajar. About twenty people were standing in the corridor, looking at the portraits of the former first ladies, including a great many Republicans, hanging on the wall. Everyone was laughing and joking, and the atmosphere was little short of riotous. It was like the first day back at high school after summer vacation. I noticed that most of the assembled company were women, and most of them were very young. One in particular, aged about twenty, had a voluptuous figure and an eye-catching plunging neckline. We exchanged glances and smiled. I discovered later that she was Chelsea's nanny. But already, it was abundantly clear that the Clintons liked to surround themselves with young people. Miniskirts had come to the White House!

The Clintons were Bill, his wife Hillary, their daughter Chelsea, Mrs. Clinton's mother Dorothy Rodham, and her brothers Hugh and Tony Rodham (Tony was later married at the White House). Also present were Bill's mother, Virginia Clinton, and his brother. The president's father was deceased but later, his stepfather Dick Kelley also came to visit the White House. They were a splendid family, including their cat Socks, a sweet, lovable creature who was adored by the press and quickly became America's most famous feline.

While the Clintons were busy taking part in the inauguration ceremonies, the staff of the new administration set about taking possession of the White House, even more rapidly and efficiently than usual, it seemed to me. Bill Clinton's people were everywhere in the offices, where furniture, chests, boxes, and packages were unpacked with disconcerting speed. The place was like a teeming anthill. The White House looked quite different. Everything happened so fast, and the changes were so radical that we began to worry that the new president might not retain the existing domestic staff. The White House had a new occupant, but that occupant was also the representative of a completely different political party. After twelve years of Republican administration, the Democrats had taken the helm once more.

Like their predecessors, the Clintons embarked on a tour of the various balls organized by the Democrats throughout Washington: eleven in total, each one with a guest list of two or three thousand people. They returned to the White House at 2 a.m., completely exhausted. For its part, the White House carried on as under George Bush, who liked to be woken at 5 a.m. with breakfast in bed. When the stewards entered the Clintons' bedroom at 5 a.m. the next day, they were greeted with: "What the hell are you doing? Can't a person get some sleep around here?"

The First Lady soon made it quite clear that she would not be confining her role to overseeing the running of the household. Nonetheless, she underwent a radical transformation with her arrival at the White House. Mrs. Clinton had visited the White House a few months earlier, between election day and Christmas, for tea with Mrs. Bush, who had doubtless given her a great deal of advice. Hillary Clinton would have to change her appearance and manners, and accustom herself to the minutiae and constraints of protocol. A graduate of Wellesley College (class of '69) and Yale (where she met Bill Clinton in 1970, marrying him in 1975), she was brilliant and had a strong personality. She assumed the role of First Lady with gusto, and a few essential adjustments. When she first arrived at the White House, Mrs. Clinton paid little attention to her clothes or hair. She was an unsophisticated "woman in the street," who transformed herself into the epitome of elegance and style. She began to pay particular attention to her hair and was always accompanied by an army of beauticians and Washington hairdressers. Over time, she adopted a personal style perfectly suited to her character. But she aimed to do more than that. Mrs. Clinton saw herself as her husband's co-worker: a true associate and colleague of the remarkable president.

To this end, Mrs. Clinton chose to take an office in the West Wing of the White House, which is also the site of the Oval Office, itself the home of the historic Resolute desk. The desk is made from wood recovered from the British ship HMS Resolute, which was discovered abandoned in Arctic ice by an American whaler and returned to Queen Victoria as a token of goodwill. When the ship was decommissioned, Queen Victoria had the desk made and presented it to President Rutherford B. Hayes in 1880. President Kennedy installed the Resolute as his work desk in the Oval Office in 1961. The photograph of Kennedy's son, John John, poking his head through the kneeboard door (which was added to the desk by President Roosevelt) was published around the world. President Reagan used the desk for the eight years of his presidency, but President Bush used it for just a few months. Bill Clinton brought it back into service. The desk was placed in front of the Oval Office windows, which were hung with new, golden yellow curtains.

Traditionally, the Oval Office's curtains and carpet are changed whenever a new president takes over. A change of president, a change of carpet. Bill Clinton was very pleased with his personal choice: a dark blue design with the Presidential Seal at its center. A dazzling collection of paintings was hung on the walls, and a marble bust of Kennedy was added as a reminder of times past. Each new president redecorates the Oval Office to his taste, marking the room with his own personal stamp.

Hillary Clinton's office was less imposing, a functional workroom where she spent a great deal of time. Many other First Ladies before her had had offices of their own, but these were mostly used for interviews with the White House's domestic staff. Mrs. Clinton took up the tradition established by Rosalynn Carter: she went to work in her office first thing every morning and generally spent the day there. Her personal administration included her chief of staff, Maggie Williams, her assistant Melanne Verveer, and a host of young women. The Clintons enjoyed young people and were always on the lookout for new blood, original ideas, energy, initiative, and daring. Mrs. Clinton had hired a good fifteen such women, in charge of planning her official visits and organizing her days, which were almost as busy the president's. Hillary's office, and her redoubtable team of female aides, soon acquired the nickname "Hillaryland."

Hillary faced her first major challenge as First Lady in 1993, at the traditional grand dinner organized for the governors of each of the states of the Union. One hundred and twenty guests were invited. Hillary was a complete novice in such matters. Her only previous experience of official dinners of this sort dated back to 1977, when she and Bill, then attorney general of Arkansas, were invited to the White House for a state dinner in honor of Prime Minister Pierre Trudeau of Canada. This lack of experience did not deter her from bringing her own personal style to White House events and festivities. Mrs. Clinton had hired a social secretary, a young woman by the name of Ann Stock, who joined "Hillaryland" from Bloomingdale's department store in Washington and whom I knew already, as I had once made a birthday cake for the store's centenary. She was a person of terrific energy, with an impeccable sense of hospitality. With her help, and that of Hillary's other aides, the dinner was a success. But Mrs. Clinton wanted to do better than that.

For quite a lengthy period, there were no more grand dinners at the White House, but smaller meals for around fifty or sixty guests. We wondered why. With hindsight, it seems clear to me that the Clinton team wanted to take time to get to know the workings of the place as thoroughly as possible and to perfect their own style of hospitality: the planning and organization, service, cutlery, tableware, and, of course, the menus. On this last point, as with everything else, we had expected some changes and surprises. We had no idea just how right we were.

Matters were decided very quickly. Mrs. Clinton was a very political animal, to the extent that we sometimes felt we had two presidents in the White House. This was the first time since the departure of Rosalynn Carter that I had seen a first lady actively involved in state affairs at the White House. Meals fell into two categories: those organized for the president and those organized for the First Lady; each had their own guest lists, and they often entertained in different rooms, at the same time. On two or three mornings each week, working breakfast meetings were held in the Map Room. I discovered later that these were generally fundraising events for the Democrats. I had no idea of the sums involved, but the *New York Times* did its sums and published the amounts raised for the party at the breakfast gatherings. I discovered that one of my patisserie creations had fetched 16,000 dollars. I was amused by the idea, and thought nothing more of it, other than the fact that I was resigned to getting up early on days when the breakfast parties were planned. The president's activities were no concern of mine, and I was not about to pass judgment. I just got on with my work as requested.

A second sphere of presidential functions began to form around Mrs. Clinton, who was extremely interested in social policy, health, and the question of medical insurance. Our early impression—that we were serving two presidents instead of one—was confirmed. President and Mrs. Clinton each hosted their respective working lunches and working dinners, at which quite different and separate projects were discussed.

The Clintons settled into the White House with a great deal less protocol than their predecessors. When they were alone as a family, without guests, they took their meals in the kitchen. On Friday nights, when they were not leaving for the weekend, they would make a meal of the week's leftovers from the refrigerators. Of the five presidential families I have served, the Clintons were the only ones who chose to eat in the kitchen.

President Clinton had allergies: chocolate, above all, and also dairy products and possibly wheat flour and pollen. When the Clinton family arrived at the White House, we took care to use chiefly silk flower arrangements in the rooms used most frequently by the president. The Clintons' doctor, Connie Mariano, kept the problem well under control but the rest of the White House staff were at something of a loss to know what to do or think. During an official visit to Paris in 1994, at a dinner hosted by François Mitterrand and his wife Danielle, Mrs. Clinton was surprised to find herself addressed by France's own First Lady: "I do hope you understand, but we couldn't possibly have a table with no flowers. Please accept our apologies, once again." Madame Mitterrand explained that she had been informed of President Clinton's allergy to fresh flowers. The extent of the condition was never entirely clear, but plenty of people worked to help the President cope with his allergies, real or imagined. Personally, I avoided wheat flour in my pastries.

On November 9, 1993, we hosted a grand reception to celebrate the engagement of Mary Matalin and James Carville, two dedicated politicians—she a Republican and he a Democrat, which must have made for some interesting pillow talk—and close friends of the Clintons. Around 300 guests were invited. I was asked to make a three-tiered cake: one layer flavored with vanilla, another with coffee (which Mrs. Clinton adored), and the third with chocolate. For the president, as always, I served a separate cake on another plate: a carrot cake made without butter, wheat flour or chocolate. The perfect cake for President Clinton! During the reception, I was busy cutting the main cake in front of the guests when the president came up and carried off a plate with a big piece of chocolate cake. I hurried to stop him, pointing out that the slice was not from his own special cake. The president was astonished and made it clear that no one was going to tell him whether or not he could eat a piece of chocolate cake. "I'm the President around here. I can eat what I like."

I apologized, but pointed out that I simply thought he would prefer to avoid an allergic reaction. "Today, I'm eating chocolate, Roland. That's all. That's how it is today, and tomorrow it will be different."

I explained that I had thought I was doing the right thing.

"Absolutely. You were quite right to point it out, but I want chocolate, so there you go."

The president made off with his bounty, and I never found out what happened after that. All I knew was that I had done my job.

Every new presidential family refurbishes the White House to their own taste, with the exception of the Bushes, who left everything as it had been under the Reagans, with just the odd coat of fresh paint here and there. The Clintons maintained the tradition, and brought in an interior decorator from Arkansas, Kaki Hockersmith. With her help, Mrs. Clinton set about making her mark on the White House, with marvelous results. She began by transforming the Jackie Kennedy Garden into what she called a sculpture garden, where numerous artists were invited to display works in stone, wood, metal, or more offbeat materials. She wanted to give American artists a space in which they could express themselves and present their work, in a prominent setting viewed by every visitor to the White House.

On March 9, 1993, just a short while after President Clinton's inauguration, François Mitterrand was the guest at a White House working lunch. I wanted to create a typically French dessert for the occasion, which would catch President Mitterrand's attention. The dish was described on the menu as dandelion wine terrine. Dandelions are a much-underestimated plant with remarkable qualities. Marinated at length in Bordeaux, they produce an interestingly flavored wine, which can be distilled to a liqueur. The taste is distinctive and highly unusual, but delicious. The terrine was served with a fruit salad decorated with sugar dandelion flowers and petits fours. President Mitterrand was indeed surprised to see dandelions on the menu, particularly as a dessert (dandelion greens are quite familiar as a salad ingredient in France), but he was not sufficiently amazed to ask to meet the pastry chef responsible. I was disappointed. I would have dearly loved to shake the hand of the president of my home country, at least once. But never mind.

After the "interim" period described above, the Clintons launched themselves into an extraordinary succession of receptions, inviting people from every walk of life, many of whom one would never have expected to see at the White House. Tents were needed to accommodate everyone, or "pavilions," as the president preferred to call them. These magnificent structures were heated in winter, air-conditioned in summer, with hardwood floors, windows, and a large stage with curtains. Just one problem: they were exceedingly drafty. The pavilions remained in place at the White House for several years—an eight-year-long garden party, consisting of an endless string of receptions and state dinners. The Clintons made an important discovery: whoever they met, whoever's hand they shook, whether they were Democrats or not, always left the White House completely under their spell. Meeting the president, experiencing his charisma at first hand, feeling the force of his extraordinary personality—when he spoke a kind word and especially when he took the opportunity to look a person straight in the eye while shaking their hand, à la Ronald Reagan—was all it took to make anyone a devoted Clinton supporter. The Clintons quickly understood that the more people they invited to the White House, the more supporters they could count on. It was a simple enough calculation, and it worked.

The Clintons found it hard to adapt to Washington life. Life as president of the United States is inevitably tougher than life as governor of Arkansas, and their temperaments were unsuited to the constraints imposed by their new duties. They were no longer free to come and go as they pleased, and this weighed heavily upon them. Mrs. Clinton liked to get out of the White House incognito for a breath of everyday life, and she often donned disguises to enable her to do so: sunglasses, a baseball cap, and worn-out black clothes. Thus attired, she would take a walk in the city, followed at the regulation distance by her secret service bodyguards, themselves dressed like ordinary folk in the street, often riding bicycles. As a further precaution, a van would also follow along, packed with armed men. Hillary Clinton liked to walk around the streets of Washington in this way, and her expeditions were so well organized that she passed completely unnoticed. One day, however, when she was walking near the Washington Monument, some tourists asked if she would take a photograph of them, using their camera. She kindly did so and overheard a boy saying to his mother that there was something familiar about her face. She melted quickly back into the crowd. Chelsea experienced the same problem: a suitable school had to be found for her, and she was escorted there by secret service agents, which she was never happy about. She, too, lost a great deal of personal freedom.

It is certainly true to say that the secret service agents didn't always exercise an especially light touch. After spending their first Easter weekend at Camp David, where they attended a service in the beautiful Evergreen chapel and spent a peaceful few days together, the Clintons returned to Washington. Mrs. Clinton decided to bring her mother with her. Dorothy Rodham, physically frail and depressed following the death of her husband, came to live at the White House. The First Lady noticed that some furniture had been moved in the presidential apartment during her absence. The apartment had been searched over the weekend. She was horrified and questioned the chief usher, who admitted that he had forgotten to let her know about the impending intrusion.

To make matters worse, Chelsea's nanny, Helen Dickey, who had remained at the White House over the weekend, and occupied rooms above the presidential apartment, reported hearing noises on the Saturday night. Bravely, she had gone down to investigate and found herself face-to-face with a group of armed men dressed all in black—secret service agents who informed her that she had no business there, they were simply doing their job, and that she should clear out quick. Mrs. Clinton was extremely displeased and could scarcely believe her ears. It appeared that the men were looking for electronic bugging devices; a suspicious amount of supposedly confidential information was appearing in the newspapers. They suspected that the presidential apartment had been bugged and decided to carry out a search. Their failure to inform the First Family was a serious mistake. Mrs. Clinton gave them a serious dressing down. She certainly knew how to make her feelings felt, and I wouldn't have liked to be in their shoes. A memorandum was issued to ensure that nothing similar ever happened again. But the incident did nothing to improve relations between the Clintons and the secret services. Often, an agent would be summarily removed and replaced without explanation.

On September 13, 1993, the White House witnessed a truly historic event: the meeting between the Israeli prime minister, Yitzhak Rabin, and the Palestinian leader, Yasir Arafat. The meeting was to coincide with the signing of the so-called Oslo peace accords, which had been secretly negotiated in the Norwegian capital. Prime Minister Rabin was the first to arrive. In discussion with the Clintons, he outlined a small, symbolic scenario designed to reinforce the significance of the long-awaited pact. The day would, it was agreed, include a public handshake between Messrs Rabin and Arafat at the moment of the signing.

The day's events unfolded in an atmosphere of great enthusiasm. Everyone was genuinely happy to see these two figures working with President Clinton to resolve their long-standing conflict and address their regional difficulties. All three men met in the Blue Room before heading for the South Lawn, where a huge podium had been erected, so that the many invited guests could enjoy a view of the ceremony, a decisive moment in world history.

I wanted to make my modest contribution to the success of the Oslo accords, with patisserie creations designed to reflect the winds of peaceful change blowing around the world. In the morning, for breakfast, I had prepared a selection of miniature Danish pastries, and was delighted to see Yasir Arafat take one, along with everyone else. Arafat did not stay to lunch at the White House. President Clinton and Prime Minister Rabin were left to eat together in the little dining room next to the Oval Office. I had been informed quite late in the morning, but the dessert I had prepared for three would do just as well for two. I had planned something very light, served on individual plates: five white doves made from lemon sorbet placed on a nest of fresh fruit, each with a sugar olive branch in its beak. President Clinton and Prime Minister Rabin marveled to see how a simple dessert could fall into step with the march of world events. It was a truly glorious day for the White House, the United States, and President Clinton, who had worked so hard to secure the accords. We all felt that we were entering a new era.

In 1994 the White House kitchen experienced a small revolution. Mrs. Clinton wanted more typically American food than that prepared by the head chef, Pierre Chambrin. This was the culmination of a series of mishaps and misunderstandings, which I will touch on only briefly here. The worst incident took place at the very beginning of the Clinton era, during the Fourth of July celebrations. Bands were playing on the esplanades, and there is always a big firework display. Mrs. Clinton had invited around twenty members of the family, and friends, for a traditional Fourth of July meal, namely fried chicken, a favorite American dish, often eaten cold at Independence Day picnics. The one absolute golden rule is that the meat must be thoroughly and completely cooked. As a Frenchman, I have learned that there is almost nothing Americans like less than lightly cooked poultry. The slightest hint of pink, and they will refuse to eat it. At the beginning of the Clinton administration, everyone was taking special care, and mistakes were strenuously avoided. For my part, the evening's dessert was particularly attractive:

picnic baskets made from meringue filled with an assortment of ice creams and fresh fruit.

I was in the habit of watching the Fourth of July fireworks from the White House roof, which had an unrivaled view. Usually, I was alone, but tonight I noticed that a number of other people had had the same idea: Mrs. Clinton's mother, Dorothy Rodham, the president's stepfather, Mr. Kelley, Chelsea, and several others. Everyone greeted me, and I learned during the course of the conversation that the fried chicken had not been a success. It had been served pink, and Mrs. Clinton had summoned one of the chefs, yelling that he was so incompetent he couldn't even cook fried chicken. I felt uncomfortable and unsure of my place up on the roof terrace with the president's family. Suddenly, I noticed a woman dressed all in black climbing the stairs. Mrs. Clinton. I hoped that she wouldn't mistake me for the chef who had ruined the fried chicken. But no. Hillary greeted me by name and thanked me for the magnificent dessert, which everyone had greatly enjoyed. "Thank you for joining us for the fireworks," she concluded. I was overcome with relief.

Shortly before this, just after President Clinton's inauguration, everyone—the full team of White House chefs and pâtissiers—was busy in the kitchen when a woman arrived whom I had never seen before. She was one of Mrs. Clinton's aides, Capricia Marshall, an ordinary-looking woman sporting a pair of bifocal glasses. But long years at the White House had taught me never to judge on appearances; power and influence often reside in unexpected places. It behooves every member of the White House staff to treat everyone else with courtesy and circumspection. Be nice to the stewards and chambermaids, and they will sing your praises to the president and First Lady. On the day in question, Capricia asked the duty chef if he would be able to put together a buffet in half an hour. Mrs. Clinton had invited sixty people from Arkansas, who had spent several days in Washington following the presidential inauguration. She wanted to serve them a brunch in the Blue Room. The chef replied that he didn't have time. I understood what was at stake and proposed a buffet of pastries, which could be ready within half an hour. Capricia Marshall must have told Mrs. Clinton about this; the First Lady was always extremely kind and pleasant to me after that. This is how reputations are made at the White House. You have to be able to improvise and conjure up the First Family's every whim, in record time. Or else.

For whatever reason, chef Pierre Chambrin decided to leave the White House after a tour of duty that had begun under George Bush. Mrs. Clinton consulted several people and eventually concluded that there was no substitute for an American chef if you counted on serving American food. Several candidates were invited along to the White House for assessment tests. Mrs. Clinton tasted their efforts herself over lunch, together with a full complement of aides from Hillaryland. The successful candidate was Walter Scheib, a chef from the Greenbrier Hotel in West Virginia. Mrs. Clinton briefed him on her project to promote American cooking and produce. French products, such as Perrier water and cheese, which had been a feature of White House menus since the Carter administration, were gradually phased out. Mrs. Clinton insisted on serving American mineral water and American wines.

Until now, meals at the White House were served on large porcelain dishes, each holding enough for ten people. The waiter made his tour of the table, and each guest helped themselves from the dish. This is known in the trade as "Russian service," and it has always been a favorite of mine. It's ideally suited to private dinners and allows the chefs to create beautifully garnished, attractive arrangements on the large dishes. Mrs. Clinton wanted to change things and serve individually plated meals, as was the practice in contemporary restaurants. Personally, I always preferred the large platters, which enabled each guest to help themselves according to their personal appetite and tastes, something which is impossible with a pre-plated meal. Mrs. Clinton agreed to make an exception for the desserts. She knew that I always did a great deal of research before a state dinner, with the relevant embassy, in order to create suitable decorations reflecting the culture of the country in question, or dishes that symbolized their customs, tastes, and values.

In the White House kitchen, Mrs. Clinton presided over a minor revolution. When the new chef took over, she invited every other chef to hand in his or her resignation. Walter Scheib could then rehire the team of his choice. In effect, everyone was hired back, with the exception of one chef who was particularly incompetent and nonetheless thought of himself as something of a leader, all of which had caused difficulties in the past. At the White House, everyone works directly for the president and the First Lady; anyone who fails to give complete satisfaction can be fired on the spot, without explanation.

The new chef made a great many changes, far too soon, with the result that many White House staff members were furious to see their familiar working methods overturned. The press took up the story, and there was even talk of "Kitchengate." A reporter from the *New York Times* poured still more oil on the flames, announcing that Mrs. Clinton was making sweeping changes in the White House kitchen, but that the pastry chef was to be spared. Mrs. Clinton had given me the green light, and I continued with my creations, my pretty desserts, as I had always done. Mrs. Clinton was always delighted with my work at the White House.

On May 28, 1994—in the middle of an otherwise tempestuous year— we enjoyed a small ray of sunshine: Mrs. Clinton's brother, Tony Rodham, married Nicole Boxer, the daughter of a Californian senator. The wedding dinner was to be held at the White House. We created a four-tier cake topped with two white doves in a sugar rose bush decorated with blue ribbons (the bride's chosen color). The result was superb, but simple and understated. In my twenty-five years at the White House, I have never created a cake for the wedding of the daughter or son of a serving president—a "proper" wedding at the White House itself, with a truly stupendous cake to match. It is one of my biggest regrets.

On June 13, 1994, the White House was the setting for an extraordinary dinner in honor of Emperor Akihito and Empress Michiko of

Japan. The meal took place in one of the pavilions installed in the Rose Garden, in front of the Oval Office. The day's dessert had a flavor of the Land of the Rising Sun, since it was inspired by the hundreds of cherry trees planted along the National Mall in front of the White House, a gift to the United States from Japan. In springtime, the trees are a sea of pink blossom and fresh green foliage. The dessert, entitled simply "Cherry Sorbet," was a sophisticated, highly refined composition served with almond ice cream and fresh California cherries. The cherry sorbet itself nestled at the heart of a huge blown-sugar cherry measuring about twelve or sixteen inches in diameter. The two halves of the cherry were stuck together with melted white chocolate, and opened to reveal a ball of white ice cream, inside which was the sorbet. The dessert also featured long stems of cherry blossom and foliage, made from sugar and baskets of sushi—made of chocolate!—with bamboo handles. Twenty-five desserts were made for 250 guests, not forgetting an array of little kumquat tarts (the attractive orange fruits are typically Japanese). The red cherry sorbet, discovered nestling in the white ice cream when this was cut open, was intended to recall the Japanese flag. It was a resounding success. At the end of the meal, Empress Michiko asked to meet me and express her admiration of my work. Protocol forbade domestic staff to meet official state guests, but it was a tremendous reward to know that the Japanese empress had been impressed by my dessert.

A great many celebrities were invited to the White House that evening, including Barbra Streisand. When the dessert arrived, Ms. Streisand got up to visit the powder room and passed through the area set aside for us to organize the food service prior to taking the dishes into the dining room. I was deep in conversation with the sous-chef, mulling over the dinner and its success. The star walked between us and we both greeted her: "Good evening, Ms. Streisand." We were completely ignored. Not even so much as a glance. We were mere flunkeys, or worse. I was reminded of the loutish French secret service personnel who had accompanied President Mitterrand. When Ms. Streisand returned from a lengthy visit to the bathroom, she ordered a new dessert and sushi basket just for her, despite the fact that everyone else had already been served some time ago. She made strident demands for her dessert, but none was forthcoming. Once the dessert is finished, it's finished, and that's that.

The dinner served on July 1, 1994, was especially problematic. We were hosting a visit from King Hussein and Queen Noor of Jordan, together with the Israeli prime minister, Yitzhak Rabin, and his wife. A table of Muslim and Jewish guests with their particular dietary traditions and requirements. I was careful to offend no one and created a dessert of nougat ice cream with almond sorbet, served with strawberries, raspberries, and wild blackberries, a passion-fruit sabayon sauce, and macaroons. I couldn't, of course, use fresh cream for the nougat or the sabayon sauce and made do with a synthetic substitute instead. The result was a delicious combination of sorbets and fresh, wild red fruits. We avoided a diplomatic incident! No member of either delegation felt overlooked, thanks to the careful combination of ingredients and produce.

My true moment of glory came a few weeks later, in September 1994. We were to receive an official visit from Boris Yeltsin, who was now president of the Russian Federation. The occasion called for another stunning dessert. I decided to make *nougatine* baskets with tall sugar handles decorated with wide sugar ribbons and bows, in red, white, and blue—the colors of both the Stars and Stripes, and the flag of the Russian Federation. Each basket was filled with molded lime ice cream covered with a second layer of my by now quite celebrated frozen vodka mousse. Around the attractive, delicate green dome of ice cream, I placed a ring of California peaches, surrounded by raspberries, strawberries, and blackberries. The whole creation was served with petits fours. When the dessert was brought into the dining room, everyone in the room applauded; a television crew was on hand to film me taking the dessert "on stage." President Yeltsin spoke to President Clinton at great length about the dessert and how it was made. The dinner was a crowning moment for me.

The Clintons' first two years at the White House had, in truth, been far from easy. Mrs. Clinton had lost her father and the president his mother. This was an especially difficult time for Chelsea, who lost a grandfather and grandmother in the space of just one year. Alone and in private, their sorrow was plain to see. In public, they carried on as usual, smiling and strong. High office often makes inhuman demands of its incumbents. Whatever happens in a president's private life, it should never be allowed to affect his public role. Of the five presidents I have served, George Bush Senior found it hardest to conceal his emotions in this way; on TV or at public events, he would sometimes seem to be fighting back the tears. The others remained stoic and steadfast in the face of adversity.

In early December 1994, Bill Clinton decided to hold the G7 summit in Florida. As a rule, we didn't accompany the president on trips such as this. This time, an exception was made and the executive chef and I, together with a team of assistants, would be traveling to Florida for the summit. This involved complex planning, since the pastry kitchen at the White House had to carry on running smoothly in my absence. We got to work in the kitchens of one of the Majestic Hotel Group's finest operations, the Biltmore in Miami. A grand dinner was organized at the hotel on December 9, 1994, for the seven heads of state and their spouses. It was up to us to take charge of the preparations. We faced the difficult challenge of working in an unfamiliar hotel with limited space at our disposal in the hot, humid Miami climate (even in winter). We brought a certain amount of equipment and accessories with us on the plane, including a set of pretty chocolate boxes for the petits fours, transported by one of my assistant pastry chefs in his hand luggage.

The dessert I had planned for the heads of state was a large swan with cherry sorbet, which Bill Clinton adored and which featured on menus throughout his mandate. The sorbet contained a filling of frozen Amaretto mousse (this delicious Italian liqueur has a marvelous aroma of almonds). The mousse was made using non-dairy whipped topping, due to President Clinton's allergy to dairy products. For me, this was an unsatisfactory but necessary compromise. The swan was served with a delicate, pale green lime sauce and decorated with exotic fruit. The bird's neck and wings were made from white chocolate, which in theory contains only cocoa butter and would therefore be safe for President Clinton to eat. The dessert was accompanied by the little chocolate boxes, each bearing the presidential seal, filled with petits fours and chocolates.

The secret service agents were omnipresent—on every floor of the hotel, in every corner, behind every door. We were issued with several different passes relating to the different areas of the hotel in which we would be working. While preparations were underway for the dinner at the Biltmore, we were also organizing another dinner, scheduled for the following day, on Fisher Island, a billionaires' playground with its own golf course, swimming pool, and every imaginable luxury. The island featured a sumptuous restaurant overlooking the sea, in a mansion formerly owned by the Vanderbilt family, the setting for the second G7 dinner. The Clintons had asked for a dessert buffet, and I created an opulent array of crisp baked apples and mangoes, an assortment of Florida fruits, a chocolate log with passion fruit and fresh raspberries, Mrs. Clinton's favorite mocha dessert, and cherry tarts, all accompanied by a host of petits fours and chocolates. In fact, the desserts were to be served not in the restaurant itself but afterwards, on board the *Virginia*, a private yacht owned by the German-American billionaire John W. Kluge. The *Virginia* was the finest boat I had ever seen. It was immense, with extraordinarily luxurious cabins, including bathrooms with bathtubs and washbasins carved from individual blocks of marble. The dining room even featured a fireplace with a working chimney.

While the guests were dining at the Vanderbilt, the yacht pulled up at the quayside, and together with my assistants, I took onboard the desserts we had made earlier at the hotel. I set up the buffet while the boat turned, ready to for the trip back. Naturally enough, no other boats were allowed into the surrounding waters that evening. While the *Virginia* was carrying out its maneuvers, the captain offered us all a glass of champagne, after which we rapidly made ourselves scarce. The heads of state and their spouses had finished dinner and were standing on the quayside ready to step aboard for dessert. We watched as the majestic yacht set sail with its cargo of presidents and heads of state. The chefs, who had finished their work well before us, were able to take the ferry back to Miami and sleep soundly in their beds, a luxury denied us. We were forced to remain on the island, waiting for the next ferry to the mainland. While we waited, the genial head chef of the Vanderbilt invited us to the dining room to sample some of his finest wines, which he opened especially for us. When the ferry finally pulled in, it was 2 a.m. and we were all fairly tipsy. The chef thoughtfully put his own car onboard the ferry to drive us the few miles back from the landing stage to our hotel. We finally fell into bed at around 3 a.m. and had to be up again at 5 a.m. to take the plane back to Washington.

At 5 a.m., I failed to wake up. One of my assistants banged on my bedroom door. The vans were waiting, I had to be up and out within ten minutes. I leapt out of bed, pulled on the first clothes I could find, and scurried down to reception without a wash or a shave. I was asked to sign my check, but in my comatose state, told the receptionist that I didn't have time and could she send it on to me in Washington? I jumped into the van and was thoroughly reprimanded for my late appearance. At the airport, all I could think about was boarding the plane for a few more hours' sleep. Back in Washington, we donned our chefs' uniforms straight away, at around 2 p.m. No time to rest or nurse a hangover, we launched straight into the string of festivities marking Christmas and New Year at the White House, with no respite until the end of December.

Christmas with the Clintons was quite an event. Over 1,500 guests were invited to the White House at the end of their first year in office, and each person was served with a selection of petits fours upon their arrival. The building was decorated with twenty-nine Christmas trees, and one or two receptions were organized every day. Their first Christmas was a difficult time for me. The pastry kitchen was extremely small, I had few assistants, and the growing number of guests at the White House was consuming more pastries and desserts than ever before. The situation remained tense over the next few years, although the means at my disposal did improve. Mrs. Clinton's management of the social calendar and kitchens often left me in an impossibly difficult situation. On the day before the First Lady was due to hold a Christmas party for the White House office staff, for example, I would be asked to prepare 20 platters, each one featuring a chocolate Christmas log, and 100 fours: 20 logs, and 2,000 petits fours, to be prepared in the space of just one day, for the appointed time. She never asked whether this was possible. She would simply ask for "twenty platters for 7 p.m." She knew that everything would be ready on time—she had complete confidence in me. The Clintons' family Christmas meal was held at the White House, since they had no second home or family compound elsewhere, other than Camp David, where they spent a private holiday afterwards. There were always around twenty or twenty-five guests present for the meal, which included a family dessert for which Mrs. Clinton had given us the recipe: an atrocious concoction of Coca-Cola-flavored jelly served with black glacé cherries. Personally, I could think of nothing more appalling, but I bowed to the family tradition. I also made lemon tartlets, a carrot cake for the president, a little gingerbread house, and a number of large sugar sculptures. The meal featured a dessert buffet with an array of ice creams and petits fours, not forgetting the traditional Christmas log decorated with stars, Christmas flowers, and little animal figures, all made by hand.

In 1993, the pressures of work were such that I began to look around for a retreat, somewhere where I could relax in peace and quiet. It was time for us to buy a house in the country with plenty of land, if at all possible. I needed a place where I could recharge my batteries. If I was to carry on in my demanding job, I needed somewhere where I could enjoy a simply, healthy life, reflect, and gather fresh inspiration.

We started looking for a house not far from Washington, and eventually chose a delightful place called Clifton, with fine grounds extending over more than five acres, in a magnificent woodland setting. Many local people kept animals. We were lucky to find a house on Willowbrook Road, all in white brick: a White House of our own, deep in the country, and big enough to enable us to invite our friends and families. There was a garden with lawns and flowerbeds, to my great delight, since I love growing roses. The property also had an enclosed courtyard, with railings and a fishpond, over which stood a statue of a woman holding vase overflowing with water. My dream home!

Left: A quiet moment in the White House garden, before serving the world leaders of the day. Private collection of Roland Mesnier.

Below left: "Topiary Valencia," a majestic dessert for the King of Spain. Official White House photograph © Ralph Alswang.

Below right: A diplomatic dessert for the fiftieth anniversary of NATO: strawberry ice cream, iced nougat, and a champagne sabayon sauce. Official White House photograph © Ralph Alswang.

With President and Mrs. Carter, my first bosses
at the White House. Official White House photograph.

President Reagan blows out the candles on a birthday cake in the shape of a star—a happy,
private moment shared with the First Family. Official White House photograph.

Posing in front of the Christmas tree with President and Mrs. Bush.
Private collection of Roland Mesnier.

Behind the scenes in the White House pastry kitchen. Private collection of Roland Mesnier.

Presenting Bill and Hillary Clinton with their anniversary cake,
in the White House dining room. Private collection of Roland Mesnier.

In the presidential apartments, a private conference between a prime minister and a pastry
chef. With Lionel Jospin and his wife Sylviane Agacinski. Official White House photograph.

Sumptuous Christmas festivities with the Clintons.
Official White House photograph.

With Mrs. Clinton, during the grand festivities for the millennium, in front of the White House, the Washington Monument, and George Washington's house, all in gingerbread...!
Official White House photograph.

The traditional "Christmas photograph" with President and Mrs. Bush,
a delightfully warm couple. Official White House photograph.

At a press conference with Mrs. Bush in front of the biggest-ever Christmas White House:
175 lbs of chocolate and gingerbread! Official White House photograph.

With my assistant Suzie Morrison, presenting President Bush with a cake on the theme of one of his favorite pastimes: fishing. Official White House photograph © Tina Hager.

The First Family leaving the White House aboard a helicopter from the Marine One fleet. Private collection of Roland Mesnier.

In California, with a pink Cadillac and a private chauffeur. My American dream!
Private collection of Roland Mesnier.

At my retirement reception. Memories, memories… Official White House photograph.

The White House cake, under construction. With the compliments of l'Académie de Cuisine and created by Mark Ramsdell for my retirement reception. Private collection of Roland Mesnier.

CHAPTER 15

Two Presidents for the Price of One

State dinners at the White House involve a great deal of forward planning and research—and careful coordination with the protocol department, whose job it is to gather detailed information, ensuring that nothing is served that could possibly cause the slightest problem.

Ahead of an official visit, the delegations from the two countries were involved in dialogue for months, sometimes even up to a year ahead, to organize the trip. The planning and organization must be perfect, no detail should be overlooked. Will the delegation need interpreters? What are the visiting head of state's culinary and musical tastes? And those of his or her family? What does he or she think about other heads of state (essential intelligence if gaffes are to be avoided)? What colors should be used for decorations during the visit, notably for the flowers? In China, white is the color of mourning. In Japan and France, chrysanthemums are the traditional flowers of mourning. Does the visiting head of state drink alcohol, and if not, will they be offended if others drink at the table? No one smokes at the White House, and guests must be informed that no one will be allowed to break this rule. Will women from Japan or Korea be able to attend in traditional dress? Many of the visiting First Ladies asked to be informed in advance of the colors Mrs. Clinton would be wearing during the visit to avoid fashion disasters: two First Ladies clad in red, green, or blue! What about the size of the presidential lecterns? Each delegation takes care to ensure that no one appears taller than anyone else, and that each speaker has a lectern of identical width. All these important details have to be settled well ahead of the event itself. This is why I have always paid such close attention to the desserts to be served. I trust the embassies to provide accurate advice and information. "Dessert diplomacy" is truly an affair of state!

Often, as previously mentioned, the visiting monarchs, presidents, or prime ministers stay at Blair House. Others prefer their own embassies or a Washington hotel. They usually arrive in Washington in the evening and are greeted at the White House. The official welcoming ceremony takes place the following morning, usually on the South Lawn, just behind the Washington Monument. The visiting head of state walks with the president along a red carpet to a small area in the middle of the lawn. Here, hundreds of invited guests are assembled to cheer and applaud the meeting between the two countries, providing a warm welcome for the presidential guest. The representatives from each delegation are also present, together with their respective cabinet chiefs, officials, and military staff representing each section of the U.S. armed forces. A crowd of journalists is always present, and the spectacle of marching soldiers and military inspections by the two heads of state is grand indeed. Speeches are made, the cannons are fired—twenty guns for a head of state, nineteen for a head of government—and the military bands play music evocative of American history and independence, notably "Yankee Doodle Dandy," except during visits from members of the British royal family, for obvious reasons. The flags tremble or flap in the wind. It's a great sight.

The Marine Band has been attached to the White House since the time of Thomas Jefferson. Its members sport a badge on their uniform bearing the legend "The President's Own." I have heard them play hundreds of times; naturally enough, they play military music, songs exalting the bravery and pride of the various U.S. armed forces: the Navy, the Marines, the Air Force, and the Coast Guard. The band's uniform is red, with dark blue trousers with a red stripe down the outside leg, a white hat with a black band, a jacket closed with brightly polished gilt buttons, and black braid for some or red for others. It has been my privilege to get to know some of the musicians and to be able to tell them that in my view, they are—in all sincerity—the finest in the world.

One of my biggest regrets in retirement is that I no longer hear their virtuoso playing on the band's brightly polished instruments.

The year was 1995. America's political parties were gearing up for the preelection campaign and the hunt for a candidate capable of the winning the race in the following year. Usually, during this period, the pace of diplomatic and official life at the White House would tend to slow down a little. But here we were, embarking on another dazzling round of receptions. There was a degree of anxiety in the air, largely due to the many minor scandals and incidents that had marked the Clintons' first term at the White House.

On February 9, we held a state dinner for the German chancellor, Helmut Kohl, and his wife. Mr. Kohl is a very tall, massively built man, with a huge appetite—thanks to which I almost ran short of desserts for the rest of the guests. The dessert, it has to be said, was quite original and delicious: coffee ice cream with grilled hazelnuts, a cinnamon and chocolate sabayon sauce, and a basket filled with assorted small macaroons. The result was attractive to look at, full of flavor, and symbolized the winter season. The chancellor adored it. One evening, President Clinton invited his German counterpart to dinner at a noted Italian restaurant in Washington, the Filomena. After a rich meal, they left in jovial mood and brought an enormous chocolate gateau back to the White House. Both of them shared a love of good food. In Helmut Kohl's case, this had resulted in a truly majestic girth, necessitating the use of a specially adapted limousine, which followed him everywhere on his travels. He was too big to get in and out of a normal taxi or car.

April 19, 1995, was a bloody day indeed. A car loaded with explosives was blown up in Oklahoma City, killing 168 people. The entire nation was horrified and grief-stricken. At the White House, the catastrophe provoked deep consternation. President and Mrs. Clinton could scarcely come to terms with what had happened. Before leaving for the memorial service for the victims of the massacre, the president and first lady planted a dogwood tree in the White House garden as a reminder in years to come of the brutality of the crime and as a symbol of the continuity of life. Dogwoods flower in springtime, when the shrub is covered with magnificent white blossoms, each one marked with a distinctive motif similar to a carpenter's nail. Christians see this as a symbol of the nails driven through Jesus' hands during the Crucifixion.

On April 25, 1995, just after the Oklahoma tragedy, we hosted a visit from the newly elected Brazilian president, Fernando Henrique Cardoso, and his wife. Naturally, I devised a dessert to celebrate Brazil on the theme of nature, in honor of that country's breathtaking landscapes, fauna, and wild flowers, which so many people travel there to enjoy. Brazil is also well known for its multicolored butterflies, and I decided to incorporate these into the design. The result was a basket of *borboleta* oranges (*borboleta* means "butterfly" in Portuguese). The Brazilian delegation was highly appreciative of my research and the dessert's Portuguese title. The basket was made from *langue de chat* cookies, and contained orange sorbets, crystallized fruit, and a Grand Marnier parfait, decorated with orange wedges dipped in sugar. Nonetheless, the conversation at dinner was somber indeed.

The year 1995 was one of violence. On November 4, Yitzhak Rabin, the Israeli prime minister and principal architect, with Shimon Peres, of peace talks with the Palestinians, was struck by three shots fired by a young, ultraorthodox Jewish extremist just as he was stepping down from a peace rally podium after delivering a superb speech in favor of the Middle Eastern peace process. His death was greeted with enormous sorrow throughout the United States. President Clinton was devastated. He had never thought such an act possible. He spent a great deal of time in prayer and reflection, and traveled to Israel for Rabin's funeral, together with his predecessors. Prime Minister Rabin was dead and perhaps with him the hope of peace in the Middle East.

A lighter moment in these dark times: a screening organized by the Clintons in their private cinema at the White House of the film *Apollo 13*, in the company of the astronaut John Glenn. The director, Ron Howard, was also present, together with an array of stars and well-known personalities: Tom Hanks, Kevin Bacon, Gregory Peck, Lauren

Bacall, Tom Cruise, Delta Burke, Meg Ryan, Morgan Freeman, John Travolta, and many more. Celebrities were always present in force at the White House.

In July 1995, the White House hosted a visit from the South Korean president Kim Young Sam and his wife. For dessert, I created a dish of pistachio sorbet decorated with sugar roses, the Korean national flower. The president told Bill Clinton that he was extremely touched. The dessert was served with strawberry sauce and chocolate truffles flavored with ginseng tea, another example of the research that goes into the dishes served to guests at the White House.

July 17, 1995, was the date fixed for a traditional ceremony at the White House when, a few years after the end of their final mandate, the former president and his spouse are invited by the new First Family to witness the unveiling of their portraits; these are placed on easels for the occasion, covered with a white cloth. Little by little, the gallery of presidential portraits has grown to constitute a history of the United States on canvas. The unveiling is the occasion for a reception for some 200 guests, and an opportunity for the White House staff to greet the former president and First Lady, usually for the first time since the end of their mandate. This time, ahead of the party, I was privileged to be given a preview of the portrait of Mrs. Bush. She was portrayed sitting on a chair with a table to her left topped with a vase with three white roses and a framed portrait of her dog Millie. Mrs. Bush wanted to be painted with the real Millie sitting on her knees, but was dissuaded by the artist. For the reception, I recreated the presentation easel in chocolate, with the ceremonial cloth left hanging slightly open, so that all could be seen of the portrait was a few white hairs—unmistakably Mrs. Bush! At the bottom of the piece, I painted Millie's hindquarters, with her tail wagging impertinently, apparently trying to get in on the picture, as Mrs. Bush had asked. I made about half a dozen versions of this model, each about eight or twelve inches high. The pieces were placed on the serving platter of pastries. When Mrs. Bush saw them, she understood straight away; there was a small tear in her eye and a big smile. After the reception, she asked me to keep the pieces safe in a box, so that she could take them back to Texas to show to her friends.

Sometimes—not often—life presents you with an opportunity to make good on past mistakes. For me, the occasion was a Mexican dinner organized on October 10, 1995, for President Ernesto Zedillo Ponce de León and his wife. The memory of the figure of the Mexican man asleep against the wall of his house still burned. This time, I created a corn-flavored ice cream, a typically Mexican specialty. The ice cream was shaped into a dome, garnished with tequila mousse and pieces of lime, and decorated with nothing but sugar ears of corn. The dessert was served with a lime coulis, small candy made from honey, and Mexican petits fours, known as "wedding cookies."

Christmas came around once again, and with it the sparkling garland of dinners, receptions, and banquets. Following on from my first gingerbread creation for the Bushes, I embarked on a tradition of Christmas gingerbread houses, but each time with a special personal touch for the first family of the day.

My first creation had been a Victorian house; Santa Claus's workshop was built against one side, peopled with elves. Santa Claus himself was represented taking off from the roof with his sleigh and reindeer: a very up-to-date Santa Claus, holding a cell phone in one hand. The piece used a great deal of marzipan to make the toys, animals, and figures. The First Family was delighted: the piece was unusual and quite unlike anything they had seen before. The following Christmas, we decided to recreate the White House in gingerbread and chocolate. The resulting piece weighed 330 pounds! Another very busy Christmas.

After this, I decided to try and produce more personalized houses, adapted to the First Family themselves. As usual, I began by doing some background research with the help of a woman who has known the Clintons for many years, since their days at the governor's residence in Arkansas: Carolyn Huber. I asked her to find me some photographs of the president's old family home in the town of Hope, Arkansas. She brought me several photographs and from these I was able to reconstruct the old house with its crooked roofline. Around the house, we placed marzipan cookies, decorated Christmas trees, and baby deer. When the piece was finished, the president was invited to the dining room to see it.

"Roland," he told me, "it's another masterpiece. I'm incredibly touched that you have made this for me. Merry Christmas! It's magnificent, really." There were tears in his eyes.

The following year, we decided to do the same thing for Mrs. Clinton. Once again, I asked Carolyn Huber to find photographs of the house where Mrs. Clinton had spent her childhood. This time, I decided to present it with a "cutaway" front, so that you could see inside. The bedrooms were equipped with miniature pieces of furniture, including bedside tables with softly lit lamps. In one room was a figure of Mrs. Clinton in bed, dreaming of her childhood toys: the theme of the piece as a whole was "childhood dreams." Outside the house, Santa Claus could be seen arriving in his sleigh, with snowmen and Christmas trees full of birds. Mrs. Clinton was very moved during her presentation of the piece to the press.

Each year, since the beginning of this Christmas "tradition," the press has been invited to a preview. I would stand next to the gingerbread house, and answer the journalists' queries, with Mrs. Clinton's help. This led to all manner of unforeseen situations, since we never knew what sort of tricky questions might arise. I experienced some difficult moments and some very funny ones, too. Photos were taken; articles were published in the newspapers. Fifteen minutes of fame!

President and Mrs. Clinton were doubly touched by these recreations of their childhood times because they came as a total surprise. I asked the staff to give nothing away when I asked for the initial photographs. The element of surprise was essential. I never told anyone what I was planning for Christmas. Plenty of people tried to find out, setting cunning traps to trick me into giving something away, but I never fell for it. A pastry chef can be involved in undercover operations, too. Huge numbers of people, perhaps 30,000 or 50,000, have been able to admire the pieces created for the Christmas festivities at the White House. Often, people wanted to take photographs of them. My gingerbread houses have earned me a quite a reputation, throughout the United States.

The following year, it was Chelsea's turn to be the subject of one of my fantastical gingerbread creations. Chelsea hadn't had a family childhood home as such: the Clintons didn't own a family property, and she had grown up in the governor's residence in Arkansas. I didn't feel that this was a sufficiently personal subject for her, but I knew that she had studied classical dance at the Kennedy Center, and decided instead to create another gingerbread White House, this time with a cutaway front, so that the interior of the building could be seen. The Blue Room was presented as a ballet studio, with a scene from Tchaikovsky's *Nutcracker Suite*. The dancers and ballerinas were all made from sugar; we even managed to recreate Chelsea's features for one of them. Either side of the house, the entrance was decorated with two giant nutcrackers made from gingerbread. Chelsea was hugely appreciative. "Look at that girl there," she said to me. "She looks like me!"

All of these gingerbread creations were made in a room on the ground floor at the White House, the so-called China Room, which contains displays of each of the table services created for the First Families since the time of George Washington himself. It's a superb room, very large and very fine, with huge windows, chandeliers, and red velvet drapes. Every year, the White House workers would remove the carpet and furniture, and lay a protective covering on the floor, so that we were free to work on the houses without fear of doing any damage. The press previews were held in the China Room, and journalists would also stop by beforehand to report on the work in progress. A film was also made each year, of the construction of the houses, to be shown on American TV before Christmas. I was pleased to be able to promote my work, and that of my team of assistants, and, above all, the prestige of the White House itself in this way. The year after the presentation of the piece featuring Chelsea as a ballerina dancing in *The Nutcracker*,

I decided to create an imaginary castle, bristling with towers, with a great door through which you could see Santa Claus loaded with presents, together with his reindeers, including Rudolph with his red nose. Outside the castle, the president's dog Buddy and Socks the cat could be seen skating together, wearing scarves floating in the wind. The entire piece, including the decorations, weighed 330 pounds.

The gingerbread house was getting bigger and bigger, and heavier and heavier, each year, so that transporting it to its place on the buffet sideboard was an increasingly delicate operation. A posse of journalists always managed to be present when we moved the house, hoping to see it collapse and crash to the floor—just in time for that night's prime time TV news. And sure enough, disaster nearly struck when we came to transport the fairytale castle. A team of six or eight people had lifted the piece onto a trolley and taken it over to the buffet, ready to transfer it across. Just as the workers began to lift it, one of the towers came unstuck and began to sway alarmingly, threatening to crash down on the walls of the castle. Luckily, this particular fairytale castle was fitted with electric lighting, and the wiring prevented the tower from collapsing completely. I stepped around the back and stood the tower back up. Phew! The press was dreadfully disappointed. The excited pack of journalists had truly believed they were about to witness their long hoped-for catastrophe.

For the Clintons' last Christmas at the White House, I paid them another gingerbread tribute. Eight houses—one for each year of the Clinton presidency—were presented with open-fronted drawing rooms, each one furnished with pieces made from marzipan and chocolate, with a chef standing ready behind the buffet and a host of invited guests. A vast amount of work went into each one.

~

Elections were held in 1996. There were two candidates in the running: Bill Clinton and Bob Dole. Naturally, we hoped that President Clinton would hold on to the reins of power. We had gotten to know the First

Family and balked at the idea of having to start all over again with a new boss. Meanwhile, there was an election to fight, and President and Mrs. Clinton devoted themselves to the campaign. There were conventions, meetings, receptions, speeches, and, as always, thousands of hands to shake. At the White House, we continued the familiar round of state dinners, albeit slightly fewer than usual.

On February 1, 1996, the White House was due to host an official dinner for President Jacques Chirac of France and his wife Bernadette. The event caused pandemonium in the kitchens, where—as I have already mentioned—the chefs were now all American. Mrs. Clinton wanted a menu using American ingredients and produce, but with a distinctly French touch. This was no easy task, but the main course was not my problem. My own challenge was to devise a dessert worthy of the finest French cuisine, but which would also symbolized a country I hold dear: I am a naturalized American but remain a Frenchman at heart. I am not one to forget my roots. And since we were to receive a visit from the president of France, I would do my very best to create something truly distinguished.

My first thought was to create a *croquembouche* composed of prof-iteroles coated in crisp caramel: a traditional French pastry centerpiece, which would be readily recognized as such by the dinner's American guests. I gave up on this idea, though. The dessert is difficult to eat, and the crunchy caramel coating on the soft choux buns isn't to everyone's taste. I decided to create a dessert that looked like a *croquembouche*, but wasn't a real *croquembouche* after all. I decided to produce what was described on the menu as a "pyramid of apple and cherry sorbets, with Calvados sauce." This would be served with a second dessert, typically American this time, so that no one's national sensibilities could possibly be offended: peanut-butter truffles, chocolate caramels, and chocolate bark. The pyramid was composed of a cone of apple sorbet, stuck all over with little sugar apples filled with cherry sorbet, each one with its own white chocolate stem. These alternated with choux buns filled with confectioner's custard, and fresh raspberries. The result was a festival of vivid colors in the shape of a *croquembouche*. In addition to this, I made choux pastry swans filled with cream and fresh fruit swimming on a "lake" of lime sauce. For the ultimate finishing touch, each pyramid was topped with a spun sugar plume reproducing that seen on the tops of the helmets of the French Republican Guard. The whole ensemble was truly impressive, both in size and scope.

The one difficulty I was faced with was a question of pastry thermodynamics: the pyramids were a combination of frozen elements and pastries, which need to be served at room temperature. Ice cream melts very quickly, so the only solution was to work as fast as possible, sticking the sugar apples and choux buns onto the pyramid at the very last minute and sending the whole straight up to the dining room, so that the choux pastry had no time to chill and the apple sorbet had no time to melt. The significant detail in all this was that there were fifteen pyramids in total. When they were taken into the dining room, all perfectly intact, many guests who had come armed with cameras started taking pictures. The desserts were greeted with a blinding barrage of flashlights, like true celebrities! Best of all, I discovered later that President Chirac had enjoyed a long conversation with Mrs. Clinton during the dinner in English. Oh, to have been a fly on the wall.

"I like a great many things about America and, above all, the food." As a student, Monsieur Chirac had worked for the Howard Johnson restaurant chain and still had a taste for American cuisine. This is very unlike his public face back home in France, where he is known as a fan of the very French country dish, *tête de veau*.

On February 27, 1996, we celebrated a happy event: Chelsea Clinton's sixteenth birthday. Chelsea was a brilliant student and a credit to her parents. She showed great kindness to all the White House staff and was always pleasant, never demanding. She had been thoroughly well brought-up by Bill and Hillary, and everyone adored her. She would become an exceptional young woman. I had great respect for her. Living in the White House at her age was not easy, despite the superficial luxuries: she was hemmed in by the restrictions of protocol, accompanied everywhere by secret service personnel, snapped by the paparazzi every time she set foot outside. I admired her for the way she handled all this, and I wanted to create a magnificent cake for her birthday, which was to be celebrated at Camp David. One morning, on my way to work, I heard a radio reporter announcing that Chelsea had asked her father if she could be allowed to take her driving test. She wanted him to buy her a car.

I decide to make a sugar driver's license, complete with a lifelike photograph of Chelsea, and a chocolate car: a violet-colored Jeep with four big, black wheels, yellow seats, and the top down. On the back shelf we placed a pair of sugar ballet shoes. The registration plate bore the words "Sweet Sixteen." The car was placed on a stretch of chocolate road scattered with hazelnuts to resemble gravel. There were sugar roses at the corners and a strip all around it reading: "Happy Birthday, Chelsea." The cake itself was a carrot cake, so that Chelsea's father could enjoy a piece, too. The cake was accompanied by a selection of ice creams. Chelsea loved it. On the night before the party, she had been to the theater in Washington to see *Les Misérables*. She enjoyed a wide range of activities with her girlfriends, many of whom were invited to the birthday party. She was touched by the trouble we had taken to celebrate her sixteenth birthday. It was an unforgettable moment.

On June 23, 1996, some 300 guests gathered in one of the garden pavilions for another state dinner, this time in honor of President Mary Robinson of Ireland. We had prepared a plated, frozen dessert. I wanted to evoke the ancient castles of Ireland. We made a series of round towers constructed from *langue de chat* cookies, measuring about five inches in diameter and five inches in height. These were decorated with an Amaretto parfait and fresh, pitted cherries.

~

The Clintons had a refined sense of public relations and were acutely aware of the importance of music, especially American music, as a way of bringing people together. They created the so-called "Internet performances at the White House," a series of concerts in the garden pavilions, featuring invited American stars. The president always enjoyed getting up on stage to play along on the saxophone, often in front of an audience of up to 1,000 people, seated at tables set for dessert, which was eaten during the show. The concerts featured a glittering lineup of stars and less well-known performers, from all over the United States. American music of every type—rock, jazz, blues—was much in evidence. Stars topping the bill included Meryl Streep, Robert de Niro, Garth Brooks, Gloria Estefan, gospel singers from Harlem, Kevin Spacey, B.B. King, Eric Clapton, Linda Ronstadt, Sheryl Crow, Aretha Franklin, Bobby McFerrin, Vladimir Horowitz, Jordan Michael Barbakoff, Liza Minnelli, Mary Chapin Carpenter, Yo-Yo Ma, Itzhak Perlman, Rita Moreno, and many more. The list was long and reflected all the dynamism, youth, and modernity that the Clintons had brought to the White House. They were very much a couple of their times, who had brought the venerable old White House well and truly up-to-date.

For the concerts, my job was to prepare desserts for tables of ten, arranged on rotating platters—individual dishes of mousse, chocolates, petits fours, pieces of orange, lemon, or crystallized ginger, candies—all decorated with musical notes or musical instruments in chocolate. On one occasion, a storm broke out during the concert. The water leaked under the canvas of the marquee, and the women guests, in evening dresses and high heels, found themselves up to their ankles in mud. Everyone had to remove their shoes, lift their skirts, and show off their legs. Personally, I found the spectacle absolutely charming, but in future years, the tents were all equipped with wooden floors.

At this period, during the end-of-year festivities at the White House, the Clintons began to host events celebrating Hanukkah, the Jewish feast of lights, and Eid al-Fitr, the end of Ramadan, with a seated dinner to which Muslim guests were able to bring their prayer rugs for use in a room set aside for the purpose. Another Clinton innovation, which has continued under President George W. Bush.

~

The White House is, of course, a place where tensions can run high, and where I operated under extraordinarily high pressure and was always obliged to create novel desserts. I simply had to let my hair down every once in a while, but one year, things went a little too far. We were at the Homestead, my former hotel, where I had had my first experience of professional life in the United States. Every year, the hotel hosted a gastronomic festival: every leading American chef was invited to take part. We were housed in fine style, with all expenses paid by the hotel, and I was happy to take a break away from the White House; happy, too, to see my old team from the Homestead, all of whom had remained firm friends.

On the Friday evening, the Homestead hosted a grand reception for around 350 people, during which each chef gave a cooking demonstration. I presented my recipe for a *crêpe soufflée*, cooked in an extremely hot pan and flambéed in Grand Marnier. The flames always shot up high, to general acclaim, and the dessert was served hot, straight from the pan, with raspberries, strawberries, and blackberries. *Crêpe soufflée* is a refined, delicate dessert, and its preparation was always a great highlight at the festival each year. I would have liked to present something different every once in a while, but was always told that I simply had to do the *crêpe soufflée*, because everyone enjoyed it so much. I was very proud, too, to return to my former stomping ground and be welcomed back so warmly.

Sunday nights at the festival were reserved for a grand dinner for which each chef prepared a special contribution. Naturally enough, I was to present a dessert, with my friend Michel Finel, who was the Homestead's pastry chef at the time, and a man for whom I have the greatest respect. In truth, he never let me help much; I was there to relax and have fun, not work, and Michel took care of everything with supreme skill.

The Homestead had a small discotheque, where we would often gather among friends, after work, for a drink or two. On the evening in question, I had gotten together with a group of former co-workers. We drank to old times, to life, to friendship. My wife Martha was tired. We had to be up early in the morning for the journey back to Washington, so she left me alone with the others and went off to bed. A big mistake. Scarcely before her back was turned, we fell to drinking more and more; so that the room danced around me like a ship tossed on the high seas. On Monday morning, I woke up in a wheelchair in our hotel room.

I opened my eyes, with a certain amount of difficulty, and a vague sense that something had happened, but with absolutely no recollection of events at the end of the previous evening. I asked Martha: "What's this chair doing here?"

Martha was a little annoyed: "You tell me. I was asleep when someone brought you back in it. You fell fast asleep. I didn't want to wake you up."

"But why the wheelchair?"

"Because they found you sitting on the floor in the ladies' room."

"What was I doing there?"

"I have no idea, given that I wasn't with you at the time."

I was seriously worried and more than a little ashamed, particularly as I couldn't remember a thing. Drinking myself into a state of oblivion on the floor of the ladies' room was not really me. And I knew that my drinking binge would be all over the hotel by now. A binge that had left me unconscious. Above all, I was horrified to have lost my self-control to such an appalling extent. It was at that moment that I realized just how badly I had needed to let go and have some fun. There was no other explanation for my behavior. I have never found out exactly how I ended up in the ladies' room, but one or two eye witnesses, somewhat embarrassed themselves, have told me that in an advanced state of drunkenness in the discotheque, I had tried to swing from the chandelier. No further details were forthcoming. I have never said much about the incident, because it was quite clear that my behavior surprised everyone, to say the least. But what's done is done. My wife fetched the car, we loaded our bags, and Martha drove us back to Washington.

We didn't talk much during the journey, mostly because I was still sleeping off the alcohol. I have never forgotten the incident, and I'm not proud of it.

In the years that followed, I continued to visit the Homestead for the gastronomic festival. It was a splendid event, where I was able to get together with old friends. I remain enormously fond of the Homestead and returned there often during my years at the White House, at the executive chef's invitation, to give patisserie demonstrations, including the flambéed desserts in the dining room. I was always delighted and not a little emotional to rediscover the surrounding countryside, a landscape that is so reminiscent of the Ognon Valley in France. The landscapes of Virginia are very like my home region of Doubs, France. There are small rivers, rocky escarpments, and, just in front of the hotel, a little ski slope covered with artificial snow each winter. There's also an Olympic-size ice rink. The Ognon Valley is not equipped with ski slopes and ice rinks, but it opens onto a mountain vista known as the Fort de la Dame Blanche. During my childhood, these hills were still dotted with wartime bunkers, which the American forces had occupied on their victorious sweep up the Doubs Valley. From there, they had bombarded the German forces further up the valley; a hail of shells fell there on the day I was born. When I was a child, we would often go to the Fort de la Dame Blanche, a chain of white rocky outcrops planted with trees. We spent many weekends there in spring and summer, picking flowers, or gathering blackberries to take home to my mother, who used them to make quantities of exquisite jam. We often came across the local wildlife: boars, deer, and hares. From the summit, the panorama extended far and wide to a distant blue horizon. The Homestead, with its mountains, forests, and wildlife, always reminded me of the Ognon Valley. Going there was a little like going home.

Election day was fast approaching, and the polls still indicated victory for Bill Clinton, with Bob Dole way behind. Bill and Hillary campaigned right up to the very last minute, traveling from state to state, and city to city, trying to secure more votes. Finally, the big day arrived.

The presidential plane landed at Little Rock, Arkansas, at 2 a.m. The President and Hillary Clinton voted in their home state, and then visited friends. There was nothing left to do but wait. Clinton's supporters were certain he would win again, and everyone else thought the same. Eventually, Bob Dole telephoned the president to offer his congratulations in the traditional way. He had conceded defeat, and we learned that Bill Clinton had won with an eight-point lead—a remarkable victory. After midnight, President Clinton and Vice President Al Gore arrived, holding hands with their wives, to greet their supporters at the Old State House, the former Capitol building, where Bill Clinton had launched his first campaign on October 3, 1991. Hundreds of party activists were waiting outside to give them a standing ovation. It's an emotional moment for any president to receive such a resounding vote of support and confidence from the American people. In his speech, the president spoke, as so often, about the year 2000, when humanity would step into the new millennium. He saw himself as a force for unity, capable of taking both American political parties forward into the future: "Now, we've got a bridge to build and I'm ready if you are. . . . America has told every one of us—Democrats, Republicans, and Independents—loud and clear: it is time to put politics aside, join together, and get the job done for America's future."

As always after an election, some members of the Cabinet were relieved of their posts—and the crushing burden of power—and found themselves free to return to everyday life. Most notably this time, President Clinton had appointed a new secretary of state, Madeleine Albright, the first woman to hold this high office. She held the job for the next four years. The appointment marked a small revolution.

And so in January 1997 the new president was inaugurated. Bill Clinton returned to the Capitol to swear on the Bible. I had prepared a great many chocolate coins for the grand reception that followed, and a selection of typically American desserts. Because this was a reelection, we felt under an obligation not only to carry on usual but to redouble our efforts and enthusiasm, to show that we could do even better than before.

Inauguration day was marked by a small family incident, which did not pass unnoticed. Chelsea came down into the White House lobby so that her mother could check her appearance before setting off to the Capitol. Any mother would do the same, I imagine. Chelsea was wearing a coat, against the winter cold. Mrs. Clinton asked her to open it, so that she could see the dress Chelsea had chosen to wear. Surprise! Chelsea was wearing a miniskirt. She looked marvelous. After the ceremony, during the march-past at the White House, all eyes were on Chelsea and not just those of young men of her own age. The press took up the story, announcing that Chelsea had blossomed into an attractive young woman. As I have said before, Chelsea is a person for whom I have enormous respect. She has always shown great dignity and self-confidence, and she has always known her own mind and behaved appropriately. She had a great sense of humor and was highly intelligent. In public, she always conducted herself like a true "First Lady."

~

After the reelection, the Clintons launched into a series of banquets celebrating the memory of Thomas Jefferson. Jefferson's influence on American cuisine is still strongly felt: thanks to him, numerous ingredients from France had found their way into American cooking. We planned to recreate a number of menus from Jefferson's time, including original dishes served to his guests at Monticello—sumptuous meals indeed. For my part, I was grateful to President Jefferson for introducing vanilla, *marrons glacés*, and small pastries to his native land. My personal homage to Jefferson took the form of little busts of the great man on small round silver dishes, surrounded by vanilla ice cream served in little shells and individual, whole *marrons glacés*. Another dessert was also served: "maids of honor," consisting of tarts made from almond shortbread. We also prepared almond macaroons, puff-pastry strips filled with raspberries, apple and frangipane tarts, and others filled with rice pudding and blancmange. These were Jefferson's personal favorites, which he always served at Monticello.

On February 23, we hosted a lunch for the Israeli prime minister, Benjamin Netanyahu. Naturally, I devised a kosher dessert: a honey soufflé made with no dairy products—only egg whites—and served with finger biscuits. On April 8, it was the turn of the Canadian premier, Jean Chrétien: chocolate truffle turbans with raspberries, lime coulis, and cranberry jellies (cranberries, deliciously sour, grow wild in Canada), accompanied by hazelnut and almond nougats.

In June 1998, the United States was once again playing host to the former G7 summit, renamed the G8 following the admission of Russia. I traveled to Denver, Colorado, where the heads of state were to meet. Two assistant pastry chefs traveled with me to prepare two different categories of receptions: those hosted by the president in Denver and those hosted by Mrs. Clinton for the other First Ladies in the Rocky Mountains.

As soon as we arrived in Denver I realized, with no great surprise, that the summit was going to require an enormous amount of work. There would be plenty of sleepless nights ahead. We arrived at the hotel around 8 or 9 p.m. and I collected my room key. Imagine my surprise, when I opened the door to go to bed, and found someone else already asleep. On closer inspection, the person in question turned out, somewhat to my disappointment, to be an African-American man who must have weighed around 250 pounds. He was, in fact, a fellow chef from the White House. I woke him up and asked him what he was doing in my room. He replied that this was the room he had been given.

"No way are we sleeping together," I said. "I like you, buddy, but not that much."

I hurried back down to reception, where I was told that there were no other rooms available. I asked to speak to the lady in charge of our accommodation, Robyn Dickey. "Find me a room, or I'm heading back to Washington right away." I pointed out that there was no way I could work like a slave for four days without so much as a room to sleep in. Needless to say, a room was quickly found.

My headquarters for the summit were in a splendid kitchen that was part of the University of Denver, where we organized a dinner for the G8 members on June 20, 1997. The chef, Raymond Liejl, was a very pleasant man, as was the school's director. Both were formidably intelligent and endlessly patient. I greatly enjoyed their company. For the dinner, I created a dessert entitled "Pike's Peak," for the perennially snow-capped mountain of the same name, part of the Rocky Mountains, which rises up as a backdrop to the city of Denver. The dessert looked just like a snowy mountain, with chocolate pine trees on its lower slopes. Slices of fresh mango and kiwi fruit were arranged around the base. The interior of the mountain was made from raspberry nougat ice cream. Everyone greatly enjoyed the dessert, including my new friends from the university. A commendable effort, with the compliments of the jury.

The heads of state all arrived in large black limousines, with the exception of Helmut Kohl, who traveled in his specially adapted minibus, as usual. We all expected him to drink beer with his meals, which he duly did. But to everyone's great surprise, the biggest beer drinker at the summit was not Mr. Kohl, but Jacques Chirac. Far from sipping elegantly at a glass of the finest Bordeaux, the French president proved to be an avid beer drinker, downing glass after glass of the frothy nectar. As is well known, in fact, the ancient Gauls were mightily fond of their national brew, known as *cervoise*. Subsequently, whenever President Chirac was visiting the White House, I reminded the butler, who marveled at my memory, to make sure that a supply of cold beer was on hand.

On the evening of the first dinner, I was left alone to take charge of the dessert while my assistants made preparations for the First Ladies' lunch, the following day. This was to take place at Winter Park, a high-altitude ski resort in the Colorado Rockies. The "First Ladies" traveling to the meal included Cherie Blair, Nina Yeltsin, Flavia Prodi, Aline Chrétien, Bernadette Chirac, and Kumiko Hashimoto. The journey to Winter Park was by car, taking a road leading through magnificent country, but which was full of twists and turns. Several of the spouses were actually taken ill on the trip. The prime ministers and presidents, for their part, took lunch at the Denver Public Library. Both meals featured the same dessert: a dome of passion fruit mousse, garnished with fresh cherries and served with an Amaretto sauce and kumquats.

On the evening of June 21, everyone met up at a delightful restaurant on the outskirts of Denver, known as The Fort, a Wild West-style building perched on a red, rocky hilltop overlooking a deep valley that extended for miles. My assistants arrived in the early afternoon to prepare for the dinner—a barbecue for around 50 people at which everyone was free to help themselves and eat at whichever table they chose. There were just two problems. Firstly, there were more guests than food. And secondly, there was Helmut Kohl, who devoured three "Apple Gooseberry" desserts with blackberry sauce and vanilla ice cream. The Italian prime minister, Romano Prodi, had already eaten two himself, and I had none left for the staff, which was very bothersome. At the end of the meal, nevertheless, we were congratulated in front of everyone.

Everyone was standing outside on the panoramic terrace in front of the restaurant. Suddenly, we heard the sound of bugles heralding a cavalry charge. The sound was coming from the valley bellow. Everyone hurried to watch. A troop of cavalrymen had launched an "attack" on the fort, bearing the flags of all the countries represented at the summit. A fantastic spectacle, followed by a parade with Native Americans. Cannons were fired, and the horses kneeled to honor the heads of state present at the dinner.

For this G8 summit, President Clinton had asked us to serve typically American food for the guests. The menus included bison—a fabulously tender meat, far more so than beef—but also rattlesnake, which had a mixed reception among the presidents and prime ministers. This last experiment was, I think, a mistake. The start of the festivities was marked by another, quite amusing, gastronomic incident. Secretary of State Albright had invited her Russian counterpart to dinner at a Denver restaurant. The menu included "mountain oysters" which happen to be deep-fried bull's testicles. The guests were more than a little surprised when their plates arrived.

On October 29, 1997, the White House hosted a state dinner for the president of China. On this occasion, the diplomatic stakes were even higher than usual. China was still largely inaccessible to the West and with such a vast country it was difficult to come up with a symbol for the dessert which was all-embracing. I created something quite original: "Orange Blossom Surprise," a dessert based on oranges, with a pomegranate sauce and mandarin tartlets, together with chocolates flavored with tea and ginger. Another quite extraordinary meal, which went smoothly from start to finish.

~

In November 1997, we were invited to the opening of the Bush presidential library in the little town of College Park, Texas. We were greeted upon arrival with a barbecue, and it was a pleasure to see the Bush family gathered together with their children and grandchildren. Barbara Bush arrived with a new dog, and I didn't dare ask what had happened to Millie. We spent three marvelous days in Texas, enjoying warm weather for the month of November. Everyone took photos. At the entrance to the library, a bronze statue stood guard next to a water basin graced with the galloping figures of four bronze horses. Wonderful! Inside were collected all the Bushes' White House souvenirs, including a model of the presidential plane Air Force One, many photos, autographs, and gifts from heads of state, which had been presented during official visits. The building included a superb penthouse apartment, which the Bushes were free to use when they visited the library for whatever reason. The apartment overlooked the surrounding gardens. The library's grounds were magnificent and the Bushes had elected to be buried there when the time came.

We enjoyed the spectacle of a parachute drop, and the parachutists landed all around us on the library lawn. Every former president was there, with the exception of Ronald Reagan who was too ill to attend, and was represented by his wife Nancy. The company included Gerald

Ford, Jimmy Carter, and Lady Bird Johnson, the widow of Lyndon B. Johnson, who had died in 1973. And, of course, Bill Clinton. Everyone gave a speech, and the tone was light-hearted. An unforgettable, nostalgic day and a wonderful opportunity to meet again the people with whom we shared so much. I was particularly touched when George Bush's daughter Doro came up to thank me once more for all I had done for her wedding party. Memories, memories.

In early November 1997, we welcomed a new member of the first family, a chocolate-colored Labrador by the name of Buddy. The first time he saw the president, he jumped straight into his arms, with scant regard for the rules of protocol. Bill Clinton decided to adopt him there and then. This was a piece of luck for the president: the dog went on to become something of a savior for him, providing a great deal of moral support and companionship in difficult times. Buddy was full of energy, and a beautiful dog with golden eyes. He and the president became inseparable. In relaxed moments, sporting a plaid shirt and jeans, and chewing a cigar which he never lit, Bill Clinton would play with Buddy in the White House grounds, tossing a ball. Buddy would race after it, and Bill Clinton would race after the dog.

The only problem with Buddy was that he bore the same name as one of the White House butlers—40 years old, married with two children—who had become the Clintons' favorite butler. He was unfailingly good-humored, even when experiencing difficult times himself. He loved his job, and the people with whom he worked. One of his children had been killed in a motorcycle accident, and President and Mrs. Clinton had attended the funeral ceremony in a village near Washington. As usual, a few forked tongues hissed with surprise that the president should waste his time attending the funeral of one of his employees' children.

Buddy bore the unfortunate coincidence of his name and that of the president's dog with his usual great good humor. When the leg of a White House chair was found to have been chewed, he said: "Not me! Blame the other Buddy." Of all the colleagues I left behind me when I retired, Buddy is the man I miss most. Every time we see each other now, we greet each other with the words: "Hey, Buddy!"

Bill Clinton also had a private photographer, by the name of Ralph Alswang, aged about 30, married, but with no children. We were very close, and always exchanged French-style cheek kisses whenever we met, which surprised people greatly, since American men never normally do this. I liked him a great deal. He was always cheerful, always had a good story to tell, and was always ready to take a photograph as requested. He took a great many of me. Sadly, whenever such people leave the White House entourage, we rarely see them again. When Bill Clinton's term in office drew to a close, Ralph disappeared from view. I still regret his loss today. We shared some great moments over the eight years of the Clinton presidency, and now we may well have said goodbye forever.

Chapter 16

The Clintons Fight Back

News of the Monica Lewinsky affair broke in January 1998. I know that I will disappoint many readers of this book when I say that I have nothing to contribute on the subject. I know no more than what was reported on the radio and TV, or in the press, and even if I did, I would reveal nothing. I have always believed that I was not at the White House to criticize the First Family, but to serve them and, in times of difficulty, to shield them. Beside which, I have always admired the Clintons, and feel that I am in no position to pass judgment. Who can honestly say that their own personal life has never been subject to inevitable highs and lows? I was very surprised when I learned of the affair. In any event, difficulties at the White House, which may be widely reported elsewhere, are never discussed by the staff. You can't always be sure just who you are talking to or that your words won't find their way back to the ears of the First Family. And so everyone keeps mum, except with very long-standing colleagues who you know you can trust. Even then, as a general rule, it is seldom advisable to confide your thoughts on anything that touches the First Family. Whenever well-intentioned souls tried to tell me what they thought and seek my opinion, I would let them know politely that it was not my job to pour oil on the fire.

Essentially, I found it hard to believe everything that was reported in the press, which was having a field day and, it seemed, prone to gross exaggeration. Whatever the truth of the matter, the sordid business cost President Clinton a great deal of time and deeply hurt the people closest to him. I felt great compassion for them. I was sorry to see President and Mrs. Clinton's lives turned upside down as the result of a minor scandal involving a star-struck girl. Each day brought new rumors and malicious gossip. I hoped that the whole sorry business, worthy of a trashy soap opera, would soon be over. But it was not to be. Certain parties were out for the president's blood, and blood attracts sharks. There were a great many sharks circling the troubled waters around the White House during those weeks.

The president and First Lady were far from radiant, but they made enormous efforts to remain dignified throughout the affair. Hillary was grief-stricken and Bill, too. He paid a heavy price for his mistake. But the Clintons rose to the challenge and overcame it. A few months later, when the affair had died down, the presidential couple was seen to smile again. They took meals together, chatted, enjoyed each other's company. The affair hadn't ruined their lives forever, but things remained difficult, nonetheless. As for Monica Lewinsky, I had, of course, come across her in the corridors of the White House and had occasionally passed the time of day. She was a very pleasant young woman. It was Buddy who first pointed her out to me: "She's called Monica. She works in the administrative offices." Quite simply, she was a very pleasant, very attractive girl.

There was one girl, however, whose conduct throughout the affair was universally admired, and not least by me: Chelsea Clinton. For summer 1998, the Clintons rented a house on Martha's Vineyard. This was perhaps their darkest hour. The family was hounded by the press, and Chelsea took matters into her own hands. It was Chelsea who spoke to the journalists, keeping them at bay in order to protect her parents, with a grace, dignity, and charm that could not fail to reflect favorably upon them in the eyes of the press.

~

I was getting to know the ways of the media. They were not necessarily ill-intentioned, or dishonest, but they were always on the lookout for the slightest defect or misdemeanor, and when they found it, they would talk about nothing else. With my strong French accent, I had to take care to pronounce everything as clearly as possible during press conferences, so that I would not be misunderstood. And I was careful to speak in short, simple sentences. There is much to be learned at the White House from watching the president and the First Lady speak to the press, day after day. During my eight years with the Clintons, I took part in eight press conferences, usually at very little notice. The executive chef and I would be called in at the last minute, and I would find myself installed in front of a forest of microphones, answering often very tricky question as tactfully as possible. I learned how to handle relations with the media during the Clinton years. I knew, for example, that if a press conference was to be given about a meal served at the White House, I would have to present a dessert, with help from my assistant Susie Morrison. When the head chef gave a conference, he always came armed with an impressive-looking folder from which he would read about the origins of a fish or some other ingredient.

I remember one particular conference, organized by Mrs. Clinton, during which we presented information about the menus served at the White House. Everyone was called up to the dining room, urgently: we were going to be on TV. I quickly put together an attractive platter of pastries and carried it up with me. The head chef had nothing on hand but a tray of small biscuits. Mrs. Clinton chose to present my pastries rather than the biscuits, and I found myself alone with her, talking to the cameras. The press quickly cottoned on to my work at the White House, and I became a firm favorite with them, the subject of many highly flattering articles. Mrs. Clinton was a great help in this: she always paid me the highest praise when she introduced me or spoke about my work to the press.

～

During all these years of hard work at the White House, laboring to create delicious, novel desserts, I took very few holidays. From time to time, however, I returned to France to visit my family. One year, my wife

Martha and I spent a month at the home of a distant cousin, Christian Paccard, at Arbois in the Jura. We enjoyed wines from the Pupillin region, *vin jaune*. In 1996, my friend and his wife stayed with us in the United States. Christian taught cooking at a college in Arbois, where he trained many young people. One day, as we were talking, we came up with a bold idea: a student visit to Washington, during which everyone would be invited to an official visit with the First Lady. I asked Christian to bring a case of wine with him, which I sent to Mrs. Clinton, with a letter from him, requesting an audience for the pupils during their trip, scheduled for 1998. Mrs. Clinton agreed immediately and became a good friend of my French friends, the Paccards.

It is worth noting that the Clintons adore France and all things French, although this might not have seemed immediately obvious when the First Lady set about banishing French products from the White House kitchen. I understood afterwards that this decision was taken for purely political reasons. When my friend Christian arrived at the White House with all his pupils, on April 30, 1998—thirty people in total—Mrs. Clinton greeted them all warmly, and we had our photograph taken all together in the Diplomatic Reception Room. The French party then moved on to the Homestead, my alma mater, and the Greenbrier, where I had worked before that. Their trip also included a visit to the major Washington cooking school, L'Académie de Cuisine. It was a splendid tour, and I was happy to have been able help with its organization, enabling a party of young people to discover the United States, and learn a great deal about American life and people. Mrs. Clinton was hugely appreciative of the delicious wine and often spoke about the visit to me afterwards.

～

On February 5, 1998, the White House hosted an official visit from the British prime minister, Tony Blair and his wife Cherie, including a grand dinner for about 250 people in the East Room. I wanted to excel myself for the occasion and began with an idea for a favorite English dessert: strawberries and cream. The dessert was presented in magnificent chocolate baskets decorated with wild strawberries and white roses in sugar. Each basket contained a dish of poached strawberries with a light lemon mousse made with Devonshire cream from England. The baskets also contained slivers of chocolate, and were decorated all around with colored chocolate flakes. I knew, too, that the Blairs and Clintons were close personal friends, and I wanted to mark their meeting with something very special.

Two weeks before the visit, I decided to accompany the dessert with platters of petits fours, including brandy snaps, nougat, chocolate caramels, and shortbread, another British favorite. As a final touch, I wanted to decorate the platters with a representation of Big Ben, London's celebrated parliamentary clock, in chocolate. I would need twenty-five chocolate Big Bens for each of the platters; I also needed a silicon mold of the tower, complete with its clock, about a foot high. Where could such a thing be found? I decided to call the pastry chef at my London haunt, the Savoy. We didn't know each other, but he very kindly agreed to send me a replica of the tower as soon as possible. Three days before the dinner, the tower still hadn't arrived. I was very worried, but I can never admit defeat. I had to pull off a culinary triumph that would be talked about all over the US and Great Britain. The Savoy pastry chef reassured me: he had sent the replica of Big Ben as requested.

The tower arrived on the morning of the dinner itself, Thursday, February 5. I had no idea what to do; it would take at least eight hours for the silicon mold to set. I decided to take the bull by the horns and invent a new way of molding chocolate. The method was as follows: I made a soft paste of flour, sugar, and butter, covered it with a thin layer of plastic film and pressed the tower into a block of the paste, like modeling dough. In this way, I could imprint the form of the tower on three sides of the block, rather than four. This wasn't a problem: the towers were then stuck onto a plaque of white chocolate, artistically cut out around the tower, and painted with a skyscape of clouds and birds. The towers were then brushed with icing sugar to highlight the details and stuck upright on a chocolate base. The same procedure, twenty-five times! We pulled off this minor tour de force thanks to a great deal of extremely fast work. Tony Blair and the other guests were touched and delighted.

~

On Thursday, June 18, 1998, the White House hosted a visit from the French prime minister, Lionel Jospin, and his wife. The event was marked not with a full-scale state dinner, but with an official lunch for a large number of guests. Dessert was *crème brûlée* with passion fruit and *tuiles*. During the morning, just before the lunch, I took a telephone call in the pastry kitchen. I was asked to go up to the presidential apartment, as Mrs. Clinton wanted to see me. I was quite surprised; such invitations were not common. When I arrived, I was greeted by the French prime minister and Madame Jospin, who had asked to meet me. I was quite overcome and very proud that Mrs. Clinton had agreed to call me. With her characteristic generosity, the First Lady spoke about my work in glowing terms. I had sent up a small platter of pastries decorated with an attractive sugar sculpture: a wineglass decorated with a small posy of hand-made sugar daisies. Madame Jospin asked me a number of questions about the piece, which she liked very much. Lionel Jospin, for his part, was plainly very proud to see a Frenchman working at the White House. He wanted to know where I was from, what I had done beforehand, how I came to get the job. At the same time, he was greatly entertained to be conducting a private interview between a prime minister and a pastry chef in a setting more accustomed to negotiations between presidents. President and Mrs. Clinton were also greatly amused, and smiled broadly at some of our comments. It seemed to me that their understanding of French was better than is generally assumed. We took photographs, which were signed for me by Prime Minister Jospin. They occupy a proud place among my souvenirs, today.

~

During all my years working abroad and at the White House, I never felt that my family back at home in France fully understood what I was doing. It was quite beyond anything they knew; they had never left Franche-Comté. Often, I would have liked to have been able to show one of them all the marvelous, extraordinary events I had witnessed throughout my life, so that he or she could tell the others. It has sometimes been a sorrow to me, to be unable to share my love of my work, and my great enjoyment of life, with my "folks back home." Now, I can talk about it in this book. But alas my parents will never read it; both are long since dead. I should love to have been able to express to them what it meant to me to meet and talk with the world's greatest leaders—me, the little boy in shorts who used to run through the fields, and loved the countryside, the farm, animals, and fishing.

~

Patisserie is, of course, an art in its own right, and one that borrows a great deal from the other arts, not least architecture. I had already produced a pastry model of Big Ben (twenty-five, in fact), as we have seen, but another, greater challenge presented itself on the occasion of a state reception for the Italian prime minister, Romano Prodi, and his wife, on May 6, 1998. The couple were both from the city of Bologna, and I decided to create a dessert reproducing the city's celebrated Asinelli and Garisenda towers, dating from the twelfth century. I recreated the two enormously tall, square brick towers using a chestnut parfait, which Italians love. The pastry towers each measured about sixteen inches high and were so solidly built that you could knock them with a spoon to serve the parfait contained within with no danger of the tower falling over. It was simply a question of following the basic rules of construction. The dessert was presented on a round dish, surrounded by a gateau of meringue and peaches, and served with a choice of chocolate or caramel sauce. The entire creation was edible, including the brick-work, and the dessert was accompanied by platters of Italian petits fours, decorated with blown-sugar swans. Once again, I had striven to outdo myself. Had I succeeded? Prime Minister Prodi and his wife were clearly delighted, and thanked the Clintons at great length.

~

The year 1998 was a dark one for the Clintons. On August 7, two car-bomb attacks were launched against the U.S. embassies in Nairobi, Kenya, and Dar es Salaam, Tanzania, leaving 260 people dead, including 12 Americans, and thousands injured. Almost all of the victims were Kenyan or Tanzanian office workers or passersby. This came just as the scandal surrounding the Lewinsky affair was in full swing. Just three days earlier, the U.S. attorney general had asked the independent counsel Kenneth Starr to investigate alleged financial irregularities during the president's last election campaign. Sometimes, the burden of power can be heavy indeed.

~

Every year, the White House holds a barbecue or picnic for Congress, to which senators, members of the House of Representatives, and their families, are all invited. The event is a great favorite with the First Ladies, who strive each year to come up with an appealing new formula, and to attract as many guests as possible to the South Lawn, usually between 1,000 and 2,000 people. In 1998 Capricia Marshall decided to try and dissipate the prevailing gloom and scandal by installing a fairground for the occasion, complete with carousels and rides, a Ferris wheel, shooting galleries, balloons, and jazz bands from Chicago and New Orleans. The food included specialties from every corner of the United States: hamburgers, candy floss, cheesecakes, and pralines, but also fried catfish from Louisiana, fried crocodile, and a host of other delights.

Needless to say, all of the desserts and pastries were produced in my kitchen. There was always work to be done! The giant outdoor party went on for several days, and everyone at the White House stopped by to join in the fun. The president, First Lady, Chelsea, and all of us took turns on the rides. The Marine Band was on hand, too, breaking into a chorus of "Hail to the Chief" every time Bill Clinton appeared.

Shortly beforehand, Mrs. Clinton had taken a few days' vacation in Austria. Not long afterwards, I received a parcel from the famous Hotel Sacher in Vienna, containing a Sachertorte, one of the celebrated chocolate cakes that have made the hotel a household name all over the world. The cake was accompanied by a note from the First Lady: "Roland, please tell me what you think of this cake." I was deeply touched. I wrote to thank Mrs. Clinton and indicated that I was especially delighted by the gift, as I had always dreamed of traveling to Vienna and visiting the Sacher. I adore the great, long-established luxury hotels of this world—the Sacher, the George V, the Savoy, and the Homestead—whose corridors are steeped in the memory of so many famous names. On the other hand, I greatly dislike many of today's modern hotels: so cold and sterile, and completely devoid of memories.

The summer of 1998 was one of surprises, including one very pleasant moment indeed: a visit to my pastry kitchen from Chelsea, together with a friend of hers from Texas, who wanted to see how my desserts were prepared. I assumed that Chelsea knew little about desserts and pastry-making, but once again, I was surprised and impressed by this remarkable young woman. She had a real feeling for pastry and knew a great deal about it. She recognized a block of frangipane on the table and knew all about choux pastry. She had decided to make her parents' favorite desserts for them: respectively, a little mocha cake, and a cherry pie with vanilla ice cream. I gave her the recipes, broke the eggs, provided her with a pie mold, which she would need to grease. Chelsea went to work, and I left her to get on with the job, asking my colleagues to keep an unobtrusive eye on things. She asked everyone a lot of questions and observed the professionals at work. At the end of the day, we took a group photograph with Chelsea and her friend. I didn't want to take advantage of her presence. The day remained a simple, friendly visit, during which Chelsea was delighted to spend time with us, while we got on with things as usual.

The next day, the girls returned punctually at 8 a.m. I had told them to be on time: "Work starts at 8 a.m. sharp and if you're late, you'll be washing the pans." Chelsea and her friend giggled over their coffee, but I made it quite clear that they could finish their drinks, then put away the cups, don their toques and aprons, and get to work. No dirty coffee cups were to be left lying around in my pastry kitchen. They both set to work without a word of complaint, busying themselves with the tasks begun the day before. The cakes were finished by midday, to be served to Chelsea's parents that evening. I guided Chelsea through the preparation of a creamy, fresh batch of vanilla ice cream, before teaching her how to make rose blooms and leaves out of marzipan. She could practice for as long as she liked, I said, but by the end of the day I wanted to see marzipan roses on the cakes, without fail. I showed her once, twice, three times. "Not like that, like this." Chelsea said: "I'm going to do it. I want to get it right. I absolutely want to present my Dad with a fantastic cake tonight, so he can be proud of me. I'm going to give it my all."

By the end of the day, both girls had succeeded in making a set of marzipan roses that bore a striking resemblance to cabbages, but the results were really not bad at all for a first try. We decorated the cakes, and Chelsea announced to her father that she had made that evening's desserts, one for each parent. When the waiter arrived carrying the cherry tart and the mocha gateau, the president and First Lady were smiling broadly. They could see that the desserts lacked the usual finesse, but they were delighted nonetheless. For my part, I was thrilled to see that the two girls had thoroughly enjoyed themselves in the pastry kitchen, and had taken great pride and pleasure in what they produced. Chelsea telephoned me afterwards to thank me for letting them come down and spend time in the kitchen. I replied that the White House was her home; she was free to come to the pastry kitchen any time she liked. We were honored to see her, and she would always be welcome.

~

Sometimes, seasonal considerations take precedence over matters of diplomacy. On September 7, 1998, we hosted the Czech president, Václav Havel—another visit loaded with significance, symbolizing a desire for greater understanding between the two countries. I wanted to create a dessert that would evoke the idea of NATO. I created a caramel, rum, and raisin ice cream covered with a pastry dome topped by a large bow made from baked, caramelized pastry. This was placed on top of the dome just before serving. Pears poached in heavily spiced red wine were arranged around the base, and the whole creation was served with little croissants and sugared vanilla pretzels. At a push, the dome could be taken to symbolize the protection afforded by NATO, but on the whole, the dessert owed more to the prevailing season (fall) than to the political climate.

I was always struck by the Clintons' unerring eye for a good party and the slick organization that accompanied such events at the White House. Birthdays are, of course, as good a pretext as any. Chelsea's sixteenth birthday has already been described, and there were many more besides, notably for the president and Mrs. Clinton, unless they were away from the White House at the time. When a member of the First Family celebrated their birthday at the White House there was always a big party. This was particularly true for Mrs. Clinton, who threw parties in her own highly individual style, including costume parties. One such event, in 1999, was on a theme of "past times." The Clintons attended dressed as James and Dolley Madison, president and First Lady of the United States from 1809 to 1817. I was dressed in a period costume from the reign of the French king, Henri IV, and the rest of the staff borrowed outfits from a host of different historical periods. I had been asked to bake a special "horror" cake for the occasion, decorated with skeletons and with smoke rising from the top. Strange, but true. Everyone had a thoroughly good time.

In 1994 Mrs. Clinton's birthday party harked back to the 1950s, the decade of her birth. Everyone came dressed in outfits from the period. The cake took the form of a jukebox, with a sugar couple jiving on the top. Large imitation LPs made from chocolate were stuck around the side, and the cake was flanked with sugar hamburgers, hot dogs, and French fries.

The following year, 1995, the theme was "the country." A tractor was installed at the entrance to the White House, and everyone was invited to come dressed "country-style." The birthday cake took the form of a bale of hay, behind which would be seen an old, run-down cabin, with a split stable door open at the top to reveal a horse's head. The ensemble included some essential American country accessories: a cowboy hat, a lasso, and a fiddle, all made from sugar or chocolate. I wore an old pair of jeans with holes, a battered straw hat, and a black and red plaid shirt. Mrs. Clinton wore a red and white striped skirt with a big red bow, a blue blouse, a curly blond wig, and a black hat. The president wore his (more or less) usual off-duty outfit: a plaid shirt and jeans. Once again, everyone had a great time.

In 1997 we celebrated the First Lady's birthday in one of the garden pavilions. The event provided an opportunity to promote Mrs. Clinton's book, *It Takes a Village*, published the previous fall. The book deals with youth and the parenting of young children, taking its title from an African proverb that expresses the idea that childrearing is the work of an entire community. The cover featured an attractive series of children's drawings. For the party, I created three life-size sugar balloons, suspended above the cake, as if floating in the air. The balloons were decorated with the words "Happy Birthday." We reproduced the book's cover in decorative sugarwork on a sheet of white royal icing.

One year, things were organized a little differently. As it turned out, Bill Clinton and Tipper Gore, the wife of the vice president, shared the same birthday, August 19. The First Lady decided to organize a joint party. I created a cake with several tiers, each with a different flavor. The top represented a golf course, with a little golf cart and golfballs. For Mrs. Gore, we created a cascade of life-size sorbet roses in a host of different colors and flavors.

We also celebrated Hillary Clinton's mother's birthday. Mrs. Rodham had reached the grand old age of eighty. She asked for a cake that would remind her of California, where she often spent her vacations, in Los Angeles, by the sea, or in the mountains. I modeled three cakes in the shape of tall, pointed mountain peaks rising up above a beach. The piece also included the sea, with boats, and a little, typically Californian cottage by the waterside. A banner was strung between the two mountains, reading "Happy Birthday, Mrs. Rodham." This little piece of California was to be transported to Camp David with exceptional precautions to ensure that it arrived intact. I made sure that the banner could be removed and put back in place after the journey. Mrs. Rodham thanked me for the cake, which represented everything she held most dear. I was, in fact, a kind of interpreter, translating people's tastes, memories, and desires into patisserie: "Say it with cakes!"

For eight years, we also celebrated the birthday of Lionel Hampton, a marvelous musician who was the first jazzman to play the vibraphone, a drummer of true genius, and a gifted improviser. For his ninetieth birthday, we created a cake in the form of a multicolored xylophone. Mr. Hampton played the xylophone, and the president accompanied him on the saxophone—a truly remarkable sight and sound.

～

In late 1998 the executive chef and I were called to Mrs. Clinton's office along with other members of the White House staff. The First Lady told us that she was planning to write a book about the White House, illustrated with photographs and featuring some of our most delicious recipes. The book would give an insight into the running of the White House, and Mrs. Clinton hoped to include a few anecdotes about state dinners. All proceeds from the book would be donated to the White House Historical Association and a portion of the publisher's profits would go to the National Park Foundation. The First Lady's legal advisers were reticent about the idea; we were forbidden to take part in any such publication while we were still in the employ of the White House. However, Mrs. Clinton insisted that we should be featured in the book. We agreed to sign a disclaimer to avoid any possible difficulties. The book, *An Invitation to the White House: At Home with History*, appeared a few years later and was a great success, a real bestseller.

~

In 1998 the organizers of the City of Washington childrens' Christmas party at the White House decided, at the last minute, to invite 6,000 people instead of 2,000. A great many children would be present, and I was asked to give a demonstration of how to produce blown and pulled sugar. My assistants decorated Christmas cookies with multicolored fondant icing: a huge amount of work. I was short-staffed and took advantage of the occasion to call up my son George, from Florida.

There were so many people in the pavilion set up for the event that it was almost impossible to get around. The press was particularly unhappy—this was a children's party, so there were no savory snacks or alcohol. Some of the journalists became frankly annoyed. Despite this, it was a very enjoyable day. The garden was decorated with huge ice sculptures by noted artists. In the marquee, the patisserie team gave a host of different demonstrations, including how to decorate Christmas cookies and Yule logs. As part of my blown-sugar demonstration, I created Christmas-tree ornaments, angels, and a host of other pretty decorations to the children's delight.

One person at the party was less than impressed: my son George. He was irritated by his visits to the White House; he knew everyone, but the majestic organization of the place, the conspicuous consumption, the lifestyles of the people who frequented the building, the way in which money was spent were most displeasing to him, a waste of tax-payers' careful thrift. George was by nature a free spirit. He did what he liked, when he liked, and preferred to walk away when he was tired of a particular job or needed a change of scene. He was ideally suited to his life as a musician, earning money by house painting between engagements. I loved having him with me at the White House. We would eat together and shared some great moments. I always took plenty of photographs of him in front of the various Christmas creations or the Christmas trees. Sadly, these visits eventually came to an end.

George was on friendly terms with everyone at the White House thanks to an annual buffet at our home, to which I invited all my colleagues—about forty people in all, including the family and friends. The party was usually held sometime between Christmas and New Year, and George always came along. It was a great pleasure to see everyone gathered together, but also a huge amount of work for us: fillet of beef Wellington, crab Louis, shrimps with cocktail sauce, smoked salmon, cold cuts, bread, salads, and cheese platters—and, of course, lots and lots of desserts. A grand dinner, but most importantly a dinner with friends.

~

The year 1999 promised to be extremely busy, with plans underway for the celebrations marking the new millennium and further festivities for the fiftieth anniversary of the signing of the North Atlantic Treaty and the creation of NATO. This was in addition to the usual heavy round of activities at the White House: state dinners and still other, unforeseen events. For some reason—the forthcoming year 2000, a general sense of uncertainty about the way the world was headed, the impending end of the Clinton mandate?—I felt anxious about the year ahead, with a vague notion that it would not be a good one for me. I would have to hold fast and steer a steady course, as always.

We began, as usual, with the Christmas and New Year parties at the White House. Immediately afterwards, on January 11, 1999, came a state dinner for the Argentinian president, Carlos Menem. I carried out my research in the usual way, collecting brochures from the Argentinian embassy to help me create a dessert that would reflect something of the country in question. Upon arriving at the embassy, I was told that the Argentinian ambassador, an extremely pleasant man, wanted to see me.

"Roland," he said, "I know exactly what you should do: decorate the desserts with bulls' heads. They'll love it." During our conversation, I discovered that because Argentina is so well known for the quality of its beef, the Argentinian people have adopted the bull's head as a national symbol. Bull's heads are everywhere in Argentina: in newspapers, magazines, and tourist brochures. I thanked the ambassador warmly for his excellent idea, but had no intention whatsoever of heeding his advice. Had I done so, it would probably have spelled the end of my White House career. If the Clintons were presented with dessert platters decorated with bull's heads, they would certainly have wondered if I was losing mine.

My own ideas took me in a quite different direction. I discovered another favorite Argentinian specialty, an extraordinarily delicious ice cream known as *dulce de leche* made from condensed milk, which is boiled for hours until it turns to a kind of caramel. This is what I would serve for the dessert. In addition, I served a dish of pineapples—an important Argentinean crop—cooked in a very special way, then arranged on silver platters topped with a kind of sweet pastry, giving them an agreeable crunchy taste. As an accompaniment, I made walnut caramels and little coconut snowballs. Having given up on the bulls' heads, I decorated the dishes with a quite different Argentinian export, the tango: sugar figures of dancing couples, each about ten inches high, were placed above each dessert, on a dance floor made from chocolate, against a backdrop of chocolate palm trees. The Argentinian president was in raptures.

CHAPTER 17

A New Millennium

As always, events brought their share of drama and sorrow. February 7, 1999, was a profoundly sad day for many Americans. King Hussein of Jordan had died. He was a great friend of the Clintons, and of the United States, a man of courage and integrity whose death was a source of enormous sorrow for the American people. I had prepared many meals for him. Presidents Ford, Carter, and Bush traveled to his funeral in Jordan, together with President Clinton and many other heads of state. Upon their return, all were invited to stay at the White House. Carter and Bush accepted, but Gerald Ford left after dinner. This was, of course, not an occasion for a formal dinner, but it was quite extraordinary for me to see four presidents, three of whom had been my employers, gathered in friendship at the White House. President Ford had lost to Jimmy Carter in 1976 and had taken his defeat very hard. Over the years, however, the former adversaries had become close, firm friends. True men of power know how to set aside their personal differences.

Shortly after this, rumors began to circulate at the White House that Mrs. Clinton was considering running for senator from the state of New York. The idea came as no surprise to anyone.

On February 24, 1999, the White House hosted a visited from the president of Ghana, where President Clinton had been warmly welcomed in the past. Ghana's hospitality was to be returned in style. I set about creating an elaborate, carefully researched dessert. As usual, the Ghanaian embassy provided information, help, and inspiration. I noted that Ghana was famous for its colorful *kente* fabrics, which were often worn by the women. The dessert was entitled "Sweet *Kente* with

Honey Ice Cream and Pineapples." We recreated the printed *kente* fabric using multicolored almond paste, and filled pineapple shells with mango and pineapple ice cream, topped with meringue. Tropical roses were arranged around the edges of the dish, made from thin slivers of mango. There was a raspberry sauce and, as a finishing touch, cocoa beans, which were in fact chocolate truffles. I discovered that Ghana was also a major source of gold, and included chocolate squares wrapped in real gold in the composition. A most exciting dessert.

NATO's fiftieth anniversary was to be celebrated in April 1999, with three days of festivities at the White House. Everything began on April 23, with a grand dinner for the NATO representatives and their spouses. The dinner was held in the East Room, at a semicircular table laid with a superb cloth, stunning silverware, and ravishingly beautiful flowers. I created a molded stand in pale blue marbled sugar, about fourteen inches in height, and a sugar dish supporting a dome of strawberry ice cream decorated with nougat. The dessert was served with a champagne sabayon sauce, little chocolate globes, and passion fruit. The dome on the stand was feather-light and was further decorated with sugar flags of NATO countries. On the following day, April 24, 1999, we hosted the anniversary dinner itself. I created a special rectangular mold bearing the inscription "fiftieth anniversary of NATO," decorated with chocolate, fresh fruit, and a coulis. The dessert, which was individually plated, was stuffed with chocolate cream and praline. Finally, on April 25, we organized a lunch for the European delegation to coincide with the Euro-Atlantic Summit. I prepared a mascarpone mousse with strawberries, raspberries, and blackberries, and pepper and ginger petits fours—a particularly interesting combination. But a huge amount of work!

Shortly after all this hullabaloo, on May 13, 1999, we hosted a visit from the Japanese prime minister, Keizo Obuchi. The visit was the occasion for a state dinner which seemed to me, at the time, to be the grandest and most formal event I would ever witness during my career at the White House. I was wrong, as we shall see later. Six hundred guests were gathered for the feast and naturally enough I created a Japanese-inspired dessert: a plate of kiwi sauce through which threaded a river floating with multicolored flowers. Spanning the river was a bridge decorated with a green and dark chocolate bonsai tree, and beneath this was the dessert itself, a timbale of assorted mousses, almond around the outside and orange within, recalling the colors and design of the Japanese flag. Orange segments were served as an accompaniment. The dessert was entitled "Bonsai Garden of Sweet Serenity."

~

Christmas was approaching as were the events marking the passage into the new millennium. We would have to work harder than ever. This year, instead of my traditional gingerbread house, we created a group of historic Washington buildings. The White House itself would be just one building among several. Others included the Washington Monument and George Washington's house at Mount Vernon. As is well known, George Washington never lived at the White House, which was built after his time in office. The display would occupy the same space as usual but would be differently arranged. The monuments would all stand very tall, even though this meant that the White House would appear smaller in relation to the others. On the eve of the festivities, everything was ready. Mrs. Clinton was very pleased with the results, and the Christmas celebrations proceeded as usual, with large numbers of guests and press, radio, and TV journalists. The only difference was that this year, there could be no question of leaving Washington after Christmas Day for my usual holiday until the beginning of January. After working hard for an entire month, we had to get straight on with preparations for the millennium celebrations, which promised to be truly remarkable.

First of all, the gingerbread monuments were given a millennial touch with the addition of chocolate fireworks, which we placed on their rooftops and a host of other special decorations. Then there were menus to devise, and thousands of pastries, desserts, and chocolates to make, without a minute to lose. This time, my son George came up to Washington for a week to provide badly needed extra help.

Festivities began on the evening of December 31, 1999, with a seated dinner for 500 people. In addition to the White House itself, we had the use of two large pavilions. The first, to the west of the building, was erected over the Rose Garden. The other was installed in the famous East Garden, renamed in memory of Jackie Kennedy. The Rose Garden pavilion served as a dining room, and the Jackie Kennedy pavilion was a discotheque. The latter garden (Hillary Clinton's sculpture garden) featured two statues I adored, a horse couched on the ground, and another standing up, both made from branches. The sculptures were lit up, and the trees and bushes were filled with tiny lights. An enchanting sight! The pavilions were heated, and carpet was laid on the floor.

An elaborate menu had been prepared for the first dinner, for 500 guests. The meal began with an oyster consommé, followed by caviar, lobster, and foie gras, before moving on to the main course: lamb stuffed with truffles served with roasted artichokes and polenta. After this, and before the grand finale (my dessert!) came a salad of beet and blue goat cheese. The dessert itself was a huge chocolate and champagne mousse in the form of a clock, with the hands set at five minutes to midnight, just before the passage into the next millennium. The petits fours, served on platters of 50 for every 10 guests (2,500 in total) were decorated with a little calendar of the year 2000 and a chocolate firework. We got to work at 6 a.m. that day, making preparations for the meal, which was to begin at 7 p.m. After the dinner, President and Mrs. Clinton headed for the National Mall, the complex of gardens and lawns extending from the White House to the Capitol. Bands were playing at strategic intervals along its length, and the Clintons joined in the mass celebrations.

During this time, we were busy preparing buffets in the White House, loaded with dishes of all kinds, and, of course, an array of pastries, ready to serve 1,500 guests. We took a break to watch the fireworks in the gardens, and then finished setting out the desserts. Many of the staff members had had quite a lot to drink by now, and the atmosphere was heating up. It was their millennium celebration, too. I had to make sure that my colleagues kept their cool and carried on with their work. I certainly didn't want to see anyone lose their temper or break with protocol. I needed eyes in the back of my head. Strict orders were issued to everyone. At around midnight, President and Mrs. Clinton returned, bringing with them the new influx of 1,500 guests. The party continued, the buffets were opened, and we were still hard at work after midnight. Then, the order was given for a further set of buffets, for breakfast this time, to be ready for 4 a.m.—eggs, bacon, ham, toasts, pastries, croissants, brioches, *viennoiseries*, for around 1,200 people who, it was estimated, would still be at the White House at that early hour. We wondered when we would be able to go home. We were told that we could go home once every guest had left, and the buffets had been cleared away.

Most of my colleagues had begun to get a little annoyed; many of them were hungry and very tired. It was getting very late: 1 a.m., 2 a.m., 3 a.m. I had to shake more than one of them awake. Panic stations! But we had to get on with our work—there were still around 1,500 people in the White House. The disco was still in full swing, and there were a great many VIPs present: Sophia Loren, Muhammad Ali, Steven Spielberg, Jack Nicholson, and many, many more. It would be impossible to list them all. It was an extraordinary evening, and one that I will remember to the end of my days.

We made it through to 6 a.m. The guests had all left, and now it was time to clear the buffets and put away the equipment. At 7 a.m. George and I climbed into the car to drive home. George was livid. He simply couldn't believe that a party could go on for so long. We had been working for twenty-five hours nonstop—something he had never done before in his life. He learned a great deal that night. I think he grew up all at once, with the millennium. When we reached home, we collapsed into bed and woke up at noon on January 1. George was still outraged by what he had seen. How could the U.S. government possibly justify spending so much money on the festivities, with everyone drinking and eating all night long? He was exhausted and took a very dim view of everything. We relaxed in front of the TV all day and enjoyed a quiet family dinner in the evening. At lunchtime the next day, we went out to an excellent restaurant. George's mood began to lift, but he still couldn't stomach the fact that he had worked for twenty-five hours without stopping.

George retained at least one happy memory of the millennium celebrations: the photographs I took with him in front of the *Crystal Tree of Light*, an extraordinary installation created for the White House by glass artist Dale Chihuly. The piece was a montage of individual, hand-blown glass elements forming a glass cone the same height and shape as a very large Christmas tree—some thirty feet tall. It was a splendid creation, using light as an integral part of the composition. A true monarch of the forests. Its beauty surpassed that of any real tree. But it was not a living thing.

～

And so we launched into the year 2000, and the start of another electoral campaign. Thinking about my future, I realized that I was extremely tired. This First Family, of whom I was so fond, had demanded a great deal of me. I was no longer capable of working as I had in the past; I lacked my former precision and in some cases—when working on pieces for which I had developed the greatest finesse and rapidity—I felt that I was operating to ninety percent of my abilities. I would have to think about what I should do. The end of one presidential mandate and the arrival of a new First Family were, as always, a source of anxiety for me, but this time my fears were exacerbated. Should I carry on in the job or not? At the same time, I had also begun to think about writing a book on the subject of patisserie, once I had retired. I was already working on the project and had begun to look for a publisher. What sort of book?

I had no idea. I took legal advice, since it was forbidden to publish any-thing while still working at the White House, and was told that once I had retired, there would be no problem. Little by little, I formed the idea for a straightforward cookbook, based on all the desserts I had created during more than twenty years at the White House. The project required a great deal of thought.

Meanwhile, the election year—which always heralded a flurry of activity in Washington and throughout the United States—promised a period of intense hard work. Knowing the Clintons, I felt sure that they would work to their utmost ability, to the very last minute, which they did. They adored people and loved meeting as many people as pos-sible, time and again. In February 2000 Mrs. Clinton announced that she would be running for the U.S. Senate, confirming the rumors that had been circulating for some time.

As usual, the start of the year was marked by the state governors' ban-quet. Among the guests was George W. Bush, governor of Texas and son of former President George Bush. The White House maître d'hôtel George Hanny, a longstanding staff member who was not noted for his timid approach to life, came over to me at the end of the meal and said he just been talking to Governor Bush (whom he referred to as "Dubya") and his wife Laura. George Junior had told him: "Keep the bed warm, we're coming back." Clearly, he was supremely confident of victory in the forthcoming presidential election. I was amused by the story.

~

On February 23, 2000, the White House hosted another royal visit, from King Juan Carlos and Queen Sofia of Spain, including a grand state dinner. In light of the strong historical ties between the United States and Spain, this was an important event. Once again, I would have to surpass myself. I carried out a great deal of intensive research, starting with the King of Spain's coat of arms, from which I created a chocolate shield on a two-inch block. The dessert was entitled "Topiary

Valencia." "Topiary" referred to its shape, a kind of montage, like a *croquembouche*, while "Valencia" was an allusion to the oranges that flourish everywhere in the Spanish sunshine. The sauce was made with glazed kumquats and there were also walnut caramels dipped in chocolate, raspberry-flavored butter petits fours, and ginger cookies. The finished dessert took the form of a square box surrounded by chocolate trelliswork and decorated on each side with the arms of the King of Spain in dark chocolate on a white chocolate background. Rising from inside the box was a tall cone of sorbets, some twenty-four inches high: lime, lemon, and orange, each one shaped like the fruit whose flavor it represented. The cone was surrounded by even taller sugar stems, sugar branches decorated with orange and lemon blossoms. The whole piece measured about three feet in height, and was extremely beautiful, with three basic colors reflecting the colors of Spain itself. Fresh kumquats and raspberries were piled around the base. It was a truly majestic dessert and greeted with compliments from all sides.

In March, President Clinton hosted a working dinner for the Egyptian president, Hosni Mubarak. This was undoubtedly the last time that President Mubarak would receive such an invitation from Bill Clinton, whose time in office was drawing to a close. I had decided that every head of state visiting the White House during this period would take with them the memory of a truly exceptional dessert. For Mubarak, we created an inverted pyramid, point downwards, in red, orange, and white chocolate. On top of this was another pyramid, point upwards, made from yellow and red sorbet (melon and raspberry). The upturned pyramid was supported by four small columns decorated with chocolate ribbons in yellow, red, and white. I was told later that President Mubarak had spoken a great deal during the dinner about the desserts he had enjoyed at the White House over the years and had been touched by our use of his country's eternal symbol.

Three months later, on June 20, 2000, we made preparations for a visit from King Mohammed VI of Morocco. I had been working at the White House for almost twenty years now, and I found it harder and harder to come up with inspirational new ideas. I lacked the necessary concentration and began to realize that it really was time to think about retiring. Even after a trip to the Moroccan embassy, I found it hard to know what to serve. All I knew was that when the dessert was brought to the table, everyone present should immediately think: "Ah, Morocco!" Still, I was devoid of ideas and quite panic-stricken. I decided to head for a little Washington bistro where I liked to drink a glass or two and think quietly, away from everyone else. The dessert would include mosaics, but also houses, plenty of houses. And minarets? Best to avoid any religious references. What about camels? Camels are everywhere in Morocco. And date palms and oases. A complete jumble. I began to work out some ideas on a paper napkin. I wanted to see if I could create a wall of blue mosaics, such as those seen all over Morocco, around the outside of the cake. The cake itself would be made of ice cream, probably orange sorbet, with date mousse. What about a round cake? No, hexagonal. On top, we would mold a dome using more orange sorbet and date mousse. The dome shouldn't be too reminiscent of a mosque, so we would decorate it with orange segments dipped in red and yellow sugar, and fine shreds of crystallized orange zest. The dessert featured the color blue, but there would have to be red, too— the Moroccan flag is entirely red with a small star in the center. We would use red pomegranate seeds. The dessert was taking shape, but it lacked an atmospheric touch. I would create a sort of sugarwork screen, made from icing sugar mixed with gelatin, which sets as hard as cement. Taller than the dessert, this would act as a backdrop on which we could paint palm trees and a caravan of camels, each one smaller than the last as they walked towards a tiny oasis in the distance. A typical desert landscape, with deep blue sky and an orange sun. Perfect! My dessert was all planned out on a cocktail napkin in a Washington bistro.

I knew that mint was a favorite ingredient in Moroccan cuisine and decided to serve the dish with a fresh mint and honey sauce, accompanied by honey cakes topped with sesame seeds, fresh dates stuffed with almond or pistachio paste flavored with orange flower water and dipped in sugar syrup for a glossy finish. I am sure that His Majesty was deeply touched by our superlative efforts in his honor.

~

Throughout the various presidencies that had marked my time at the White House, we had served thousands of desserts, dinners, lunches, cocktail parties, and teas; I had begun to feel quite exhausted. And yet I had no choice but to carry on. I took plenty of exercise, went for walks in the country, tried to watch my diet, got to bed early, and slept well. I would carry on until it was time to retire; there was no question about it.

The desserts I created became more and more opulent. It's in my nature to fight back with all guns blazing when I feel under threat. I had also imagined that after the most recent, extraordinary succession of dinners and celebrations—with official visits from Japan, Spain, and Morocco, not forgetting the millennium—the president would slow the pace a little. We had reached the end of his mandate, and the electoral battle between George Bush and Vice President Al Gore was intensifying. Whenever I met Vice President Gore, as I sometimes did around the White House, I made a point of being as pleasant as possible. It seemed to me that he had a very good chance of taking over. My humble background and experience had taught me that a man should never forget on which side his bread is buttered. In fact, the election promised to be a very close race: the polls stood at fifty-fifty, and no one knew how it was going to turn out.

During this period, I was presented with another huge challenge—there is no other word for it: a state dinner for 800 people in one of the garden pavilions. When I heard the news, I admit I was close to tears. I felt like a man who had been flogged for years, and hoped for a little respite, only to discover that the punishment was about to start all over again, but worse. Eight hundred people! Not only that, but the dinner was in honor of India, in the person of the prime minister, Atal Bihari

Vajpayee. India, like Morocco, Japan, and Pakistan, is a difficult country in terms of patisserie, since its national cuisine doesn't feature many typical desserts, and I didn't feel qualified to re-create those that existed. Once again, I felt hemmed in, under pressure. But I would triumph. I began, as usual, by telephoning the Indian embassy, who sent me a hefty package of brochures and literature. It took me a good week to read through them all and decide what I was going to do. The brochures were superb, and I realized just what an extraordinarily beautiful country India is. I was full of admiration. The lotus flower was everywhere: its center is a hemisphere roughly the size and shape of a large walnut. There are pale pink petals around the base, all rising up high around the center of the flower. I was enchanted by it and wondered how it could be reproduced for a dessert. I had to keep a firm grasp on the practicalities of the situation—800 people constituted a veritable horde, nothing like the "small" groups of 150 or 200 to which I was accustomed. The same brochures also featured pictures of India's superb white tigers, an endangered species that has become something of a national symbol. There were sacred cows, too, but that was a ridiculous idea. I would stick with the lotus flowers and tigers. How to incorporate them into a dessert? Should I prepare individually plated desserts or platters for ten? The latter seemed the obvious answer. I would create the center of the lotus flower using a bowl to obtain the hemisphere, which could then be upturned with the flat part facing upwards. I would hollow little holes in the dome and fill these with melted chocolate. Except that the president didn't want any chocolate in the dessert. His flower would have to use raspberry jam instead.

I would also have to draw on the colors and flavors of India: banana mousse garnished with preserved fruits on the inside and mango sorbet on the outside to create a vivid saffron yellow. But how could I attach the pink chocolate petals? I would make them first, then see. With two rows of petals per flower, I needed around 3,200 petals. I planned to mold them inside large plastic spoons. With so many to make, it seemed preferable to start straight away: order the chocolate, buy the plastic spoons, recruit help. This was mass production, factory-style. We succeeded in making the 3,200 petals, and I attached each of them to a chocolate base.

I wanted the platter of petits fours accompanying the dessert to be just as redolent of Indian culture; which is where my white tigers came in. I had bought one—a miniature made from rubber—at the Washington zoo and used it to create a mold from which I made eighty white chocolate tigers. The dark stripes on their fur were painted by hand in liquid chocolate.

In the White House's so-called "chocolate room," I had a team of six pastry chefs working on the production of the white tigers. Another six-person team was working on the ice cream. The creation and assembly of the pieces took around six weeks. Afterwards, it was a race against time to see whether or not these desserts, preserved in dry ice, in special drawers, would arrive at the tables at the right temperature. I calculated that they would take exactly forty minutes to reach the perfect temperature. Allowing twenty minutes for the salad and twenty minutes for the main dish that preceded it, I would have to take them out just as the main dish was being taken to the dining room. Nothing could be allowed to disrupt the service, and everything was calculated down to the last minute. The tigers and petits fours posed no particular problems: we could set them on the platters two or three hours before the dinner. As a final touch, we had modeled trees with drooping foliage: one tree per tiger, with each tiger lying beneath a tree. The dessert was entitled "Mango and Banana Lotus," with the subtitle "Majestic Tiger's Delight."

Everything went smoothly. The eighty dishes decorated with large lotus flowers, eighty boats of raspberry sauce, and eighty dishes with the white tigers resting under their trees all arrived safely. They were greatly appreciated by the 800 guests, many of whom took the white tigers home with them as a souvenir.

~

The fateful day of the elections was upon us in early November 2000. The entire country was holding its breath—no one knew what would happen. The two candidates were literally neck and neck in the polls, after a bitter, no-holds-barred campaign. That evening, I watched anxiously as the results were announced from each state. At around 10 p.m. it was announced that Al Gore had won Florida, a Bush fiefdom, and hence the election. I went to bed thinking that Gore would be my next boss. The count wasn't over, but the press had more or less given the presidency to Gore. It was with great surprise, the following morning, that I discovered George W. Bush had been elected president. But his election was to be hotly contested.

CHAPTER 18

The Bushes are Back

Al Gore continued to believe and declare that he had won the election. There followed a period of extreme confusion, when votes were counted and recounted in the two states where the result had been decided by a razor-thin margin. People blamed a lack of clarity in the design of certain ballot papers, which were overly complicated and may have encouraged some Republican voters to vote Democrat by mistake or vice versa. There was panic in both camps, and the lawyers were quick to enter the fray. I had never seen anything like it.

While all this was going on, the Clintons continued to receive guests at the White House. On November 9, 2000, we organized a dinner for 250 people to celebrate the 200th anniversary of this unique presidential palace. We were asked to prepare a menu similar to the one that had been served for the inauguration of the first president to occupy the building. This was not, as I have already mentioned, George Washington, the first American president and father of the nation, who never lived at the White House, but at his farmhouse in Mount Vernon on the outskirts of Washington. The White House's first tenant was his successor, John Adams, who moved in with his wife Abigail in November 1800. A period menu was what was needed, and I set about discovering as much as I could about Mrs. Adams's personal tastes. To my surprise, I discovered that she often served *oeufs à la neige*, a very European dessert. I would serve the same dish with a sophisticated twist. Each plate was garnished with cream, in which floated two halves of meringue, one white, the other covered with ganache and chocolate. Each plate also featured a plaque of white chocolate bearing a reproduction of the prayer written by Adams in a letter to his wife Abigail on his first night at the White House (he was alone, and she was to join him sometime later). The prayer is still carved on a marble plaque above the chimney-piece in the White House dining room: "I pray Heaven to bestow the best of Blessings on this House and all that shall hereafter inhabit it. May none but honest and wise Men ever rule under this roof."

With this somewhat unusual version of *oeufs à la neige*, we served raisin cookies and one of Mrs. Adams's favorite pastries: lemon-flavored "matchsticks." In this way, the Clintons joined hands with their distant predecessors across 200 years of history.

The Christmas festivities were approaching, the last for the Clintons at the White House. I have never witnessed the end of a presidential mandate without a tug at the heartstrings. I had admired this First Family very much and had greatly enjoyed working for them, even though the experience had sometimes been very difficult. Several times during this period, I ran into President Clinton around the White House. He had begun to relax, sporting his plaid shirts and jeans more and more often, and chewing on his cigars, which were never lit. Several times, he shook me by the hand and told me how much he had appreciated my efforts to serve the First Family throughout their years at the White House.

On November 7, 2000, Mrs. Clinton was elected senator for the state of New York with a high score—fifty-five percent, compared with just forty-three percent for her rival. The election was tantamount to a personal coronation. Mrs. Clinton was delighted by the result. One day, after discussing various other matters, she gave me a victorious "high five," beaming. Naturally, I presented my compliments on her electoral victory and wished her luck in her new adventure. My own (very) small contribution to her electoral campaign came when I managed to procure a huge cake for one of her receptions, at very short notice, from my friend André Renard, the pastry chef at New York's Essex House. Later, another, even bigger cake was ordered for a birthday party for Mrs. Clinton to be held at a Washington hotel. I was unable to take part in the preparations, since the party was not taking place at the

White House; I was, however, able to present my friend Henri (the pastry chef at the hotel in question) with a portrait of Mrs. Clinton, painted on a plaque of royal sugar icing, which I had prepared in secret in my fourth-floor office at the White House.

On December 9, the result of the presidential election was finally validated. George W. Bush was confirmed as the forty-third president of the United States. And so I took my decision. This new administration would be my last. I even doubted whether I would continue to the end of the new president's mandate. I planned, as I have already mentioned, to write a book about patisserie. The time had come to make a serious start on the project. When I had finished it, I would be able to retire and publish the book in the United States, freed from my obligations as a member of the White House staff. I had chosen an agent, Angela Miller, secured a contract with Simon & Schuster and my editor Sydny Miner, and found Lauren Chattman to work with me on the book—a trained pastry chef and Yale graduate, she was ideally equipped to become an excellent writer on the subject in her own right.

The Christmas festivities proceeded without a hitch, as usual. The Clintons spent the holidays at Camp David and remained there for New Year's. Then, on January 3, 2001, Mrs. Clinton was sworn in as senator for the state of New York, placing her hand on the Bible and promising to uphold the Constitution of the United States of America. She was now one of the congressional representatives of a city that symbolized American power worldwide, with over 9 million inhabitants and a population of 16 million in its greater metropolitan area.

A few days later, at the White House, the First Family threw a grand reception for everyone who had worked with them over the past eight years. There were both tears and laughter. We had come to the end of an era, upon which the doors of history were closing forever. Everyone had a heavy heart. And so began the traditional hustle and bustle that inevitably accompanies a change of presidents. In Washington, a new pavilion was built for the inauguration ceremony. At the White House, the many items of furniture that the Clintons had brought with them were moved out to their new home in Chappaqua, New York. Buddy, the president's beloved chocolate Labrador, was moved, too. He died a few years later after being run over by a car. And on January 20, 2001, in the time-honored fashion, the Clintons had coffee with the new president, George W. Bush, and his wife Laura, the new First Lady. The handover followed a strict, well-established routine, but I could never get used to it. The departure of "Eagle, Evergreen, and Energy"—the secret service code names attributed to Bill, Hillary, and Chelsea, to be used whenever they were mentioned in telephone conversations (similar codes are adopted for each successive First Family)—left me sunk in very real sorrow. I was not alone. On the morning of January 20, when the Clintons went down to the dining room to say goodbye to the White House staff, taking care to thank each and every one of us personally for our efforts, I swear there was not a dry eye in the house.

The various ceremonies accompanying a presidential departure were always extremely moving and sad. Each time, the atmosphere was little short of funereal. I told myself that this was probably the last time I would witness the process and this helped me to keep a sense of perspective. President Clinton came over, gave me a big hug, and told me: "Don't worry Roland, everything will be fine. I am enormously grateful for what you have done for me and my family." Mrs. Clinton and Chelsea endorsed his words. I replied that I had been honored to enjoy their trust and confidence and thanked them for allowing me to continue working for them throughout the past eight years. I wished them a safe journey and good luck. A lasting memory of the Clinton years—among many others—are my two Siamese cats, bought with my wife Martha at the beginning of the Clinton presidency when we moved into our new home and whom Martha chose to name Willy (after William Clinton) and Al (after Al Gore).

George W. Bush's arrival, or more precisely Bill Clinton's departure, was nonetheless rather turbulent. The staff of the outgoing president found it hard to come to terms with the idea of a Republican, rather than a Democrat, at the White House. Some of the Clintons' younger staff were visibly overcome when it was time to leave the great building. Some even turned quite nasty, in complete contrast to the longstanding tradition by which defeat is accepted gracefully and without bitterness. One day, on leaving the White House to go home, I encountered a young man I had never seen before. He was furious at the prospect of George W. Bush at the White House and hollered his discontent at me. Bush had been handed the election on a plate. It was a scandal. He would stay in office for just four years and then "we'll kick his ass out of here." The Bush presidency would be a dreadful time for the United States, he said. Bush was not at all the man for the job. "We'll get him out, you'll see." I let him have his say and said nothing myself. In the offices, some members of the outgoing staff had gone so far as to sabotage the premises. Pieces of furniture had been broken. The White House had never before seen anything of the kind. It was a generational issue. The senior staff members conducted themselves with perfect dignity, but the younger people did not. Nor did they mince their words. Bill Clinton complained about their conduct on several occasions.

The traditional inaugural ceremonies went without a hitch: the Capitol, the swearing-in on the Bible, and the military and other parades that fill the streets of Washington throughout the day, with their bands, pompoms, uniforms, and flags. While all this was going on, we were once again busy making the chocolate and sugar figures that are traditionally presented to the new president's guests. The only difference was that now, the Democrat donkeys had been replaced by the Republican elephants. Once again, we were preparing for some radical changes around the White House. The Clinton mandate was a fantastic period for me. Bill and Hillary had pushed me to my limits; I had given the job my all, just as under Mrs. Reagan in her time. Thanks to them, I had grown in professionalism and learned a great deal—there is always more to discover. And now I was ready to take on another new presidency.

A great many people at the White House imagined that the new Bush family would be much like the last and that Laura Bush would be a person very much in the image of her mother-in-law, who had served as First Lady before her. They had failed to understand that every president, and even more so every First Lady, wants to make their personal mark on the White House. Laura Bush was a charming lady with a perfect sense of dress and decorum. She had great charisma and was extremely kind and pleasant, none of which prevented her from leaving her distinctive personal stamp on the White House. Laura Bush's style was utterly elegant and restrained. She loved things set in straight lines and was equally direct in her dealings with people. She hated cluttered tabletops, little vases, and framed photographs scattered all over the place. With her, every item had its place and was displayed to its best advantage. Everything had to be in order, and she had little patience for the way things were organized at the White House. Laura Bush made her preferences quite clear, even down to the style of the flowers. The huge displays favored by the Clintons, often so massive that little else could be seen, were replaced by restrained, simple, elegant arrangements. Elegance and simplicity were Mrs. Bush's watchwords.

President Bush, for his part, carried a heavy burden as a result of the way in which the election had been won. The country was still split down the middle, and problems had arisen on the global political scene, too. He had his work cut out, but this suited him fine—he was a fighter by nature. A fighter with an irrepressible sense of humor. During the election campaign, he was asked what had motivated him to run for office and replied that the White House had a fantastic pastry chef: he couldn't wait to try some of my desserts.

The Bushes arrived with their twin daughters Barbara and Jenna, one brunette, the other blonde—charming girls, like all young women of their age, who had no desire to remain shut up in the gilded cage of the White House. They wanted to have fun, get on with their lives, express themselves. They chose not to stay in Washington full-time, hoping in this way to avoid the attentions of America's detestable celebrity newshounds.

The family had arrived together with two dogs and one cat. One of the dogs was a female by the name of Spot, whose birth I had witnessed at the White House when Barbara Bush was First Lady; I had held her in my hand when she was no bigger than a chicken's egg. The other dog, by the name of Barney, was making his debut at the White House. He was black, young, extremely frisky, and enjoyed playing around. Strangely, both dogs suddenly adopted a very presidential code of behavior after their arrival at the White House. This is a phenomenon I witnessed time and again during my years of service, which never ceased to amaze me. Pets arriving at the White House seemed to take the new constraints imposed on them by the rules of protocol completely in their stride. The presidential cat, Willy, was black with green eyes, and never left the president's private apartment, where he kept Mrs. Bush company. Barney and Spot had fun strolling on the White House lawns, but always in presidential style, since their favorite game consisted of running after balls thrown for them by the president, as far as possible down the magnificent sweep of grass. They also enjoyed chasing squirrels, birds, and other creatures: anything that jumped, flew, or climbed.

Mr. and Mrs. Bush's brothers and sisters, and their children, also returned to the White House, visiting their uncle and aunt this time, rather than their grandparents. We hosted a great many family members. Clearly, there would be plenty of birthdays, receptions, and pool parties ahead, in direct proportion to the number of young people in the family. Once again, the venerable old White House would ring with their laughter, jokes, and joie de vivre.

President Bush and the First Lady quickly settled into a presidential style of their own. We soon noticed that they greatly enjoyed receiving visits from other heads of state, either at Camp David, or on their own ranch at Crawford, Texas—a vast property that I never visited. It was cloaked in the greatest secrecy, and very few pictures of it have ever been published. The Bushes went there for privacy, but they also invited many heads of state and friends, serving simple meals prepared by local cooks: often dishes of fish or beef and Texas's famous pecan or apple pies. I was often asked to send down decorated cookies, reflecting the tastes of the visiting presidents and prime ministers, and their countries' culinary traditions. For Japan, I was asked to come up with a creation on the theme of baseball, a sport adored by both the Japanese president and President Bush. If the guest enjoyed riding, we would make petits fours in the shape of a horseshoe. And so on.

A great many heads of state were also invited to Camp David. President Bush hosted more heads of state than any other president before him, in the space of just two years, especially during the period following the attacks of September 11, 2001. But these visits were not usually marked by grand state dinners—President Bush organized less of these than his predecessors, in fact. Mostly, the visits featured working meals for about twenty people: cabinet members, party representatives, members of the invited president's staff. There was much talk of world affairs. And world affairs did not look pretty. Storm clouds were gathering: Iraq, Afghanistan, and the threat of terrorism.

Together with fellow staff members at the White House, I began to observe and understand the new First Family's preferences and ways of doing things. February 5, 2001, marked a first essay under the new regime, with a visit from the Canadian prime minister, Jean Chrétien. I created a chocolate and hazelnut terrine with vanilla sauce decorated with the flags of the two nations. Early days!

On February 25, 2001, the British prime minister, Tony Blair, was welcomed at Camp David. President and Mrs. Bush enjoyed variety, and liked to make use of all the different means at their disposal when entertaining heads of state. For the occasion, I created a dessert entitled "Catoctin Mountain" after the location of Camp David: a hot peach and blackberry cobbler with a rich sauce and a crisp, buttery topping, served with whipped cream.

The following dinner was in honor of the Japanese prime minister, Yoshiro Mori, on March 19, 2001. With spring on its way, we prepared a refreshing salad of oranges with orange sorbet. The sorbets were shaped into domes topped with sugar figurines of geishas in ceremonial dress and floating ribbons. Shortly afterwards, on March 23, came the traditional state governors' banquet, the first grand dinner of the new presidency.

I wanted to create a quintessentially Texan dessert for the occasion, symbolizing the state of which George W. Bush had been governor until so very recently. My research highlighted one constant feature of the Texan landscape—the distinctive masses of fine, dry branches that are blown across the plains, or along country roads, by the wind. They are an essential feature of any cowboy film, rolling menacingly by just as the hero and his adversary are locked in their final showdown. They are commonly known, of course, as tumbleweed. I thought it would be fun to incorporate them into the dessert. The resulting creation was entitled "Chocolate Tumbleweed with Honey Parfait and Poached Pears, in a Grenadine Sauce." The initial version was served with strawberries dipped in chocolate. When the dessert was served to Mr. and Mrs. Bush in private, for their approval, the president adored it. It was sensational—Texas to a "T." Mrs. Bush was less enthusiastic, however. She explained that for as long as she and her husband occupied the White House, she never wanted to see strawberries dipped in chocolate, which were always the first thing every pastry chef thought to prepare for them wherever they went. "They think we'll be delighted. But please think of something else." And so I replaced the strawberries with pears poached in grenadine, which proved to be the perfect complement to the chocolate, and the honey *parfait*. The colors were delightful, and the dessert looked splendid. The president was pleased and proud to show the state governors that he remained a Texan at heart.

On March 27, 2001, President Bush hosted a working dinner with the South Korean president, Kim Dae Jung. I prepared pineapple sorbet with ginger parfait and orange sauce—a simple, understated dessert in keeping with the tone of the occasion. The next day, there followed a lunch for 130 people. I decided on a baseball theme. The base took the form of an upturned chocolate baseball glove, holding a meringue in its palm, shaped exactly like a baseball, but filled with chocolate mousseline and a mascarpone and passion-fruit mousse. The president applauded when it was brought to the table—a splendid home run for the pastry chef.

So far, so good. The president had a great deal on his plate, as it were, but he was plainly an extremely pleasant, likeable man. For my part, I was happy and satisfied. The First Family knew me well already. I had the pleasure of meeting George Bush Sr. and Barbara Bush once again, together with their other children; everyone came to say hello. I felt as if my own family was back at the White House. I adored these people. Everything was going fine; I was working hard on my book. Life was sweet.

On June 30, 2001, we hosted a visit from the Japanese prime minister, Koizumi Junichiro, this time at Camp David. Personally, I was tired of the familiar journey up into the mountains. At first, I enjoyed the excursions—I was always driven there in an official car. But often, when it was time to leave, my driver would have disappeared somewhere with his friends. It would take me a good hour to track him down, and we always returned to the White House very late, after which I had to unload all my equipment, arriving home at about 1 or 2 a.m. I had asked to be allowed to drive there in my own car: the camp, in Maryland, is about a ninety-minute drive from Washington. It's a very pleasant trip, especially if you take a particular, winding mountain road following a trout stream, passing wild deer looking up calmly to watch the car drive past—always very slowly and carefully for fear of running into one of them. But as time went by, I began to tire of the trek. We had to load up the car, drive to the camp, pass through the entry points, unload the car, and drive back the same evening. After twenty-two years of shuttling back and forth, I was exhausted. For once—and this was the very first time—I decided to let the Camp David chefs serve my desserts. A buffet was planned, and my presence was therefore not essential. The pastries and desserts were all ready: orange and Grand Marnier ice cream, a strawberry mille-feuille, crème caramel, a fruit salad, and chocolate and ginger mousse. I gave a long list of instructions to the cooks as to how and in what order the desserts should be served.

The most difficult thing at Camp David was getting in and out of the place. The security regulations were stricter than at the White House, and visitors had to pass through two or three barriers, open their cars, and allow the sniffer dogs to inspect the contents, which caused minor catastrophes since the animals were, of course, incapable of distinguishing between what was fragile and what wasn't. The guards would open the trunk and the hood, searching everywhere. It was incredible! We were treated like public enemies. On several occasions, tempers frayed. I would protest that I had come from the White House itself and was there to serve the president his meal. Back at the White House, I explained, I had a pass that allowed me to go anywhere I pleased, whenever I liked, but at Camp David I had to stand by while my car was all but taken to pieces. One day, they would be lifting it up on jacks to take the wheels off—I was furious. I was, of course, reprimanded for my outbursts. This was no way to speak to "security." It was worse still when we made ready to leave at the end of the evening. And yet these people were our colleagues. They worked for the president, just like us, but we were treated like terrorists! I was ashamed to have to submit to their humiliating checks and searches, and had no desire to be put through the experience yet again. I'd had enough of Camp David. Unfortunately, this time, the driver of the truck containing my desserts parked it on an incline at the camp, so that the wonderful strawberry mille-feuilles toppled over and were ruined. A lesson to me never to entrust my desserts to anyone other than a pastry chef. Next time, I would send my assistant, Susie Morrison.

I had absolute confidence in Susie. Before coming to work at the White House full-time, she had served as an "extra hand" for six years and quickly became my second in command. She had previously worked at the Washington Ritz Carlton Hotel with another French pâtissier and in the kitchens of the U.S. Senate on Capitol Hill as well as in several Washington patisseries. Chief among her many qualities was her impeccable turnout: she was always spotlessly clean and unfailingly pleasant, agreeable, good-humored, and respectful to boot. She never broke a plate or knocked into a piece of kitchen furniture. Neither did I—this was something I was always careful to avoid. In twenty-five years in the White House pastry kitchen, we never broke a single plate or damaged a single item of equipment. Nothing! Not so much as a scratch!

On June 26, 2001, we hosted a visit from Thabo Mbeki, the president of South Africa. For once, my research had totally failed to come up with any favorite dishes, and I made do with a simple plum terrine served with peaches and raspberry sauce.

Summer 2001: a summer like any other. The President spent his summer holiday at his ranch in Crawford, Texas. I continued working on my book and began making plans for a trip to France in the near future. There were so many people I wanted to see again, especially my family. I missed them all greatly, and it would do me good to go back home for a while. Until then, it was business as usual. Everything carried on as normal. Everyone returned from their holidays early in September, and we began making plans for the Congress barbecue, scheduled for September 11, in the South Garden at the White House. This was expected to be a very big event, with around 1,000 guests. Everyone wanted to greet the new president. The Bushes decided to bring in a specialist caterer, their Texas friend Tom Perini, a well-known personality and organizer of barbecues, who often appeared on television. Tom was about fifty years old, a genial man with whom I greatly enjoyed working, always impeccably turned out, and never without his huge cowboy hat. He brought his own equipment, special barbecue ovens, and grills mounted on small trailers—an impressive sight. At the same time, we were in the middle of preparations for a state dinner on September 5, in honor of the Mexican president, Vicente Fox. I had planned a delightful dessert, with typically Mexican decorations, including hibiscus flowers, which are something of a symbol in both Texas and Mexico. The dessert also featured sugar figures of tropical hummingbirds, magnificently beautiful creatures with red breasts and green moiré plumage.

On September 4, we were hard at work in the pastry kitchen, making the sugar hummingbirds, when suddenly the elevator door opened to reveal Mrs. Bush in all her splendor. The first lady had come down to say hello and find out how the dessert was coming along; she was accompanied by a flock of reporters. Mrs. Bush has always shown me the greatest kindness and this was yet another thoughtful gesture, greatly appreciated.

For the Mexican state dinner, I telephoned my friend David Berkley in Sacramento, California. David supplies the finest fruits anywhere, and I always call on him when I need something extra-special. I asked him for the last peaches of season, of the highest quality, and was promised a superb batch of branch-ripened fruit with the sweetest flesh and a characteristic red "halo" around the stone, specially picked for the White House. The peaches would arrive on September 3. This particular variety is known as O'Henry, a splendid fruit which we were proud to serve for the Mexican president. The dessert also featured *nougatine* stands about ten inches tall, behind which were arranged tall sugar branches decorated with hibiscus flowers and the flock of hummingbirds plunging their delicate beaks deep into the heart of the blooms. The result was magnificent, and thoroughly Mexican. Everyone was delighted.

We faced a heavy workload and a packed calendar. On Saturday, September 8, there was breakfast for 200 guests, with a suitable array of pastries. On September 10, a working lunch with the Australian prime minister. I created a very pretty dessert: a puff pastry croustade in the form of a large scallop filled with a ginger and vanilla mousse, and served with lemon sauce. The dish was garnished with raspberries, blackberries, blackcurrants, and redcurrants. At the back stood a decoration reminiscent of Australia's Great Barrier Reef: large fronds of sugar seaweed, dotted with little colored fish. The sauce represented the waves of the sea. The result was quite spectacular and met with great acclaim from the heads of state gathered for the lunch. That was not all. On September 13, we were due to host a reception with a pastry buffet for 200 people, followed by another Mexican fiesta for 200 people with accompanying pastries on September 14. On September 16, President Bush was to host a game of Tee Ball at the White House, a personal initiative that transformed a corner of the White House lawns into a miniature baseball diamond twice a year in spring and autumn (weather permitting). The White House Tee Ball tournaments are open to Little League teams and Challenger teams for children with a physical or mental disability. The president would join in with the children for hours on end. He was a big-hearted man; more so, in fact, than some of his predecessors.

Tee Ball games were always accompanied by large quantities of cookies in a host of flavors: whole-wheat, peanut butter, chocolate chip, walnut, raisin or coconut. One thousand six hundred cookies were needed for the event to be served freshly baked. Next, on September 17, was a reception for 200, followed by a state dinner on September 18 for President Jacques Chirac of France. This was a strenuous, complicated schedule with a great many preparations (the only way to make sure we weren't completely overwhelmed). In addition to all this, George Bush Sr. and Barbara Bush were due at the White House on September 9 and were scheduled to leave on the morning of September 11.

On the morning of September 11, 2001, everyone arrived for work as usual and set about their business. I was working with my assistant Marlene and one other person in the so-called "chocolate room" on the ground floor, near the exit. Our task for the morning was to hollow out and decorate a series of large watermelons for the barbecue that afternoon. The melons were to be decorated with cattle horns—Texas longhorns—and some were destined to be transformed into old-fashioned covered wagons. When the time came, they would be filled with fresh fruit, ready for the Western-style barbecue. On the floor above, in the pastry kitchen, five or six people were working on a special dessert using a recipe provided for us by Tom Perini—a pudding made from cubes of bread steeped in crème caramel-like mixture and baked in the oven with raisins and other goodies. We had decided to produce a good number of these desserts.

I stepped outside several times to take a breather in the gardens and at around 8 a.m., I saw President Bush senior and Barbara Bush get into their car to drive home. George W. Bush was already in Florida, where he was visiting a group of young schoolchildren to read books with them and promote his initiative to improve the U.S. public school system. Mrs. Bush had also left early, for the Capitol, where she had been invited by the Congress wives.

There was no one left at the White House, then, apart from the staff. Everyone was getting ready for the barbecue, which was due to start at around 4 or 5 p.m. I came back to work at 8.30 a.m. and began cutting my fruit. Suddenly, just before 9 a.m., Marlene called me: "Roland, look!" Just next to the pastry kitchen was a television, which we kept on all the time, to follow the news. "Look," Marlene insisted. "A plane has just crashed into one of the Twin Towers in New York." I came to take a look, but I wasn't really paying attention, because I was so busy and because the tower didn't look at all as if it was likely to collapse. I got back to work. It was then that Marlene called me again, this time in a toneless voice: "Roland, a second plane has just crashed into the second tower." Dear God. I hurried to the TV and saw people running, smoke blackening the sky. This time, I understood that something very serious had happened. I was sure the barbecue would be canceled. I called the chief usher's office and was told that for the moment they had no information. We should carry on. But at 9:18 a.m. precisely, Claire, one of our colleagues in the ushers' office, burst into the chocolate room and said, "Roland, we have to get out. Right now." Everyone was running to evacuate the White House. What was happening? I thought of my colleagues upstairs in the pastry kitchen and picked up the phone to tell them to switch off the ovens, leave everything where it was, take nothing with them, and evacuate the premises as quickly as possible. Alas, the line was engaged, and I could speak to no one. I had no idea what to do—the pastry kitchen was a long way from where I was, and no one would let me go up there. The secret service agents had to restrain me forcibly, wrapping their arms around me and dragging me out: "Get out of here, don't worry about a thing." I shouted back that they should call 54319 right away and keep calling until someone answered and tell them to get the hell out of there with not a moment to lose. I must have shouted this a dozen times to a dozen different secret service agents, all while running for the door with my two assistants from the chocolate room. We were told to hurry up—a plane was headed for the White House and would be crashing into the building in a matter of minutes.

Of course, I had no time to change out of my pastry chef's attire. I wanted to be sure to keep my chef's toque so that my staff would be able to find me once we were outside. There were a great many of us. We were directed to Lafayette Square, opposite the White House, and crossed it to get as far away as possible. The crowd looked like a mass of terrified ants. I had no cell phone, and none of my staff had theirs, either. Happily, one of the secret service officers—who had promised me he would call the pastry kitchen—told me that he had done so and got no reply. I had to hope that everyone was safe. We stood waiting for the impending threat from the sky, disorientated and with no idea what to do. Everyone had left their workplace, leaving their personal belongings behind: purses, car keys, wallets. Suddenly, a plane roared in very close to the White House. Everyone covered their heads and ears. It wasn't headed for us, apparently, but for the Pentagon, as we found out later. From where we stood, we couldn't see anything except the smoke rising up into the sky. At around 9:30 a.m. we were told to move further away because another plane was on its way, this time headed straight for the White House. It was coming from Pennsylvania, and would reach Washington in just ten minutes.

We scoured the sky for minutes that seemed like hours. It was a brilliant blue, so bright that it was hard to believe that the worst had actually happened. Rumors began to circulate. Vehicles were driving around Washington with bombs on board, which the terrorists were planning to explode in the middle of crowds of people. There were about 1,000 of us standing on the edge of Lafayette Square. No one panicked—a sure sign that in spite of everything, God was on our side that day. By now, I had gathered all my staff, or rather, they had spotted me in the crowd, thanks to my chef's toque. I shouted angrily at them: "What the hell were you doing on the phone? Are you stupid or something? Didn't you see the people running? Didn't you look out of the window?"

One of them said that they had seen people running, but thought they were panicking for nothing. Lynne, one of my assistants, had been on the phone to her husband, talking about they would have for dinner that night, or something of the sort. Everyone was safe and sound, and I was very happy to see them.

Time passed, and we were still standing there with no idea what to do. No one had any information, and there was no news of our bosses, the president and First Lady. We knew that Mrs. Bush was safe, at least, that the president was a long way away, and that his parents had left that morning. But faced with such an uncertain situation, when it seemed as if the world—our world, at least—was falling around our ears, many people broke down completely. I saw the White House chambermaids sobbing uncontrollably. They were still in the upstairs apartments when the plane landed on the Pentagon and had a clear view of everything: the impact, the flames, the spectacle of death itself plummeting from the sky.

Finally, around noon, after an unbearable, three-hour wait in the hot sun, Lynne, the assistant who had made her untimely phone call home, suggested that we all go back to her home. She was the person who lived nearest to the White House. From there, we could telephone and make arrangements to get home. Lynne's home was perhaps the nearest, but it was still about four miles from the White House. My feet were covered in blood—I was still wearing my white chef's clogs, which are not used for walking long distances. We crossed Key Bridge, over the Potomac River. From there, we had a clear view of what had happened at the Pentagon: the destruction, the smoke, the plane debris scattered across the ground. A crowd of people was working to clear the wreckage. On the bridge, I met several people who knew me; they had no trouble spotting me in the crowd, thanks to my chef's uniform. "Hey Roland, how's it going? What do you make of all this?" I had no idea what to say. There were lots of cars around, but those that were out were unable to move due to the thousands of people thronging the streets of Washington. It looked like a mass exodus. After a long walk, we arrived at Lynne's home, where she immediately switched on the TV, made sandwiches, and served beer. We sat down to recover and watch the reports, trying to get some idea of what had happened. It was a disaster. In the meantime, both of the World Trade Center towers had collapsed, and the numbers of dead were rising inexorably. The TV channels were showing rolling footage of the appalling scenes, notably the poor people who had chosen to throw themselves into the void to escape the fire, preferring one death to another. And then the spectacle of the two towers, the symbols of American power, collapsing with a kind of appalling slow motion, like houses of cards in a cloud of dust.

We were able to telephone our friends and families. I called my wife Martha, who was still at work at her school in Oakton, a town near Washington, but which straddled the state border with Virginia. She wasn't entirely clear what had happened, like many people who took a while to find out and then to fully realize the enormity of events. Martha had absolutely no grasp of the gravity of the situation. I asked her to meet me in a shopping mall on the outskirts of Washington. Those of us who had come home with Lynne did the same. We recovered ourselves, drank a few beers, ate some sandwiches, and set off with her in her car. Lynne dropped each of us off in turn at our meeting points with our families. By now, the streets were deserted. There was no one around at all. When I arrived at the mall, I climbed into Martha's car. "How come there are no cars out on the streets?" she asked. She had no idea why the parking lots were all deserted, why everyone had headed home. I got angry: "Have you any idea what has happened?" Now it was Martha's turn to fire up. We were at complete cross purposes until we got home and turned on the TV. And then Martha understood. But for her, like me, and so many other Americans, it took days and days before we truly came to terms with what had happened. It was one thing to see the pictures, hear the reports, and the commentaries. It was quite another to truly comprehend a catastrophe on that scale, in your heart, mind, and body.

The next day, I contacted the White House chief usher. Of course, the barbecue had been canceled. On the other hand, everyone was called in on September 12 to decide on the future course of action. No one had the slightest idea of how to proceed. I traveled to work on the subway, having left my car in the White House parking lot on September 11.

I admit that for weeks to come, I suffered extreme anxiety and felt very nervous, especially every morning when I took my shower. I found it hard to think about what had happened. Every time we turned on the TV, I was transported back to the heart of the disaster. So many dead! Possibly the worst aspect of the whole event, for me, was that for hours on end we were unable to get back in touch with the White House and with that, the realization that the White House was essentially unprepared for an attack of this sort, that the staff had been more or less left to their own devices, that there was no emergency action plan, no security program covering an event of this kind.

If the plane that crashed into the Pentagon that day had landed on the White House, I would not be here to tell the tale. In fact, I firmly believe that the plane in question, which was flying from Dulles Airport, was indeed destined for the White House. Several reporters were of the same opinion. The pilot, or more accurately, the terrorist who had taken the pilot's place, was dazzled by the low morning sunshine; it seems clear to me that when he finally spotted the White House, which is hidden behind a line of fine, 100-year-old trees, it was too late, and he decided to fly to the Pentagon. Not forgetting flight 93, which may also have been headed for the White House, but which crash-landed in Pennsylvania because its passengers, with extraordinary heroism, decided to rise up against the hijackers.

Inevitably, the events scheduled for the following days at the White House were canceled: the receptions, the Tee Ball, the Mexican fiesta. It was unthinkable that such events could carry on when the dead were still lying unrecovered in the wreckage of the Twin Towers in New York. The First Family was deeply affected. The president, who normally displayed such exemplary self-control, often appeared to be fighting back the tears on TV. And whenever he spoke, the line of his jaw showed only too clearly how deeply he had been touched by this act of indescribable savagery. Like his father before him, he was a deeply sensitive man, albeit generally better able at keeping his feelings hidden in public. It was at this moment that he swore to wage war against the terrorist perpetrators of the attacks and to track them down to the very last man. I hope he succeeds. I am sure that he will.

In the weeks that followed the September 11 attacks, many employees at the White House could be seen walking around, heads lowered and blank expressions, in the grip of deep anxiety. Everyone feared what would happen next. Would another plane try to crash into the White House? The chief usher decided to call in a team of psychiatrists to help those who found it difficult to live with their fear. Personally, I decided not to do this. I had lived in Paris under the almost daily threat of terrorist strikes, and I didn't feel the need for extra reassurance. Some time later, I was asked to come and record everything I had seen, felt, and thought. I was very happy to have the opportunity to do this. I recognize that September 11 changed my life and my attitude towards life. I am far more cautious now than before and more careful when I have to travel late at night. I am more observant of what is going on around me and ready to react if I notice anything out of the ordinary.

The entire country was in mourning. The president set about rallying international support for the United States in its fight against international terrorism. A succession of heads of state passed through the White House, beginning with Jacques Chirac, who arrived as planned on September 18. I had the honor of meeting him and shaking his hand, having been invited up to the dining room by President Bush. I was very pleased to able to do so and proud to find myself in the company of "my" two presidents. Naturally, we adapted our service to the tone of the occasion. At a time of national mourning, there could be no question of imaginative, opulent desserts. For President Chirac's visit we prepared nougat and raspberry ice cream with poached pears filled with almond cream and cherry chocolates, which were served after the meal. The next day, on September 19, saw a visit from the Indonesian president, Megawati Sukarnoputri: papaya with lime mousse and strawberry sauce. On September 20, another dinner with Tony Blair: a triple chocolate *marquise* with praline sauce. On September 24, Jean Chrétien of Canada: *tarte Tatin* and ginger ice cream. The next meal was a working lunch with Silvio Berlusconi of Italy: passion fruit *vacherin* with seasonal fruit.

After this, President and Mrs. Bush left for a tour of Asia and were absent for most of the month of October. We began making preparations for Christmas—the Bushes' first at the White House and the first since 9/11. The presidential couple returned from their tour and things seemed to get back to normal. We began to host one or two parties and receptions: I created a very pretty cake for Mrs. Bush's birthday on November 4. The next day, November 5, was their wedding anniversary—another cake and another family get-together, as always. On November 6, Jacques Chirac returned for a lunch. I prepared an apple sorbet filled with frozen Calvados mousse served with hot cider sauce and petits fours. The next day, November 7, saw another visit from Tony Blair. Life at the White House was gearing up once again. On November 14, the president's Prairie Chapel Ranch in Texas was the venue for a visit from Vladimir Putin of Russia. We sent down an array of pecan pies and vanilla ice cream. Other visits followed, from the leaders of India, Turkey, and Spain. The Spanish prime minister, José María Aznar was invited to lunch. We served a hot clementine savarin with a Grand Marnier sabayon sauce and vanilla ice cream. On December 3 it was the turn of Ariel Sharon of Israel: another lunch, this time with cherry strudel and vanilla ice cream. And so it continued, with heads of state lining up to visit George W. Bush. It seemed as if the entire world was rushing to the bedside of the stricken United States. That year's Christmas celebrations, under the shadow of the 9/11 tragedy, were far less brilliant than usual. The receptions were shorter; there were fewer guests and less opulence.

The year 2002 was devoted to the increasingly problematic question of international affairs. There were still a great many visits, but with the exception of one or two new figures, such as Hamid Karzai of Afghanistan, the same heads of state visited again and again. January began quietly enough, with muted New Year festivities. On January 31, we hosted the new German chancellor, Gerhard Schröder to a working dinner for twenty: peach meringue gateau with a strawberry sauce. The day before, on January 30, the White House hosted a grand dinner for the artists who had worked on the refurbishment of the Oval Office. We allowed ourselves a modest, celebratory, symbolic dessert: an oval chocolate cake whose top was decorated with a reproduction of the new carpet designed for the president's office, bearing the presidential seal with its famous eagle. We also made tiny shortbread sofas and a reproduction of a quite well-known painting, presented to the president by a Texan artist. On February 10, 2002, for the first time, the White House hosted a visit from the president of Pakistan, Pervez Musharraf. We served a mango charlotte with baked apples and frozen yoghurt. The visit was a significant event, since relations between the two countries had traditionally been somewhat strained.

The annual state governors' dinner was approaching once again. I felt that in light of the recent catastrophe, we needed a dessert that would please everybody. The symbols of America's two main political parties are, as we have seen, a donkey for the Democrats and an elephant for the Republicans. I made a series of elephants and donkeys in blown sugar, sitting on their hind quarters, with their front legs outstretched, holding a sugar tray bearing the frozen dessert, garnished with fresh seasonal fruit. The gimmick proved highly entertaining for the guests: the Democrats set about decapitating the elephants, and the Republicans retaliated by guillotining the Democrat donkeys, so that many of my little animals returned to the kitchen minus their heads. A few moments of fun when everyone could set aside their respective grudges.

The lineup of visitors continued throughout the month of March. A great many guests, plenty of dinners, a great deal of work. But once again, I was in a reflective mood and felt that for me, the end was in sight. I would have to start getting out and about, away from the White House. Years had passed, and I had not made the most of life beyond my work. In March 2002, I was invited to visit Tunisia as the guest of the Tunisian government. Things were relatively quiet mid-month and on March 18 I decided to accept their invitation. I was not disappointed: Tunisia is a magnificent country. I enjoyed Tunisian specialties and wonderful hospitality from the Tunisians themselves, who are generous, open-hearted, and welcoming, like so many Mediterranean peoples. I still have many happy memories of the trip.

April 2002 and the United States was still shrouded in a veil of sorrow. In New York, work continued to clear the wreckage from Ground Zero, the former site of the World Trade Center. It takes a long time for a great city, an entire nation, to recover its aplomb after such carnage. Buildings are easier to repair and rebuild than the damage done to people's hearts and minds. On April 21, I was due to host a visit to the White House by America's World Pastry Cup team, who had won the gold medal for the first time in Lyon, in January 2001. This was a terrific victory for America and all the more so in that disastrous year. I had arranged for the victorious team to visit the White House and have their photograph taken with the president in the Oval Office. On the same day, a Tee Ball game was scheduled on the South Lawn, for disabled teams in the Challenger League. Sadly, Washington was brought to a near stand-still that day by massive protests. Thousands of people had taken to the streets, and the threat of violence was imminent: the city was hosting that year's spring meeting of the World Bank and the International Monetary Fund. Understandably enough, under such conditions, the president was unable to honor his photo call with the pastry chefs. But I was greatly disappointed nonetheless. It had taken a great deal of ingenuity and cunning to incorporate it into his busy schedule. But that's fate. There was nothing to be done.

On May 3, the Spanish prime minister, José María Aznar, was invited to a dinner at Camp David. On May 17, we celebrated Marshall

Bush's sixteenth birthday at the White House. Marshall was George W. Bush's niece, the daughter of his brother Marvin. The event was the occasion for a small family meal, and I prepared a very pretty cake. Marshall had two dogs, two little boxers, one black and one white. I recreated them in chocolate, with floating ribbons, roses, and a host of other decorations. Marshall thanked me and gave me a kiss.

I told her: "Marshall, you probably don't remember, but I made your third birthday cake, when you came to the White House to see your grandparents."

Birthday or no birthday, I made cakes for all the Bush children, including the older members of the family, who rediscovered a little of their childhood at the White House. Fifteen years earlier, I had known them all as young boys and girls; I had kept all the photos I had taken with them then, together with the colored crayon drawings they often did to thank me, like children everywhere. It was a nostalgic time. Marshall, at sixteen, wrote to thank me. I received her letter in July 2004, just before leaving the White House. It had taken two years to reach me.

We had reached June 2002, the occasion for another Congress barbecue, in place of the 2001 event, which had been abandoned amid the desolation of 9/11. The event proceeded smoothly, but many of the 1,200 guests were, inevitably, somewhat nervous and afraid. I was not. I knew that the president had worked hard to protect his country. Building on the experience of the previous year, exceptional security measures were now in place. I felt safe in the United States.

June 2002 was another month packed with events of every sort: Tee Ball—a firm favorite with the children—and a host of dinners, receptions, and private family meals. It was a pleasure to see things getting back to normal. I made plans for another trip to France, my last as executive pastry chef at the White House. I wanted to visit several colleagues and, above all, my family. Time was limited, and the trip promised to be busy and tiring. For this reason, Martha decided to stay behind in Washington.

Meanwhile, we celebrated Independence Day on July 4—a national party which, by jogging the calendar a little, would also be made to coincide with the president's own birthday festivities (George W. Bush's birthday is July 6). I decided to create a spectacular cake: he deserved it, after the many challenges he had endured. I would recreate the presidential seal in chocolate, flanked by flags and all its other attendant paraphernalia. The dessert itself would be the president's favorite cake, featuring seven layers of cake and seven layers of chocolate cream. I carried the cake into the dining room with the help of my assistant, Susie Morrison. There were candles to blow out. President and Mrs. Bush both posed for an official photograph in front of the cake with Susie and me. Another memorable evening. I was moved to tears to see how much the First Family appreciated the time and effort I had devoted to the piece.

On Tuesday, July 23, as arranged, I left for Paris, where I spent the next two days revisiting old friends and memories at the George V. The palatial hotel had been entirely refurbished and the chef, Philippe Legendre, gave me a royal welcome. Next stop the Élysée Palace and a visit to my friend Joël in his perennially gleaming kitchens. He had decided to retire in 2004 as well, and I gave him a signed copy of Mrs. Clinton's book, including my own modest contribution, to be presented to Madame Chirac. Finally, I called in at the Lutétia, to visit another friend, Monsieur Brideron, the pastry chef. After this, on July 27, I headed for Besançon and my home village of Bonnay. The aim of the visit was to see my family, but I was swept off by my friend Christian Paccard on a trip to Morzine, a pretty ski resort in the Haute-Savoie, full of wooden chalets and hotels decked with flowers. We spent five days there—a very pleasant outing, were it not for the anti-American sentiments expressed by a great many French people. Personally, I found this very hurtful. In Paris, at the start of the trip, several people I encountered stated that in their opinion, the United States had got more or less what it deserved on September 11. Some people plainly loathed George W. Bush, and everyone regretted the demise of Bill Clinton, who had been, in their view, "nice" and a good, capable president. In Morzine and Bonnay alike, I saw further proof of a horrible, growing animosity for the United States among French people. I had experienced nothing like this in the United States. President Bush had never made the slightest unpleasant remark about France or the French. My American colleagues had never turned against me as a Frenchman. But in France, I was personally insulted. People would confide, discreetly, that they genuinely felt America had brought the 9/11 attacks upon itself. It was America's fault. I was dumbfounded. I simply couldn't understand this. In Bonnay, these people had been my friends. I had no idea what to say to them. Everyone has a right to their own opinion, and I wasn't going to fight with them over it. But I was very saddened by the snide remarks, the unpleasant looks, the implications. In Morzine, when I was introduced in restaurants as the pastry chef of the White House, I was invariably greeted with cries of: *"Ah oui! Le pâtissier de Darbleyou,"* this being the French for "Dubya." Everywhere I went, *Darbleyou* was the subject of unpleasant jibes of all sorts. I was hurt to see just how badly the American president—my president, too, after all—was perceived in France and how cruelly people felt able to speak about him. Not everyone, however. I met other friends, including Christian, who were pleased to see President Bush at the helm. Plenty of other people took the opportunity to tell me so, too. On balance, it seemed to me that popular opinion on the subject in France was probably split straight down the middle.

I gave an interview to the newspaper *L'Est Républicain*, with my friend Danielle Robert, who devoted a long article to my French visit, as she did every time I journeyed home. All things considered, this was a splendid trip. I saw many old friends, and I visited my family, as I had dreamed of doing for years: my sister Geneviève, with whom I stayed, and all my brothers and sisters. In particular, I saw my brother Jean again, the pastry chef who had guided my first steps in the profession. A few years earlier, he had been the victim of a serious stroke, causing him to collapse on the floor of his pastry kitchen, where he was found by his wife Thérèse at 2 a.m. He had just managed to pick up the telephone to call for help, but found himself unable to speak. My brother, who was older than me, was one of those people who could never imagine giving up his work. He would start his day at midnight or 1 a.m. (2 a.m. on Saturdays and Sundays). There was no one to help him in his pastry kitchen; Thérèse ran the accompanying shop. He adored his work. The stroke left him paralyzed down one side of his body and badly affected his powers of speech and comprehension. It upset me deeply to see him in this state, as it was Jean who had initiated me into the patisserie trade, and I had so enjoyed our many conversations on the subject. He had always been a source of new ideas for me and had given me the courage to carry on working and to advance in the profession. Now he was reduced to a state of near helplessness. Fortunately, his wife Thérèse took tremendous care of him, driving him wherever he wanted to go. She had rebuilt her life around him, and he was extremely lucky to have such a devoted partner at his side. But his career was finished, and he was inconsolable. At home, he had an album of photographs of his finest patisserie creations. I asked Thérèse if he took pleasure in looking at it. She replied that he would look at it from time to time, then throw it aside in disgust. I think he must have felt that his work was to blame for what had happened to him. He regretted not quitting in time to enjoy a few years of happy retirement. This was not the happiest episode of my trip home; but I was very glad to have seen him all the same.

A great deal of work awaited me on my return to the States. First, there was my patisserie book to be finished, ready for publication in 2004—not a moment to lose. I began to travel back and forth between the White House and Long Island in New York State, where my writer Lauren Chattman lived. Lauren would come and get me at the airport, after which it was an hour's drive to the pretty little town of Sag Harbor, where she lived. She was married with two little girls, and her husband worked, liked her, as a food writer. Lauren had a superb, very well-equipped kitchen, where we able to test some of the recipes. We would work on the book for two or three days at a time, after which I would head back to the White House. Whenever my schedule permitted—for example when the president and First Lady were away from Washington—I would return to Sag Harbor to work on the book. I stayed in a little hotel known simply as The American Hotel, a long-established place with a fine reputation, elegant, eighteenth-century-style bedrooms, and a fine restaurant frequented by stars such as Billy Joel. The owner, Ted Conklin, was an extremely amiable man, oozing class and with arguably the finest wine cellar in New York State. I was fortunate to find such an agreeable place to stay, which could only help me as I struggled to finish the job. We were running behind schedule and worked very hard to try and complete the book on time.

On July 17, just after my trip to France, we hosted a state visit from the president of Poland. The month of August was relatively quiet. President Bush spent much of the time at his ranch. But Christmas would be coming soon, and we wasted no time in preparing the traditional gingerbread houses, decorations, and desserts. Mrs. Bush, who liked to organize small birthday parties for her staff, had planned such an event for one of them, a woman with a fine head of auburn hair, which she always wore up in a huge bun. I made a bust of white chocolate, and arranged a mass of hair made from cotton candy tied in a spectacular bun. When the cake was brought in, everyone burst out laughing.

The round of visits from heads of state intensified. On September 7, we hosted another visit from Tony Blair; on September 14, it was the turn of the Jiang Zemin of China to visit the president's ranch. On November 4, it was Mrs. Bush's birthday once again. I decided to create an extra-special cake decorated with her portrait, painted with food coloring on a plaque of white royal icing. All the family was gathered for the occasion. Barbara Bush took me to one side: "Tell me, Roland why did you never paint my portrait like that when I was at the White House. Was it because I was so old and ugly?" Everyone exploded with laughter. I reminded Mrs. Bush that she had always detested celebrating her own birthday, which brought more gales of laughter. Barbara Bush greatly appreciated the joke.

December was upon us, with a busier-than-ever schedule of receptions and parties. Thousands of petits fours and pastries, hundreds of desserts. We produced a little more each year and shouldered three weeks of hellish work. Now, as always in early December, I thought seriously about my retirement. We were navigating our way, as best we could, across a veritable ocean of work. Time was ticking away, day by day, and it would soon be 2003. There was a great deal happening on the political scene, but I am not qualified to talk about that here and it is not my role to do so. For us—the White House staff—the mounting international tension was measured in the number of visits from world leaders. It seemed to me, once again, that the building was truly the nerve center of the world.

An interlude: on January 21, 2003, we celebrated the birthday of Maestro Plácido Domingo, the world-famous tenor and artistic director of the Washington Opera. I had the honor of making his birthday cake, decorated with a representation of the stage at the Kennedy Center in Washington, graced with a black and white portrait of Plácido himself. He thanked me and shook me warmly by the hand. I was touched and honored: he is an artist whom I greatly admire.

In February and March, the threat of war loomed large. Saddam Hussein refused to collaborate with the United Nations, and President Bush decided to launch an American and British military operation, known as "Operation Iraqi Freedom": the Second Gulf War. The outbreak of hostilities split the world into two camps: those who favored the expedition and wanted to take part, and those who didn't. I admit it seemed obvious to me at the time that everyone would side with Operation Iraqi Freedom. I couldn't see how anyone would possibly stand back from it. When I learned that both France and Germany—a country where I had worked and spent a good deal of time in my youth, and which I greatly admired—would not be taking part in the war, I was somewhat disappointed, even angry. I didn't like to see my home country left standing on the sidelines either. Many Americans found it incomprehensible that France, which had been liberated from the Nazis by the Americans in 1944, should refuse to support the United States now. I had little to say on the matter. It was best to remain neutral in such circumstances, particularly in my job. In America, and particularly in Washington, I saw a few attempts to boycott French products. French wines were banned in many restaurants, but this did not last long and never assumed the proportions described by the French media. American bitterness towards President Chirac is still keenly felt today, however, and will take time to fade.

On April 2, 2003, we organized a state dinner for the Philippines' president, Gloria Macapagal Arroyo. As usual, I strove to create a quintessentially Filipino dessert, inspired by lei, the garlands of fresh flowers often presented to travelers visiting the islands when they step out of the plane. I created a composition based on mango and coconut, in the shape of an iced cup decorated with the lei, made from magnificently colored sugar flowers. The dessert was accompanied by a dish of baked pineapple with a sesame crust, and petits fours.

On June 11, we honored the memory of Anne Frank in conjunction with the organizers of an exhibition devoted to this young Jewish girl, whose diary is such an overwhelming testimony of World War II and life under the Nazi occupation. I created a simple dessert, since Anne Frank's story is a sad one: a frozen vanilla soufflé with strawberry sauce and a mixture of blackberries and raspberries. Delicious, but very plain—ideal for a rather poignant evening.

On July 4, we celebrated Independence Day and, two days ahead of the actual date, the president's birthday. This time, I began preparations well in advance, hoping to do my very best to create something extra-special. Millions of TV viewers had seen footage of the president landing in a U.S. military aircraft on the deck of an aircraft carrier, and there were widespread accusations that the president was using the war to boost his personal ratings. The criticisms were, to my mind, quite ridiculous. I decided to recreate the aircraft carrier in "military green" chocolate using a scale model. Behind the boat was a plane—the president's plane—coming in to land, and large banner reading "Happy

Birthday Top Gun," in reference to the film of the same name. Sitting on the boat were figures of the president's two dogs and cat watching the plane's approach. The whole piece was made from chocolate and marzipan, and placed on top of the president's favorite chocolate cake, served with praline and pecan nut ice cream. The president marveled at it, and when the cake was brought into the dining room, where his friends and family were all gathered—a party of about seventy—everyone burst into applause and began chanting my name: "Ro-land! Ro-land! Roland!" I was touched more deeply than anyone there could have imagined because I knew that the end of my time at the White House was fast approaching. It was nevertheless a very happy moment.

A few days later, on July 16, 2003, we celebrated the ninetieth birthday of Jimmy Carter's predecessor at the White House, President Gerald Ford. He was still in excellent health but fragile, like many very elderly people. There was no question of him trying to blow out ninety candles! Instead, we created individual, rectangular cakes, each bearing the inscription "Happy Birthday." Each plate was also decorated with a medal representing a bust of President Ford, decorated with red, white, and blue ribbons, on a little cookie. Everyone was quite moved.

On September 18, 2003, we hosted a visit from the new king of Jordan, Abdullah II, and his wife, with a small dinner for twenty-five people and the first family. I prepared a milk chocolate terrine with dates, a salad of fresh oranges and mint, and almond *tuiles*. Each dessert was decorated with little crowns made from white chocolate as a sign of the homage paid by the American republic to the Jordanian monarchy.

October 6, 2003, was the date of my last state dinner at the White House. The guest was Daniel arap Moi of Kenya. I wanted to create something truly astonishing for my last presentation piece, something that would reflect every aspect of our guest's home country. We modeled dozens of little cups in white chocolate, painted with typical big game animals in dark chocolate: elephants, giraffes, and tigers. These remarkable vessels were filled with coffee ice cream and a Tia Maria parfait. I also created a coffee ice cream coffeepot and, inside it, a coffee liqueur parfait. Guests could enjoy the coffee, and eat the coffeepot, too! All the little cups were presented on a tray, surrounded by caramelized bananas and pineapples. I also created little pulled-sugar sculptures of galloping giraffes, which were quite exquisite. These were served with coconut truffles, and dates filled with almond-paste flavored with cardamom, plus mango jellies. The result was like a firework burst of colors and flavors. Everyone was delighted, and I received a great many compliments. *Bravo l'artiste!*

Meanwhile, work was progressing on my book, *Dessert University*. I traveled to Sag Harbor more and more often, to speed things up. The manuscript was delivered to Simon & Schuster, and we went to work to produce the photographs that would illustrate the finished book. These would be recreated in the studio to ensure the greatest possible accuracy. Work on the photographs took place during the summer of 2003, in a studio in Oakland, California. The photographer was Maren Caruso, a talented young woman who specialized in food photography (patisserie in particular) and had already illustrated several works on the subject.

Her Oakland studio was located in a high-risk area, as she warned me before we began work. Not only that, but Oakland had a reputation as the murder capital of California. Maren's studio was protected with grilles at the windows, multiple locks, alarms, and other protective accessories. None of which was particularly reassuring. My hotel was a thirty-minute drive away. Maren advised me to rent a car, but I am never happy about driving in an unfamiliar city. I asked Maren if a taxi could pick me up in the morning and take me back to my hotel at night. But taxi drivers refused to venture into Maren's district after 3 p.m.—it was too dangerous. Finally, Maren found someone who would come and get me in the morning and take me back to the hotel in the evening. What was more, the arrangement cost next to nothing, just ten dollars per trip, twenty dollars a day. The only problem was that this was no ordinary car. It was a stretch Cadillac, like something straight of the movies, so long that when it turned a corner, you wondered if the back end was ever going to catch up with the front. I told the chauffeur that this didn't bother me at all. What about the car's color? Bright pink! No problem.

Imagine the scene: every morning at 9 a.m. a pastry chef dressed in a white jacket and toque stepped out to install himself like a pasha in the back seat of a huge pink Cadillac and drove off from the hotel to an unknown destination. Every evening he returned, wearing the same outfit. What was he up to? Probably a movie star. On the first morning, I was photographed by curious passersby in a barrage of popping flashbulbs.

The driver, who quickly became a firm friend, was a terrific young man. He worked as a restaurant waiter by day and had teamed up with a colleague to buy the pink monster secondhand, to rent for special occasions and events. With a price of 100 dollars for one person, 120 dollars for two, he would drive people to the restaurant so that they could get themselves noticed and make a big entrance. The car was nicknamed "The Pink Lady"—what else?

Driving through town in this car was really very "cool." Murder capital or not, Oakland was certainly a very lively place. Whenever we stopped at a traffic light, people would cluster around the smoked-glass windows, wondering who was riding in the back. I felt like a real star. For four days!

CHAPTER 19

Adieu, Monsieur le Président!

My plans were taking shape. I had given a great deal of thought to my departure from the White House. The most likely date was mid-summer 2004. My book was due out in September, and I would have to be completely free at that point to travel, promote the book, and attend signings. In the United States, if you want to sell something, you have to be prepared to get out there and meet people.

Meanwhile, I began preparations for Christmas, my last Christmas at the White House. We created a chocolate eagle with wings unfurled, in front of which was a small arrangement of fruit modeled in marzipan and a bunch of grapes. The symbolic bird presided over the dessert buffet for three weeks. Next, as always, came the traditional gingerbread house. And the following year, Mrs. Bush wanted to do something on the theme of children's books. She lent me a book I had never heard of, called *Charlie and the Chocolate Factory*, an entertaining story about an eccentric hero, Willy Wonka. Willy Wonka is in charge of production and makes everything tick, but he is helped by an army of little people with orange faces, green hair, brown knitted sweaters, and shorts with white suspenders: the Oompa Loompas. The book is full of wonderful objects and inventions, and extraordinary characters: enormous sugar lollipops and gumballs which are fed into the machines, a little boy who manages to get into this dream factory and a little girl, Violet, who turns into a giant blueberry with a tiny head and feet.

I read the book again and again, and when everything was clear in my mind, I took a pencil and went as mad as Willy Wonka, conjuring up my very own factory with old pipes, funnels, bottles, and chocolate towers. I still had to find the right molds for the chocolate components and scoured Washington's hardware stores looking for plastic utensils of all sorts. Using colored chocolate (purple, blue, green, and black) I began to mold extravagant machines with huge wheels and furnaces. The factory took shape. It was quite superb. Departing a little from the story, I created two large chocolate pulleys placed either side of it, which kept the production line operating, pouring chocolate directly onto two large "pretend" cakes colored white. Willy Wonka was depicted at work over his hot ovens, with two huge copper cauldrons made of chocolate. Violet was represented as a big purple ball in blown sugar, like all the other characters. I greatly enjoyed creating this magical factory, and Mrs. Bush loved it.

This was to be my last Christmas at the White House, although Mrs. Bush didn't know this yet. I planned to announce the news very shortly. And so I took special care over the desserts planned for dinners with friends and members of the presidential family. Four such meals were arranged, with around 100 guests on each occasion. The first was on December 5. I created snowmen made from pear sorbet with a chocolate filling and kiwi sauce. The "backdrop" was a little mountain with a miniature gingerbread house on its slopes. For the second dinner, on December 11, I created a chocolate cake in the form of a Christmas present, decorated with sugar ribbons and served with hazelnut mousse. For the third dinner, on December 14, I created a series of chocolate sleighs running down a chocolate-cake hillside, filled with Grand Marnier parfait. The presents inside each sleigh were iced petits fours, decorated with ribbons. The whole dessert was served with clementine quarters, arranged around the edges, and raspberry sauce. Finally, for the fourth and last dinner, on December 19, I prepared an English-style plum pudding served with bourbon sauce and ginger ice cream, together with a little *nougatine* dish containing a sugar cube soaked in alcohol with which to flambé the pudding. This requires extreme caution. Everyone at the White House remembers the time—during the Clinton administration—when a flaming Christmas pudding set fire to a guest's fox fur collar, as she leaned over the buffet. When I told my boss that I was planning to flambé the puddings he became very anxious but allowed me to go ahead, knowing that this was to be my last Christmas at the White House.

I handed Mrs. Bush my official resignation just before the start of the Christmas festivities. We met in the Map Room, a setting loaded with history. I told Mrs. Bush that I would be leaving the White House to concentrate on my book. I also told her that I was extremely tired and looked forward to a few years in which I would be free to enjoy life while I was still able. I had devoted twenty-five years of my life to the White House and worked for five different presidents. I had served the most prestigious guests: two French presidents, kings and queens, heads of state. I had "done my time," and now it was time to retire. Mrs. Bush took the news with perfect grace. She was, quite simply, terrific about it.

A few days later, I met the president, who took a somewhat dimmer view of my resignation. He said: "Roland, are you sure you won't reconsider your decision? What are you going to do out there? And what if your book flops? You think you can just come back to the White House? Better stay here in the first place. Why leave? There's no point, stay with us. Everything's going fine. We're very pleased with your work. What's your book called, *How to Kill a President with Calories?* No? Well then, I just don't understand. Think about it, Roland. There's nothing forcing you to leave."

I explained that I was sorry, but my decision was made. I enjoyed working for the president and First Lady, I adored their family and adored serving them, but the time had come to leave.

"Roland, you're a great guy, a very good man. I have enormous respect for you. You're an artist. You have always created the finest and most beautiful desserts any president could possibly hope to have at his table, and I thank you for that. But reconsider your decision. You understand? Reconsider it. Think about it."

When I handed Mrs. Bush my resignation, she asked my advice on the future of desserts at the White House and how to proceed. She was very worried and wondered what would happen next. How could we ensure continuity between myself and my successor? I suggested that an excellent candidate was already working in the White House pastry kitchen: my assistant, Susie Morrison. Susie was a skilled professional and a devoted member of the White House staff. Why not give her a chance? Mrs. Bush agreed. The family had a very high opinion of Susie, an extremely talented young woman. She came across very well in public and always spoke with confidence and poise. She invariably won the respect of the White House social secretaries, who were not always the easiest of people to work with. She was respected by the other pastry chefs—mostly male, and considerably older than her. She was, in short, exemplary. Mrs. Bush said: "I would like Susie to let us know when she prepares the dessert for a meal, so that we can know in advance what she is planning, see how she goes about it, and observe her way of working." We began immediately, with preparations for the Christmas festivities. Mrs. Bush had organized a small meal for fourteen of her friends; we decided to make Christmas wreaths, using lime and grenadine sorbet, and vanilla ice cream. The sorbets were served on an apricot sauce, decorated with slivers of gold and accompanied by Christmas petits fours. The wreaths were decorated with chocolate and green sugar Christmas-tree branches, on which we placed little snowmen, snowflakes, ribbons, and red Christmas berries. Each guest was served an individual wreath. Susie really went to town on the dessert, and Mrs. Bush was absolutely delighted. She could hardly believe her eyes and greatly admired the finesse of Susie's work. Another resounding success, but this time the glory was all Susie's. I fervently hoped that she would take my place as executive pastry chef. In the months that followed, she created numerous desserts, which she presented to the First Lady.

Spring 2004 was a very busy time, as always. There were no state dinners—I had served my last such presentation to Daniel arap Moi of Kenya—but there were still a great many meals, receptions, and lunches for special occasions. I applied myself to the task even more than usual.

I wanted to be sure to leave a good impression. My last dessert would be the finest! I would see the job through to the very end, and I refused any special treatment in my last months at the White House. I would end on a high note, with no mistakes or disasters.

Unlike his predecessors, President Bush was in the habit of inviting me up to the dining room very often to meet his guests, and these occasions were always accompanied by colorful stories. Both he and Mrs. Bush showed me a great deal of affection during my last six months at the White House—six terrific months for me. I was sorry to be leaving them, but at the same time I was increasingly tired, and impatient to lay down the heavy burden I had carried for so long.

The next World Pastry Cup was due to be held in Lyon on January 22, 2005. I would be able to take part, as I would no longer be at the White House. I helped with preparations for the event, a welcome opportunity to renew my longstanding friendship with Gabriel Paillasson, a pâtissier in Saint-Fons on the outskirts of Lyon. My adventures at the World Pastry Cup had begun with Gabriel back in 1988. It was he who had traveled to Washington to help me select the team we would send to the first competition in 1989. Our team came fourth, which wasn't bad for a first attempt. Back then, Gabriel had visited the White House and shaken hands with President Reagan. In 1991 he had appointed me as president of the international jury, consisting of four representatives from each participating country. The various national juries were responsible for selecting which of their country's creations would go forward to represent them in the final, to be judged by the international jury. I was responsible for drawing up the list of winners from a host of champion pastry chefs from all over the world. It was a great honor, and I was also greatly surprised to see these experienced professionals competing with daggers drawn, frequently breaking down in tears when they failed to win a prize which they felt was rightly theirs.

Sure enough, the 1991 competition was marked by an unpleasant incident. I was eating breakfast with the other members of the international jury, when one of them told me that one of the competing countries had doubtless cheated by bringing in items prepared in advance, a practice which is expressly forbidden in the rules. We would have to investigate. I discovered that the country concerned was France, which put me in a very difficult situation. It fell to me to accuse the French team of cheating and to furnish the proof! I talked the matter over with Gabriel. He assured me that there was no problem: we would gather the parties concerned in the competition tent and discuss everything as openly as possible. Gabriel convened a meeting with the Meilleurs Ouvriers de France, who were taking part in the competition as France's national judges, and the other members of the international jury. I revealed what I had been told: the members of the international jury had all told me personally and quite clearly that they had seen suspicious containers arriving at the competition site, doubtless concealing the forbidden preparations. Needless to say, the Meilleurs Ouvriers de France took the accusations very badly. Some members of the delegation were furious, ready to throw themselves at me in anger. I told them quite simply that as president of the international jury it was my duty to follow up any accusations of cheating reported to me by the other jurors. The French competitors fought their corner, swearing that there was no truth in the accusations. I appealed to the other members of the international jury, who were present at the meeting, and was astounded to hear three-quarters of them retract the accusations they had made in private over breakfast. That evening, I arranged a meeting at our hotel and asked them to explain their actions. I was told that they couldn't be entirely sure; they didn't really know what they had seen after all. I told them: "Either you have proof or you keep your mouth shut."

The next day, several members of the French jury who had been particularly aggressive towards me came to present their apologies. We shook hands. I explained once again that I had simply been acting on information and had done my job as president. It was a difficult, unpleasant incident nonetheless, but one that was quickly forgotten when we tasted the desserts entered for the final of the competition. For me, in spite of everything, it was an extraordinary, highly symbolic moment. As always at times like this, I saw the little railway house by the grade crossing where it all began. I felt proud to have come so far. And I was enormously grateful to my friend Gabriel, a truly great pâtissier, himself a Meilleur Ouvrier de France, the author of three works on sugar sculpture and the art of decorative patisserie, a true lion of Lyon, and a tireless champion of the integrity and status of our profession. We remain close friends and often speak on the phone.

My departure was drawing nearer and had been announced in the newspapers. It was now April. Easter at the White House was traditionally marked by an impressive chocolate creation. For the past two years, Susie and I had made two giant Easter eggs. The first one was decorated with a scene showing the president's two dogs running on the White House lawn, with Spot holding a tennis ball in her mouth. The second egg, made in 2003, featured a scene with Spot on her own and a separate chocolate figure of Barney wearing a hat and sunglasses, holding a brush, in the act of painting his girlfriend Spot's portrait. The result was very charming, and Mrs. Bush took a souvenir photograph of the piece. This year the president and Mrs. Bush had other concerns; we did not make the usual Easter pieces.

During the month of May I was surprised to learn that Susie would not be taking over from me as executive pastry chef. She knew only too well the enormous workload that awaited her. She told me: "Roland, you've been doing the work of five people for twenty-five years. I just don't have the strength. I would rather carry on as assistant pastry chef."

It was May already and still my successor had not been appointed. June went by, too. I began to worry, although my departure date had been carefully set after long deliberations with my employers. Initially, I had planned to bow out in April for the launch of my book. We were due to start promoting it in time for Mothers' Day, and Simon & Schuster were pressuring me to be ready and available. I was not allowed to leave, however, and had to stay on at the White House until July 30.

In June, George W. Bush hosted a great many lunches and receptions for noted figures from Afghanistan and Iraq. The President invited them in order to discuss their countries' very great difficulties. These talks took up a great deal of his time and that of the First Lady, too. They were fighting a war, after all.

On June 14, 2004, the Clintons were invited back to the White House for the unveiling of their official portraits. Together with Chelsea and her boyfriend, they enjoyed a pastry buffet featuring all of their favorite desserts, just as I had prepared them during their time in office. There was Mrs. Clinton's mocha cake and Bill Clinton's cherry pie. I also created their portraits in chocolate. Mrs. Clinton asked me to come up to the dining room for a moment. She and Chelsea both hugged me warmly. Chelsea made me promise to make her wedding cake, "like one of those cobblers that Dad liked so much." I told her that she had only to let me know when she was ready. Mrs. Clinton invited me to the opening of the Clinton Presidential Library at Little Rock that November: "You'll be retired, you'll have plenty of time!"

She told me that I would be greatly missed at the White House and that she and her family would never forget all I had done for them. Afterwards, we lined up for a photograph with all the staff on the White House steps.

June 15 was the date set for another Congressional barbecue and picnic, my last. I invited some of my fellow pâtissiers and friends for the occasion, so that they could have the honor of working at the White House before my departure. These included my old friend and colleague Yvon Hézard, who had succeeded me as an apprentice with the Maurivards. I wanted him to be able to say that he had worked at the White House, and he had already come to help during the Christmas preparations, too. Towards the end of the barbecue it began to rain. The president, who characteristically continued to make his rounds and shake hands with everyone he met, was completely soaked. He came to shelter under the tent erected over the buffet, and persisted in his belief that I wasn't really going to leave: "So Roland, this won't be your last picnic now, huh?"

But it was. I hadn't changed my mind. President Bush had his photograph taken with all the staff, including Yvon and me. Yvon was very excited.

On June 21 came the annual lunch for the senators' spouses. For this final event, I produced a dessert that I had been keeping back for the right occasion: a very special *marquise*. Based on the figure of an elegant lady of the French Ancien Régime, the dessert is in fact the pannier skirt of her dress, in this case a dome of pistachio gateau with fine layers of chocolate and fresh raspberries. The dress was decorated with piped butter-cream flowers, and the marquise's head and torso were modeled in blown sugar, with her hair piled high and decorated with little ribbons. The *marquise* was placed on a stand made of ice, lit from underneath, and surrounded by little balls of chocolate. The dessert was a great success. Mrs. Bush invited me up to the dining room and announced that after twenty-five years of desserts, my last creation was reserved specially for the senators' spouses. She held me by the hand throughout her speech. It was a very proud occasion for me. This time, I really had reached the end of my career at the White House. Even when such momentous events are almost upon us, they never seem real. We carry on, floating on a cloud, in another world. Mrs. Bush paid me a great many compliments, and everyone stood and applauded. It was difficult to hold back the tears.

During this intensely busy month, Chief Usher Gary J. Walters came to see me to ask for help recruiting my successor. He wanted me to suggest some names. But time was short; my departure was fixed for July 30, and I had begun to take a step back from work at the White House, to finish my book, so that it would be ready for publication on schedule. The book was being talked about in the media. I didn't have time to embark on a quest for my perfect successor. Nonetheless, I consulted a great deal with Susie—whoever replaced me would have to be sure to show her the greatest respect. I tried to sketch a profile of my ideal candidate: a person of impeccable integrity, an excellent pâtissier, a consummate professional, capable of rising to any and every challenge, a thoroughly decent individual.

And so three names presented themselves: Tom Vacero of the Casino Hotel in Atlantic City, Dennis Miller from the Gaylord Palms in Florida, and Thaddeus DuBois. Gary Walters told me that we would call them in one by one to make "test" desserts for the first family. Mrs. Bush would choose the successful candidate. My role was to provide the chefs with any ingredients they might need. Before the practical tests, I would interview them, then pass them on to the chief usher, and finally to Cathy Fenton, our social secretary. I had corresponded with each of them on the subject and had drawn up a provisional roster of my personal preferences: my first choice was Dennis Miller, second came Thaddeus DuBois, and finally Tom Vacero. There was not a moment to lose: my departure was imminent. On July 8, I met with Joe Bradley, who was taking care of the paperwork for my retirement. I was beginning to feel quite melancholy. At the same time, I knew that a huge burden would soon be lifted from my shoulders and that a new door was opening for me: the door I had always dreamed of seeing, standing half-open onto a world where I was free to do exactly what I wanted, when I wanted, without having to ask permission. I celebrated my sixtieth birthday on July 8, 2004.

July 8, 2004, was indeed my sixtieth birthday. Curiously, George W. Bush's birthday fell on July 6, the same day as Nancy Reagan. We were all born under the sign of Cancer, fighters to the last.

On July 12, Tom Vacero arrived at the White House for his dessert test. I greeted him and showed him around; he had never set foot in the building before. I watched his reactions closely: to me, the White House is a revered institution to be visited respectfully, as one might a church. Many other people think of it as a kind of smart hotel. I don't see it that way. The White House is a consecrated residence, and it is our job to care for the presidential couple who live there: the most powerful couple in the world. In my view, at least, the two most powerful figures in the world are the president of the United States and the Pope.

And so Tom Vacero arrived to take his test. The first problem he encountered was with the serving dishes. Like all chefs accustomed to working in great hotels, he assumed that he could choose from any number of different items of silverware. At the White House, space is limited, and things have to be organized differently. I told him that he would have to use only whatever dishes were on hand. I also made it clear that I was not there to influence him in his work in any way; no one would be available to help him. Unfortunately, he got off to a bad start by ordering Susie to "do this, do that." I stopped him right away. "Susie is not here to act as your assistant today. All the candidates are on an equal footing. You were told in advance that you would be provided with whatever ingredients you required, together with dishes big enough for an attractively presented dessert. But Susie is not here to do your work for you."

The candidates had to create a family dessert of the type served for everyday meals, and a more sophisticated piece, suitable for a state dinner. Tom Vacero prepared his menu. I made no comment, but stayed on hand throughout the day to provide him with whatever he needed. Susie waited until the evening to help him take the desserts up to the dining room. Talking to Tom, I realized that he thought the job was "in the bag." He was looking for a school for his children and was asking about apartments in Washington. He was, I thought, jumping the gun somewhat.

The following day, Dennis Miller arrived at the White House. This was the candidate at the top of my list. Once again, I was greatly impressed by his professionalism. He was very open and pleasant, and as an added advantage: he had worked with Susie before in various hotels. He clearly understood the very particular circumstances of the White House and knew exactly what he was doing once he got to work. No problem at all. His desserts were, it seemed to me, a great deal tastier than those prepared by Tom Vacero. I learned later that Mrs. Bush had enjoyed them very much and had asked for a portion to kept aside for the president, who was unfortunately absent and would be returning the next day. This was a great shame. With hindsight, I feel sure that the president's absence played an important role in the final decision.

We interviewed the third candidate, Thaddeus DuBois, on July 16. I greeted him as I had the others and showed him around. Our conversation produced one or two comments that gave me pause for thought. When I showed him a trolley loaded with 1,600 cookies ready for a Tee Ball game on the South Lawn, Thaddeus asked if Susie kept the recipe for them, explaining that he hadn't made cookies in a long time. It was crucial that a future White House chef knew how to make cookies. Not only that, but DuBois had insisted I provide him with the finest peaches, as fresh and ripe as possible, to be on hand as soon as he arrived. I had bought an entire case. That evening, it being Friday, I took two days off and left until Monday morning. On Sunday, I gave a talk to students at a cooking school in Connecticut. On Monday morning, I was keen to find out what DuBois had done with his fabulous peaches. He had put them in a pie, with raspberries, cut into pieces and baked in the oven. It seemed a shame to use such perfect fruit in this way, but in any event, his desserts seemed to please the First Family. Nonetheless, I told the social secretary what I felt would be the best course of action: invite all the candidates back one more time, when the president was sure to be at the White House and ask them to create desserts on a theme. The president had been absent for Dennis Miller's test, and I felt this had tipped the scales unfairly against him. Mrs. Bush decided to call back just one chef, Thaddeus DuBois, to make another dessert. Thaddeus was chosen for the job. For my part, I was satisfied that I had done everything I could to help appoint my successor.

On Friday, July 30, I wanted to slip quietly away from the White House with no fuss, just as I had arrived. I would finish my working day and head home. But things didn't happen quite that way. The president and First Lady were not scheduled to be at the White House on July 30. Indeed, I had hoped they would be somewhere else on that day. But on the eve of my departure, July 29, they insisted that I invite everyone with whom I had worked over the past twenty-five years to a farewell party. When Martha and I arrived, there were about forty people gathered to greet us. I was delighted and enormously proud. Then we were told that the president would be landing on the White House lawn in five minutes' time and that we should all step out onto the balcony. I was told to stand in the middle at the front, wearing my white chef's uniform and toque with a glass of champagne in one hand to salute the president, who came to join us right away. A delightful gesture! The chief usher Gary Walters presented me with my wooden worktable from the pastry kitchen—the one I had worked on for a quarter of a century—and which now bore a splendid plaque engraved with my name. I was enormously touched. There were tears in my eyes. I made a heroic effort not to break down completely. The president began to recount some of his memories and humorous anecdotes. He was laughing and asked me how my pastry book was progressing.

"How's the book going?"

"Well, it's about to come out."

"We'd better get you some publicity!"

I suggested that when he attended his forthcoming Republican National Convention in New York, he might like to urge everyone to buy Roland Mesnier's patisserie book for Christmas.

"Sure," said the president. "I'll do my speech about the Iraq war and finish by saying, 'Hey! And don't forget to buy Roland Mesnier's book.' You cannot be serious!"

Everyone roared with laughter. The banter was friendly and very funny. We shook hands one more time. Mrs. Bush hugged me and thanked me for everything I had done for them. She assured me that I would always find a warm welcome at the White House.

I was presented with a plaque bearing portraits of the five presidents I had served: Jimmy Carter, Ronald Reagan, George H.W. Bush, Bill Clinton, and George W. Bush. A truly memorable day. The crowning moment of my forty-eight-year career. Naturally, a great many friends wanted to take me out for a meal in the days that followed to talk about old times and the fun we had shared. One of my team members at the

White House organized a wonderful party at her home, for forty people, to say goodbye.

July 30 had arrived. My last day at the White House. I went into
work as usual. I could tell something was up, but I had no idea what. I
said to Susie: "At 2 p.m. it'll all be over. My official departure from the
White House."

From around 1:30 p.m. I was overcome with sadness. The end of
twenty-five years in this glorious home, twenty-five years of marvelous
patisserie creations, twenty-five years bringing pleasure to the leading
personalities of our time. The memories came flooding back, of good
times and bad, and my first steps in the trade: the bosses I had worked
for as an apprentice and, above all my parents, my childhood, the Ognon
Valley, where I would run in the fields, meadows, and woods, as free as
the wind. I remembered the dark days I had shared with the people
of the United States: September 11, 2001. And the fear and anxiety of
those closest to me—my family and, above all, my wife and son, who
had wished I would leave the White House, because it was no longer
safe to work there. I had always replied that I couldn't give everything
up on the pretext of being scared or nervous. My work was at the White
House and whatever happened, I would stay there and serve the first
family to the end. I was absolutely determined in the matter and proud
not to have left my post.

When it was time to leave, I walked all around my kitchen one last
time, touching the ovens, turning the knobs, lighting and extinguishing
the gas, checking the fridges to make sure there was enough butter in
reserve, enough flour, enough sugar—enough provisions for Susie to
carry on because my replacement had not yet arrived, doubtless due to
the lengthy investigations being carried out by the secret service into
his character. I could leave safe in the knowledge that everything was
in order.

I changed out of my chef's uniform in my office and went downstairs
in the elevator. There was no one around. Everything was quiet. Not
a soul in the kitchens or the corridors. Until, at the top of the main

passage leading to the exit, I found myself face to face with the entire staff, lined up as if for a review of the troops: the carpenters, electricians, painters, stewards, waiters, and cooks and, of course, dear Susie in floods of tears, to whom I was unable to say goodbye for fear of bursting into tears myself. We were always brought up that way in my family: never let your emotions show.

At the door, I handed in my security badge to Chief Usher Gary Walters, the head of the White House staff. The badge I had worn for twenty-five years. I walked out to my car. And I left the White House for the last time. *Adieu, messieurs les présidents. Adieu, mesdames les First Ladies.*

Epilogue

A Call to Duty and Final Farewell

It's March 2006 and I am entering my second year of retirement, having just returned from France after a two-week tour to promote the French edition of this book, *Sucré d'Etat*. The book was very well received in France. I am still working on a "cake book" and continue to tour the United States promoting *Dessert University*, my first book since leaving the White House. I tour the country, giving demonstrations, lecturing and consulting, and generally enjoying life and retirement with my wife Martha and our son George.

On March 9, I had an appointment about a consulting job at Café Leopold, located in Georgetown. It was a great meeting and I was tempted to go for it. I was just thinking about how very happy I am with my life right now and how I was finally able to disconnect myself totally from the White House. After all, the White House had been my life for many years and it felt very good finally to feel free. I totally unwound and returned to a more peaceful life.

March 11, 2006. It was a beautiful morning—sunshine and all. I was up at 7:00 a.m. and after a cup of coffee and a glance at the newspaper, I went to the office and checked my e-mail and phone messages. Around 10:00 a.m. the phone rang and my wife answered as I was outside in the backyard working on my roses. My wife told me that Lea Berman, the White House social secretary, called and asked that I call her back, which I did. She was very nice on the phone and told me that the new White House pastry chef was leaving already. Mrs. Bush asked Lea to contact me about coming back until a new pastry chef was hired. My reply was: "Of course!" I had promised Mrs. Bush at the time I handed in my notice (Christmas 2003) that if she ever needed me I would be just a phone call away. So the call came, and I was very honored to help out.

Monday, March 13. I got a call from Chief Usher Gary Walters to work out the security details. The following day, I started a series of meetings at my house with the White House assistant pastry chef, Susie Morrison, to talk about reorganizing the staff situation, making sure all shifts would be covered, revising menus, and coming up with new desserts and recipes. I wanted Susie to brief me about everything that was going on so that I could take action. Saturday, March 18, was my first day back into the White House compound. At lunch time, the butler informed the president and First Lady that I was back in the pastry kitchen. Right away, they asked to see me in the dining room while they were having lunch with their daughter Jenna and two other guests. My heart started to beat really quickly—as it did many times before. Déjà vu! I had been called into that dining room by other presidents and First Ladies. I entered the dining room, and everyone stood up and applauded me. I felt so nervous and humble. I still cannot forget where I come from. The First Lady gave me a hug and the president shook my hand. He reminded me that he had told me before I retired that I would be back to the White House someday. I replied that I did remember: he was right, and it was nice to see the First Family once again. I told him that I would do my best for them, thanked them, and left the room. After leaving the dining room, I felt as if I had never left the White House. Now it was up to me to swing between my commitments and White House events. The following days, I met on several occasions with Lea Berman and Gary Walters. Lea is very nice and easy to work with; it was the first time I had met her. I like her style. I was also working very closely with the assistant pastry chef, Susie Morrison, to devise a dessert for the retiring Supreme Court justice, Sandra Day O'Connor, using the scales of Justice as a part of the presentation for the dessert. We designed a special Napoleon for Lebanon. We worked on a state lunch for 160 people for the China delegation. We made a three-melon sorbet with orange zest and toasted sesame seeds, presented on an ice sculpture in a carved melon as the Chinese love melons, watermelon in particular. Then there was a state lunch for Ghana, and we were told to make it extra special as the president and Mrs. Bush had just visited the country and had been very well received. There were many other lunches and dinners. On May 16, we had a state dinner for Australia. There were nearly 200 people for dessert. The dessert was called "The Australian Black Pearl." It was served inside a white chocolate seashell with chocolate seaweed in the background with a lot of small chocolate fishes attached to the seaweed. Following that was the Congressional barbecue for 1,000 people and a state dinner for Japan on June 29. The name of the dessert was "Sweet Serenity—Bonsai Garden." The dessert composition was a sour-cherry sorbet filled with almond mousse with tiny macaroons and pieces of nougat, fresh peaches, and fresh cherries filled with kumquat puree. Of course, on July 4, we celebrated the president's birthday with 200 guests. We created a huge chocolate cake with chocolate decorations celebrating his entire life right up to the presidency.

Many things had changed since my departure in July 2004. A major change was that there was a new executive chef, who was appointed by Mrs. Bush. Her name is Cristeta Comerford. I worked with her for nearly ten years, and I am a great fan of her cooking and admire her as a human being. She is upstanding and respects the presidency and the White House. I was pleasantly surprised after my return to see how she had totally changed the main kitchen. She had brought back the integrity and stability of that great place. Her staff seems to be very happy, and her management style is all about quality work and serving the First Family well. Her organizational skills are superb.

After drawing up a list of potential candidates for the pastry chef position, I am planning my second retirement from the White House, as time does not permit me to work there any longer. It has been quite an honor to serve again and to see all my friends at the White House. I would like to wish my successor the best of luck. May he or she have as much fun as I have had serving the great leaders of the world.

Ten Golden Rules for my Successor

- Never forget where and for whom you are working.
- Create the greatest desserts in the world for the great and good of this world.
- Use the finest possible ingredients.
- Always be available for the First Family and their guests.
- Stay hopeful and keep smiling, even when it hurts, when it really hurts.
- Don't put yourself on show. If people want to see you, they know where to find you.
- Stay on your guard and watch what you say. Choose your words carefully.
- Don't let a compliment go to your head. Remain humble.
- Never forget, whatever your professional title, that you are simply a servant at the White House.
- Take care of your colleagues on your way up, you may find you need them on your way down.

The Presidents' Favorite Recipes

Honey Custard (Crème Caramel with Honey)
for Jimmy Carter

Serves 8

½ cup (120 g) sugar
½ cup (60 ml) water
6 large eggs
2 large egg yolks
1 cup (250 ml) honey
1 quart (1 liter) 2 percent milk
2 vanilla beans, split lengthwise
3 cups (750 ml) cut-up seasonal fruit (bite-size pieces)

Combine the sugar and ¼ cup of the water in a small saucepan. Bring to a boil and cook until the mixture turns dark amber. As soon as the syrup is uniformly amber, remove the pan from the heat. At arm's length, slowly pour the remaining ¼ cup water into the pot. Be careful—the water may splatter and the caramel will bubble up. Stir with a long-handled wooden spoon or ladle until smooth. Pour the caramel into an 8-inch (20-cm) savarin mold or eight individual 6-ounce ramekins, and set aside to cool completely.

Preheat the oven to 375°F (190°C). Whisk the eggs, yolks, and honey together in a large bowl. Pour the milk into a medium saucepan. Use a sharp paring knife to scrape the seeds from the inside of the split vanilla beans. Add the seeds and the beans to the milk. Very slowly bring the milk to a boil over medium-low heat. Remove the pan from the heat and let rest for 5 minutes to extract all of the flavor from the vanilla pods and seeds.

Slowly whisk the hot milk into the egg mixture. Pour the custard through a fine-mesh strainer into the savarin mold or ramekins.

Line a large roasting pan that is at least 2 inches (5 cm) taller than the custard mold with a few sheets of brown paper. Carefully place the custard dish(es) in the pan, and place the pan on the rack in the oven. Add enough hot tap water to the pan to reach three-fourths of the way up the side of the dish(es). Place an upside-down sheet pan or cookie sheet over the roasting pan to cover it. Bake until the custard is set around the edges but still a little wobbly in the center when gently shaken, 25 to 35 minutes for a large savarin mold, 15 to 20 minutes for ramekins.

Pull the pan from the oven and let the custard cool in the water for 45 minutes. Then remove the dish(es) from the roasting pan. Serve slightly warm or at room temperature, or cool completely and refrigerate, uncovered, for at least 4 hours or overnight. Let the custard return to room temperature before serving.

To unmold and serve: Run a sharp paring knife around the edge of the mold or ramekin. Place a serving dish upside down on top of the mold, invert the two together, and gently shake to release the custard and caramel. (If the custard won't come out of the mold, carefully lift one side of the inverted mold from the serving plate and insert a finger between the custard and the mold to break the suction. Remove your finger and gently shake again to release.) Arrange the fruit on the serving dish around the custard, and serve immediately.

Silky Chocolate Cream Pie (Tarte au Chocolat)
for Jimmy Carter

Serves 10

6 tablespoons (90 g) sugar
¼ cup (40 g) cornstarch
8 large egg yolks
1 quart (1 liter) whole or 2 percent milk
8 ounces (240 g) semisweet chocolate, finely chopped
4 tablespoons (80 g) unsalted butter, cut into small pieces
1 prebaked 9-inch (22-cm) pie shell
1 ½ cups (350 ml) heavy cream, chilled
2 tablespoons confectioners' sugar
1 teaspoon pure vanilla extract
1 lb (500 g) chocolate shavings

Whisk the sugar and cornstarch together in the bowl of an electric mixer. Add the egg yolks and beat on high speed until thick and pale, about 4 minutes.

Place the milk in a saucepan and bring to a boil over medium-high heat, whisking frequently to make sure the bottom isn't burning. Whisk about one-third of the hot milk into the egg mixture, and return the egg mixture to the saucepan. Cook over medium-high heat, whisking constantly, until the mixture reaches a full boil, 3 to 4 minutes.

Remove the pan from the heat and whisk in the grated chocolate and butter until melted. Scrape the pudding into the pie shell and cool completely. Cover and refrigerate until completely chilled, at least 2 hours or up to 1 day.

Two to 3 hours before serving, place the heavy cream, confectioners' sugar, and vanilla in the bowl of an electric mixer and whip until the cream holds stiff peaks. Smooth the whipped cream over the pudding. Scatter the chocolate shavings over the whipped cream, and serve.

Pecan Bourbon Pie
for the Carter family

Serves 10–12

For the pie dough:
3 ½ cups (350 g) cake flour
⅓ cup (75 g) sugar
pinch of salt
½ cup (120 ml) water
1 ½ cups (300 g) solid
   vegetable shortening

For the filling:
1 ½ cups (180 g) chopped pecans
1 cup (120 g) whole half-pecans
4 eggs
½ cup (120 g) sugar
6 tablespoons (100 g) melted butter
6 tablespoons (100 ml) bourbon
½ cup (115 ml) molasses
pinch of salt
½ cup (115 ml) dark corn syrup
whipped cream or ice cream, to serve

To make the pie dough:
Combine the flour, sugar, salt, water, and shortening in the bowl of an electric mixer fitted with the paddle attachment. Mix on low speed until the ingredients are well combined and the dough is smooth. Divide the dough into two pieces and press each piece out to form a 6-inch (15-cm) disc. Wrap them in plastic wrap and refrigerate the dough for at least one hour and for up to 1 week. This will give you enough dough for two pieces or one double-crusted pie. Pre-heat the oven to 375°F (180°C) and bake the pie "blind" in the oven at for 30 minutes to form a pre-baked shell.

Place the chopped pecans in the pre-baked shell. Neatly arrange the half-pecans on top. Whisk the eggs and sugar together. Add the melted butter, bourbon, molasses, salt, and dark corn syrup into the egg mixture. Pour gently over the pecans, making sure not to disturb the arrangement of the half-pecans. Bake at 350°F (180°C) for 45 minutes. Check whether the pie is done by pressing slightly on the pecans in the center; if any liquid appears, bake it some more. Serve with whipped cream or your favorite ice cream.

Quick Chocolate Mousse with Crystallized Ginger
for Ronald Reagan

Serves 6

4 ounces (110 g) semisweet or bittersweet chocolate, finely chopped
1 cup (250 ml) heavy cream, at room temperature
2 teaspoons finely chopped crystallized ginger
6 individual chocolate shells (optional)

Pour 2 inches (5 cm) of water into a medium saucepan and bring to a bare simmer. Place the chocolate in a stainless steel bowl that is big enough to rest on top of the saucepan, and place it over the simmering water, making sure that the bowl doesn't touch the water. Heat, whisking occasionally, until the chocolate is completely melted. Remove from the heat and let cool until the chocolate is just warm to the touch, between 95 and 100° F (35–38° C) on a candy thermometer.

Whip the heavy cream with an electric mixer until it holds soft peaks. Add the whipped cream and the ginger to the chocolate all at once, and quickly whisk together. Scrape the mousse into a large serving bowl or individual goblets, or pipe it into chocolate shells if desired. Sprinkle with the crystallized ginger and serve immediately, or refrigerate, uncovered and without the ginger, for up to 1 day before serving.

Orange Flourless Chocolate Cake
for the Reagan family

Serves 10–12

1 ½ sticks (170 g) unsalted butter, plus extra for greasing
flour, for dusting
6 ounces (170 g) bittersweet chocolate
1 cup plus 2 tablespoons (220 g) sugar
zest of one large orange
4 eggs plus 2 egg yolks
½ cup (55 g) unsweetened cocoa powder
10x confectioners' sugar, for dusting
candied orange peel and vanilla ice cream, to serve

Preheat the oven to 375°F (190°C). Butter and flour a 10-inch (25-cm) round cake pan. Line the bottom of the pan with parchment paper, then butter and flour the parchment paper. Gently melt the chocolate over a double boiler. Stir the butter into the chocolate to melt, and stir until smooth. Remove from the double boiler and whisk the sugar and orange zest into the chocolate mixture. Add the eggs and egg yolks and whisk well. Sift the cocoa powder over the chocolate mixture and whisk the batter until totally smooth. Pour the batter into the pan and bake for approximately 35 to 40 minutes, or until the top has formed a good crust. Cool the cake in the pan on a rack for 10 minutes. Invert the cake onto a serving platter. Dust with confectioners' sugar and serve with candied orange peel and vanilla ice cream.

Baked Apple Soufflé
for George H. W. Bush

Serves 12

3 pounds (1.3 kg) Granny Smith apples, peeled, cored,
   and cut into 1-inch (2-cm) cubes
1 cup plus 2 tablespoons (225 g) sugar,
   plus extra for decoration
½ cup (100 ml) Cointreau or other orange-flavored liqueur
½ teaspoon pure vanilla extract
1 tablespoon cornstarch
5 large egg whites, at room temperature
whipped cream, for serving

Preheat the oven to 375° F (190°C). Place the cubed apples on a rimmed baking sheet and bake, turning two or three times to ensure even cooking, until tender, approximately 25 to 30 minutes.

Meanwhile, butter two 4- to 5-cup (1-liter) soufflé dishes and sprinkle them generously with sugar.

Puree the baked apples in a blender. Measure out 3 ½ cups (350 ml) of the apple puree and place it in a large bowl. (Set aside any remaining puree for another use.) Stir in ¾ cup (180g) of the sugar. Combine the Cointreau, vanilla, and cornstarch and add to the puree.

Whip the egg whites with an electric mixer on high speed until they hold very soft peaks. Whipping constantly, add the remaining 6 tablespoons sugar in a very slow stream until they hold stiff peaks.

Stir about one-third of the egg whites into the apple mixture to lighten it. Gently but thoroughly fold the remaining egg whites into the apple. Divide the mixture between the two soufflé dishes and smooth the tops with a spatula.

Pour 1 inch (2.5 cm) of hot tap water into a large roasting pan. Carefully place the soufflé dishes in the pan, and place the pan in the oven.

Bake until the mixture is set and the soufflés have risen and are firm to the touch, 30 to 40 minutes. Remove them from the pan and let them cool on a wire rack for 10 to 15 minutes.

Place a serving dish upside down on top of one soufflé dish, invert the two together, and gently shake to release the soufflé. Repeat with the second soufflé dish.

Serve immediately, with whipped cream.

Chocolate Chip Cookies
for George H. W. Bush

Makes around 70 cookies

3 cups plus 3 tablespoons (450 g) all-purpose flour
1 teaspoon baking soda
¼ teaspoon salt
2 sticks (250 g) unsalted butter, softened
1 cup (240 g) granulated sugar
⅔ cup (130 g) packed light brown sugar
2 large eggs
¼ cup (60 ml) molasses
1 tablespoon pure vanilla extract
one 12-ounce bag / 2 cups (350 g) semisweet chocolate chips
1 cup (220 g) chopped walnuts

Combine the flour, baking soda, and salt in a medium mixing bowl. In the bowl of an electric mixer fitted with the paddle attachment, cream together the butter, granulated sugar, and brown sugar until thoroughly combined. Beat in the eggs, molasses, and vanilla, scraping down the sides of the bowl once or twice as necessary. Stir in the flour mixture until just incorporated. Then stir in the chocolate chips and walnuts. Place the bowl in the refrigerator and allow the dough to chill for 1 hour.

Preheat the oven to 400°F (204°C). Line several baking sheets with parchment paper or Silpat pads.

Drop heaped tablespoons of the dough 2 inches apart on the prepared baking sheets, flattening them slightly by hand. (Balls of dough may be placed next to each other on parchment-lined baking sheets, frozen, transferred to ziplocked plastic freezer bags, and stored in the freezer for up to 1 month. Place frozen cookies on prepared sheets as above, and defrost on the counter for 30 minutes before baking.)

Bake for 8 to 10 minutes, until just light golden. Cool the cookies for 5 minutes on the baking sheets before using a metal spatula to transfer them to a wire rack to cool completely. The cookies will keep in an airtight container for 2 to 3 days.

Christmas Spiced Fruit Bars
for the George H. W. Bush family

Serves 10–12

2 ½ cups (450 g) sugar
1 ½ sticks (170 g) butter
½ cup (115 ml) molasses
pinch of salt
1 teaspoon lemon rind
1 teaspoon mace
1 ½ teaspoons cinnamon
3 teaspoons (15 g) baking soda
⅓ cup (8 ml) water
4 eggs
2 ¼ cups (220 g) bread flour
½ cup (85 g) sliced almonds
½ cup (85 g) currants
⅓ cup (60 g) candied lemon peel
⅓ cup (60 g) candied orange peel
melted chocolate and nonpareils, to decorate

Cream the sugar, butter, molasses, salt, lemon rind, mace, and cinnamon together. Add to this mixture the baking soda dissolved in ⅓ cup (80 ml) of water. Gradually add the eggs, one at a time. Mix the bread flour into the above mixture. Add the sliced almonds, currants, candied lemon peel, and candied orange peel, stirring well. Allow the mixture to rest overnight in the refrigerator. Using a number 8 plain piping tube, pipe strips 4 inches (10 cm) apart onto parchment paper on a baking sheet. Bake at 350°F (180°C) until firm. Allow to cool and brush on chocolate and decorate with nonpareils. Cut into slices 1 ½ inches (4 cm) wide. These will keep in the refrigerator in zip lock bags for several weeks.

Bananas in Raspberry Cream
for Bill Clinton

Serves 8

8 ripe bananas
3 tablespoons fresh lemon juice
1 ½ cups (500 ml) Raspberry Sauce (see page 332)
2 cups (500 ml) heavy cream, chilled
1 tablespoon confectioners' sugar
1 teaspoon pure vanilla extract
3 tablespoons (50 g) sliced almonds, toasted
marzipan holly leaves (optional)

Cut the bananas into ¼-inch (2.5-cm) -thick rounds. Place them in a large bowl and toss with the lemon juice so they don't turn brown.

Whip the heavy cream with an electric mixer until it holds stiff peaks. Place 1 cup (250 ml) of whipped cream in a bowl and set it aside. Fold 1 cup (250 ml) of the raspberry sauce into the remaining whipped cream, being careful not to deflate the cream.

Set aside 16 banana slices. Arrange a third of the remaining banana slices in a serving bowl or compote dish that is approximately 8 inches (20 cm) in diameter and 6 to 7 inches (15 cm) deep.

Spread one-third of the raspberry mixture over the bananas. Repeat twice more with the remaining bananas and raspberry cream, so that you have 3 layers of each. Smooth the top with a small offset spatula.

Gently fold the confectioners' sugar and vanilla extract into the reserved cup of whipped cream. Spoon the sweetened whipped cream into a pastry bag fitted with a #6 rosette nozzle, and pipe 16 rosettes of cream around the edge of the dish. Place a banana slice upright in each of the rosettes. Pour the remaining ½ cup (150 ml) of raspberry sauce in the center of the dish so that it covers all of the raspberry cream. Sprinkle the sauce with the toasted almonds, and garnish with marzipan holly leaves if desired. Serve immediately or refrigerate, uncovered, for up to 8 hours before serving.

For the Raspberry Sauce: in an electric blender, combine 1 ½ pounds (150g) of fresh raspberries (or two 12-ounce bags frozen unsweetened raspberries, thawed) and ½ cup (150g) of sugar until smooth. Push the mixture through a fine-mesh strainer into a bowl, and set aside until needed .

Carrot Muffins
for Bill Clinton

Make 12 large muffins or 36 mini muffins

1 cup (150 g) all-purpose flour
1 teaspoon baking soda
½ teaspoon ground cinnamon
2 large eggs, at room temperature
¾ cup (200 ml) sunflower or canola oil
1 teaspoon pure vanilla extract
1 cup (240 g) sugar
1 ½ cups (200 g) shredded carrots (about 4 medium carrots)
½ cup (60 g) coarsely chopped pecans
Cream Cheese Frosting (see page 342)

Preheat the oven to 350°F (180°C). Line a 12-cup muffin pan, or a 36-cup mini muffin pan, with paper liners.

Combine the flour, baking soda, and cinnamon in a medium bowl.

Place the eggs, oil, vanilla, and sugar together in the bowl of an electric mixer fitted with the whisk attachment, and whisk on high speed until the mixture resembles a runny mayonnaise, about 5 minutes. Stir in the flour mixture until just combined. Stir in the carrots and pecans.

Divide the batter among the muffin cups, and bake until a toothpick inserted into the center of a muffin comes out clean (about 18 to 20 minutes, or 8 to 10 minutes for mini muffins). Cool in the pan for about 5 minutes, then invert the muffins onto a rack, re-invert them onto another rack so they are right side up, and allow to cool completely. (Carrot Muffins may be individually wrapped in plastic wrap and then in foil, and frozen for up to 3 weeks.) Frost with Cream Cheese Frosting if desired.

Cherry Pie Crumble
for the Clinton family

Serves 10–12

For the filling:
2 ½ pounds (1.1 kg) frozen black
   pitted sweet cherries,
   thawed and the juice reserved
1 cup (200 g) sugar
3 tablespoons (40 g)
   quick cooking tapioca
1 ½ tablespoons (25 ml)
   Amaretto liquor (optional)
pinch of salt

For the topping:
½ cup (40 g) old-fashioned
   oats
¾ cup (75 g) all-purpose flour
¾ cup (150 g) golden brown
   sugar
¾ teaspoon ground cinnamon
pinch of salt
1 stick (115 g) unsalted butter

prebaked pie shell (see page 323)

whipped cream, to serve

For the filling, mix the cherries and their juice, the sugar, tapioca, Amaretto, and salt in a bowl. Let the mixture stand until the tapioca looks translucent. (This should take 45 minutes to 1 hour).

For the topping, blend together the oats, flour, sugar, cinnamon, and salt in a large bowl. Use your fingers to rub the butter into the mixture to form coarse crumbs. Preheat the oven to 400°F (200°C). Fill the pie crust with the cherry mixture and spread the crumble over the cherries. Bake for approximately 30 minutes, or until the cherry filling is bubbling and the topping is brown and crisp. Allow to cool for 45 minutes to an hour and serve with whipped cream.

Buttered Brioche Pudding
with Dried Blueberries and Lemon Sauce
for George W. Bush

Serves 10

one 8 × 4-inch (20 × 10-cm) brioche loaf
4 tablespoons (60g) unsalted butter, softened
1 ½ cups (330g) dried blueberries
6 large eggs
pinch of salt
¾ cup (180g) sugar
1 quart (1 liter) whole milk
2 vanilla beans, split lengthwise, or ½ tablespoon pure vanilla extract
1 ½ cups (350 ml) Lemon Sauce (see page 336)

Preheat the oven to 350°F (180°C). Cut the ends off the brioche loaf and discard them.

Slice the brioche into ten ¾-inch (2-cm) -thick slices. Trim the crusts from each slice and cut each slice in half. Butter one side of each piece of brioche.

Butter a 7 × 12-inch (18 × 25-cm) baking dish and arrange the blueberries in an even layer on the bottom of the dish. Arrange the brioche slices, buttered side up, overlapping them slightly, over the blueberries.

Whisk the eggs, salt, and sugar together in a medium bowl. Set aside.

Pour the milk into a medium saucepan. Use a sharp paring knife to scrape the seeds from the inside of the split vanilla beans. Add the seeds and the beans (or the extract) to the milk. Very slowly bring the milk to a boil over medium-low heat. Remove the pan from the heat and let rest 5 minutes to extract all of the flavor from the vanilla pods and seeds.

Slowly whisk the hot milk into the egg mixture. Pass the custard through a fine-mesh strainer over the bread. Press the bread down with the back of a large spoon so that it is completely soaked.

Line a roasting pan with a few sheets of brown paper or newspaper. Place the dish in the pan, and carefully transfer the pan to the oven. Add enough hot tap water to the pan to reach halfway up the sides of the dish. Bake until the custard is set around the edges but still a little wobbly in the center when gently shaken, 30 to 40 minutes.

Transfer the pan to a wire rack and let the brioche pudding cool for 15 minutes. Then remove the baking dish from the roasting pan and let it stand for another 10 to 15 minutes. Serve warm with Lemon Sauce (see below).

For the Lemon Sauce: In a saucepan, mix 1 tablespoon cornstarch and ½ cup (120 g) sugar together in a small saucepan. Whisk in 1 cup (250 ml) boiling water. Place the pan on the stove and bring to a boil over high heat. Boil until thickened, about 2 to 3 minutes. Stir in 3 tablespoons lemon juice, 1 teaspoon grated lemon zest, and 2 tablespoons unsalted butter. Transfer the sauce to a bowl, and cool to room temperature.

Chocolate Crêpes
for George W. Bush

Serves 8

2 tablespoons sugar
1 ½ cups (350 ml) Ganache (see below)
16 Basic Crêpes (see pages 341–342)
1 pint (1 liter) vanilla ice cream, slightly softened

Preheat the oven to 350°F (180°C). Butter a heatproof serving platter and sprinkle it with sugar.

Spread 1 ½ tablespoons of Ganache over a crêpe, leaving a ½-inch (1-cm) border all the way around. Fold the crêpe in half and place it on the prepared platter. Repeat with the remaining crêpes, slightly overlapping them on the platter. (At this point you can cover the platter lightly with plastic wrap and let it stand at room temperature for up to 8 hours before baking.)

Bake for 3 to 4 minutes or until the chocolate begins to melt. Serve immediately, with the ice cream on the side.

For the Ganache: Place 12 oz (340g) semisweet chocolate chips (or bittersweet or semisweet chocolate, chopped) in a heatproof bowl. Bring 1 cup (250 ml) heavy cream to a near boil in a small saucepan. Pour the hot cream over the chocolate and whisk until smooth. Cool to room temperature.

Rhubarb Parfait
for the George W. Bush family

Serves 10–12

1 quart (1 kg) of frozen rhubarb
½ cup (120 g) sugar

For the topping mixture:
½ cup (100g) sugar
1 cup (100 g) all-purpose flour
generous stick (140 g) butter
1 tablespoon (15 ml) vanilla
pinch of salt

For the cream filling:
1 cup (200g) 10x confectioners' sugar
1 cup (240 g) mascapone, at room temperature
1 ⅓ cup (230 ml) plain yogurt
1 ⅓ cup (230 ml) whipping cream

Cook and simmer the frozen rhubarb with the sugar until the rhubarb is soft and has reduced a little.

For the topping, mix the sugar with the flour and salt. Work in the butter and vanilla with your hands, to make a dough. Crumble the mixture into small pieces on a cookie sheet lined with parchment paper. Bake at 425°F (220°C) until golden and crispy.

For the cream filling, mix the confectioners' sugar into the mascapone, and then fold in the yogurt. Whip the whipping cream to a stiff peak and fold into the mascarpone mixture. In a pretty glass bowl, place a layer of rhubarb, then the cream, and then the crumble on top. Repeat one more time and finish the top with the remaining crumble. Sprinkle the top with confectioners' sugar and serve warm or at room temperature.

SOME BASIC RECIPES

Fruit Salad "Surprise"

Serves 10

4 cups (1 liter) mixed fresh fruit, cut into bite-sized pieces
2 cups apple juice
½ cup (120 ml) honey
3 cups (1 liter) vanilla ice cream, softened.
1 cup (250 ml) apricot jam
4 tablespoons Cointreau, or other orange-flavored liqueur
1 cup (250 ml) cake crumbs
Meringue Topping (see page 340), freshly prepared
confectioners' sugar
Raspberry Sauce, optional (see page 332)

Setting aside any delicate fruit or fruit that may discolor the salad, combine the remaining fruit with the apple juice in a bowl, making sure that all of the fruit is covered with the juice. Place the bowl on a rimmed baking sheet. Loosely cover the bowl with two layers of plastic wrap, making sure that at least 5 inches (12.5 cm) over-hang the rim. Put a 2-inch (5 cm) layer of ice cubes on top of the plastic wrap. Refrigerate for up to 2 days.

When you are ready to serve the dessert, gather the edges of the plastic wrap together, taking care not to let the melted ice drip into the bowl, and discard. Pour in the honey, and stir well. Gently stir in any reserved fruit, and set aside until ready to use.

Line a 6-cup (1.5-liter) soufflé dish with plastic wrap so that 1 inch (2.5 cm) hangs over the edge. Pack the ice cream into the dish and smooth it with the back of a spoon to make an even layer. Put the soufflé dish in the freezer to firm up, about 2 hours.

Remove the dish from the freezer, and remove the ice cream disk from the dish by pulling on the edges of the plastic. Transfer the molded ice cream to a baking dish and return it to the freezer until ready to use. Set the soufflé dish aside to use later.

Preheat the oven to 450°F (230°C). Position the oven rack at the bottom of the oven.

Stir the apricot jam and the Cointreau together in a small bowl. Stir this mixture into the fruit salad until the fruit is well coated.

Place the fruit in the soufflé dish, and place the ice cream disk on top of the fruit. Sprinkle the cake crumbs over the ice cream in an even layer. Place the mixture back in the freezer while you make the Meringue Topping (see below), but for no longer than 15 minutes.

Mound Meringue Topping on top of the ice cream, forming a dome shape. Place the remaining meringue in a pastry bag fitted with a #7 or #8 star tip and pipe arcs of meringue from the edge of the dish to the center point of the dome. Dust heavily with confectioners' sugar. Bake until golden, 1 to 1 ½ minutes, turning the dish every 20 seconds for even coloring. Remove the dish from the oven and serve immediately, with Raspberry Sauce, if desired.

For the Meringue Topping: Combine 2 large egg yolks, 1 teaspoon grated orange zest, and 2 teaspoons cornstarch in a small bowl. Using a sharp paring knife, scrape the seeds from a vanilla bean, split lengthwise, into the bowl. Lightly beat together. (Reserve the vanilla pods for another use.)

Place 8 large egg whites in the bowl of an electric mixer fitter with the whisk attachment, and whip on high speed until just about to hold soft peaks. With the mixer still on high, pour in 1 ¼ cups (250g) sugar in a slow, steady stream. Whip until the meringue holds stiff peaks. With the mixer on low speed, slowly pour the egg yolk mixture into the bowl, mixing until just combined. Use immediately.

Basic Crêpes

Makes about 20 crêpes

1 large egg, at room temperature
1 large egg yolk, at room temperature
¼ cup (60 g) sugar
3/4 cup (110 g) all-purpose flour
1 ¼ cups (350 ml) whole or 2 percent milk, at room temperature
½ teaspoon pure vanilla extract
4 tablespoons (90 g) unsalted butter, melted and cooled,
  plus a little more for greasing the pan
pinch of salt

Combine the egg, egg yolk, 2 tablespoons of the sugar, the flour, and ½ cup (250 ml) milk in a medium bowl. Stir until it forms a smooth paste. Add the remaining ¾ cup (175 ml) milk and the vanilla, melted butter, and salt. Stir until smooth. Pour the mixture through a fine-mesh strainer into a measuring cup or bowl. Let the batter rest for 1 hour, or refrigerate for up to 4 days. Warm the batter slightly over a pot of barely simmering water before using.

Sprinkle a rimmed sheet pan with the remaining 2 tablespoons sugar. Fill a shallow bowl or cake pan with cool water.

Heat a nonstick crêpe pan or 6-inch (15-cm) skillet on medium-high heat until a few drops of water drizzled onto the surface sizzle and evaporate. Brush the bottom of the pan lightly with some of the extra melted butter.

Use a small ladle to pour 2 tablespoons of the batter into the pan. Quickly tilt the pan to the right and then in a circular motion to coat it completely with the batter. Cook until the edges begin to color, about 30 seconds. Carefully lift the edge of the crêpe with a sharp paring knife and grasp the edge between your thumb and index finger. Carefully flip, and cook for another 30 seconds. Invert the pan over the sugared sheet pan so the crêpe will fall out flat. Dip the bottom of the pan into the cool water. Repeat with the remaining batter (it's not necessary to butter the pan after every crêpe).

Rather than stacking the crêpes one on top of the other, overlap them slightly so that they are easier to separate. Let the crêpes cool to room temperature. To keep them nice and moist, place a clean, very damp kitchen towel over the crêpes until ready to use, up to 8 hours; or refrigerate for up to 2 days.

If you want to keep them longer, wrap the whole sheet pan, including the towel, in plastic wrap and freeze for up to 2 months. When you need the crêpes, remove the plastic wrap and place the pan in a 375°F (190°C) oven with the towel still in place; bake for 5 to 7 minutes, so the towel just becomes hot to the touch. The towel will release some steam onto the crêpes, making them very pliable and easy to work with as they thaw. Carefully lift the defrosted crêpes from the sheet pan and fill as desired.

Cream Cheese Frosting

Makes enough to frost 12 large or 36 mini muffins

8 oz (250 g) cream cheese, softened
½ cup (100 g) confectioners' sugar
1 teaspoon pure vanilla extract

Combine the cream cheese, confectioners' sugar, and vanilla in the bowl of an electric mixer fitted with the paddle attachment, and mix until smooth.

Acknowledgments

I owe a deep debt of gratitude to my wife Martha
and son George for their unfailing support.

My deepest thanks also go to:
My brother Jean, a consummate professional and a passionate
pâtissier, who introduced me to the profession and passed
on the sacred flame. I owe my whole, lifelong adventure to him.

My other brothers and sisters: Gabriel, Lucien, Geneviève, Bernard,
Serge, René, and Marie-Thérèse.

My father and mother, with whom I would have liked to be able
to share this book.

Thierry Billard, for guiding me on the right path.

Jean Mauduit, for knowing how to appreciate my sweet passions.

Christian Malard, for persuading me to write this book.

President Jimmy Carter and First Lady Rosalynn Carter,
for hiring me as pastry chef at the White House.
President Ronald Reagan and First Lady Nancy Reagan,
for the eight extraordinary years we spent together.
President George Bush and First Lady Barbara Bush,
for showing me the human, private face of life as the first family.
President Bill Clinton and Senator Hillary Clinton,
for their remarkable eight-year presidency:
an endless firework display.
President George W. Bush and First Lady Laura Bush,
whom I was deeply sad to leave.

A thousand thanks are also due to the employers who saw me through
my apprenticeship: Monsieur and Madame Paul Maurivard, and
Monsieur and Madame Raymond Ligney.

A big thank you to the many great hoteliers and chefs
who have guided me throughout my career.
And to all my friends, including Dr. Louis Arnaud,
who suggested the original French title for this book, *Sucré d'état*.

Thanks, too, to Yvon Hezard, to whom I often speak.

I tip my toque to Sophy Thompson and Katie Mascaro, and all at
Flammarion for their hard work on the English language edition,
particularly Louise Rogers Lalaurie for her elegant translation.
With thanks to Grace McQuade from Goldberg McDuffie
Communications for organizing the publicity and book tour.

And finally, to Patrice Olivon, who initiated me into the mysteries of
how to use a computer, Bernard Duclos, Valrhona chocolate—adored
by pastry chefs the world over—and Brian Maynard
and Justin Newby of KitchenAid, whose products are treasured
by cooks the world over.

A Note on the Type
This book was typeset in Adobe Jenson Pro,
a typeface designed by Robert Slimbach
and based on the late 15th-century typeface
by Nicolas Jenson.